Sexting Panic

A list of books in the series appears at the end of this book.

Sexting Panic

Rethinking Criminalization, Privacy, and Consent

AMY ADELE HASINOFF

UNIVERSITY OF ILLINOIS PRESS

Urbana, Chicago, and Springfield

Library of Congress Control Number: 2014958126
ISBN 978-0-252-03898-3 (hardcover)
ISBN 978-0-252-08062-3 (paperback)
ISBN 978-0-252-09696-9 (e-book)

Contents

Illustrations

Acknowledgments

I cannot possibly thank everyone who contributed to this book. But I will start at my current institution, the University of Colorado Denver, where the support at all levels has been exceptional, including a grant supporting the last stages of this project. My new Communication Department colleagues provided a wonderful intellectual space in which to complete this manuscript. Thanks to Sonja Foss for her generous and incisive feedback, and to Stephen Hartnett, Lisa Keränen, Sarah Fields, Michelle Médal, Hamilton Bean, Brian Ott, Brenda J. Allen, Jim Stratman, Larry Erbert, Gordana Lazic, and Yvette Bueno-Olson, among others, for helpful comments, guidance, and a warm welcome. I thank a number of other UCD colleagues for valuable feedback on my final drafts: Sarah Tyson, Gillian Silverman, Lucy Mcguffey, Andy Rumbach, Carrie Makarewicz, Kelly Palmer, and Margaret Woodhull. Finally, thanks to a number of UCD and Denver friends who have offered crucial advice and support: Sarah Hagelin, Dawn Comstock, James Fiumara, Colleen Heineman, John Tinnell, and Marjorie Levine-Clark.

Carrie Rentschler introduced me to feminist media studies when I was an undergraduate student at McGill, and her research, mentoring, and teaching has been a model for me ever since. When I returned to McGill to work with her as a postdoctoral fellow, her brilliant insights and questions challenged me to develop this book into its current form. She also offered crucial professional support and made the Institute for Gender, Sexuality, and Feminist Studies a vibrant, welcoming, and exciting place to develop this project during my time at McGill. The Girlhood Studies symposium was a particular highlight, and I thank the participants for their comments, particularly Catherine Driscoll, Sarah Banet-Weiser, Marnina Gonick, Claudia Mitchell, and Caroline Caron. I also thank a number of other people connected to the IGSF, including Liz Groeneveld, Alison Fyfe, Samantha Thrift, Caili Woodyard, and Lena Palacios. The Art History & Communication Studies Department at McGill likewise offered a wonderful set of colleagues. I owe particular thanks to Jonathan Sterne for generously showing me how to take a broader view of technology and new media studies and for patiently providing answers to my endless questions and requests for advice. The writing group he organized was particularly fruitful, and I thank its members for their indispensible feedback: Dylan Mulvin, Li Cornfeld, Anna Candido, Lilian Radovac, and Max Ritts.

During my time at McGill, this project also derived huge benefits from conversations with many other colleagues including Darin Barney, Gabriella Coleman, Will Straw, Tina Piper, Becky Lentz, and Laila Parsons. Discussions with a number of other colleagues and friends based mainly in Ottawa, Toronto, and Montreal also played a vital role in this project, and I thank Kate Cairns for helpful comments on a number of drafts, Lara Karaian for her sexting research and wonderful in-depth conversations about the topic, Ummni Khan, Leslie Regan Shade, Tamara Shepherd, Nicole Cohen, Andrea Slane, Yasmin Jiwani, Rena Bivens, and Ian Kerr. Thanks as well to researchers in the United States and elsewhere for key suggestions and insights: Kate Crawford, danah boyd, Alice Marwick, Laura Portwood-Stacer, Fred Turner, Mary Beltran, Nora Draper, Karma Chávez, Rachel Hall, Yvette Taylor, Mary Celeste Kearney, Mara Mills, Mary Bryson, Anna Feigenbaum, Jessalynn Keller, and Jessica Ringrose. I also thank those who offered exemplary kindness and friendship: Maryam Ehteshami, Sherwin Tjia, Lana Goodrich, Robin Michaels, Sean Michaels, Miri Freidowitz, and Anne Rousselot.

I began my graduate studies at the Institute for Communications Research at the University of Illinois at Urbana-Champaign. There, and to this day, I benefited from Shoshana Magnet's generous guidance, tremendous empathy, and delicious vegan cooking. I also thank members of reading and writing groups I participated in at UIUC, including Aisha Durham, Kevin Dolan, Carolyn Randolph, Michele Rivera, Myra Washington, Celiany Rivera-Velazquez, Jillian Baez, and Himika Battacharya. Other friends and colleagues connected to Urbana-Champaign likewise formed an important scholarly and social community, including Julilly Kohler-Hausmann, Kwame Holmes, Natalie Havlin,

John Gergley, Anna Kurhajec, Ian Hartman, Desiree Yomtoob, Kelly Gates, Rachel Dubrofsky, Victor Pickard, Anthony Sigismondi, Melissa Prentice, Erica Alane Hill, Alice Filmer, Robert Smith, Sasha Mobley, Steven Doran, Shantel Martinez, Robert Mejia, and Meijiadai Bai.

Sarah Projansky guided my training at UIUC and provided uncannily insightful feedback. Her remarkable ability to understand and support my goals helped me move forward when it seemed impossible. Paula Treichler's exemplary feminist media studies scholarship, vital feedback, and challenging questions were also essential. A number of other UIUC faculty members shared their research with me and offered crucial advice and scholarly insights: Kent Ono, John Nerone, Shefali Chandra, Siobhan Somerville, Mimi Nguyen, Fiona Ngo, Norm Denzin, Cameron McCarthy, Lisa Nakamura, Angharad Valdivia, Isabel Molina Guzman, James Hay, Maria Mastronardi, and Ruth Nicole Brown.

Thanks to series editor Carol Stabile for supporting this project and to editor Larin McLaughlin and the staff at the University of Illinois Press for shepherding it through the process. I thank the Social Science and Humanities Research Council of Canada and the Fonds québécois de la recherche sur la société et la culture for financial support that had an immense impact on this project. Sincere thanks are also due to all the audiences who heard parts of this work and offered critical and often lively responses, especially at the National Communication Association, the National Women's Studies Association, the Association of Internet Researchers, the Canadian Communication Association, the Canadian Women's Studies Association, Concordia University, Carleton University, Eastern Kentucky University, and the University of Wisconsin–Madison. Thanks as well to editors and reviewers at *New Media & Society* and *Girlhood Studies* for the space to develop two articles that now form the basis of chapter 4, and to the *International Journal of Communication* for brief parts of chapter 5.

I would also like to acknowledge my parents, Brian and Shelley, and my brother Sam, for their unconditional support in more ways than I can count, and for always encouraging me to ask questions and challenge common sense. Special thanks are also due to Shelley for diligent copyediting. Finally, I want to acknowledge Brandon Mills, whose patience and support has made it possible for me to even undertake this project. He has generously helped me work through some of my toughest intellectual problems, and with love, gratitude, and admiration, I dedicate this to him.

Sexting Panic

Introduction

Sexting is often seen as a technological, legal, sexual, and moral crisis. Widespread concern about sexting emerged in U.S. mass media in December 2008, when a national survey was released reporting that 20 percent of teenagers had sexted.[1] The term *sexting* refers to the creation and sharing of personal sexual images or text messages via mobile phones or internet applications, including Facebook, Snapchat, and email. Teen sexting is often framed as a form of child pornography or as part of a cyberbullying epidemic, and adult sexting is often discussed in terms of celebrity infidelity or political scandal. Yet for many people, the practice is a form of interpersonal intimacy and communication. According to one popular women's magazine, "The best sexts are like great foreplay" ("Sexting: Naughty Text Ideas," 2013). Though adults and teens alike engage in sexting, most of the anxiety and discussion about sexting is concentrated on the images that teenage girls create of themselves.[2]

Sexting raises key questions about privacy and consent in networked digital social environments,[3] but these vital issues can get buried beneath the widespread anxiety about girls' sexuality. The common sense ideas many people hold about technology, sexuality, and youth can lead to responses to sexting that are largely ineffective, such as strict sexting abstinence policies and the criminalization of consensual sexting. Such reactions often ignore privacy violators while implicitly erasing girls' sexual agency and blaming them for sexting in the first place. For example, in one case in Seattle, two cheerleaders were suspended for sexting while the boys who distributed their private images without permission were not punished at all (Blanchard, 2008). This book explores how the responses to sexting illustrate larger issues and debates about privacy in digital media, including the standards for consent, information ethics, and the nature of participation and agency in an information economy.

Along with all their benefits, new media also offer novel ways for people to harm one another. Distributing personal sexual images without permission can be a serious violation of privacy, sending unwanted sexual images or messages to other people can be harassment, and creating sexual images of people without their knowledge or consent can cause significant trauma. Longstanding gender and sexual norms that demonize teen girls' sexuality can exacerbate these kinds of violations, as teenage girls who sext consensually are often blamed, harassed, and humiliated by peers if someone distributes their private images. Likewise, when well-meaning adults prohibit sexting, they can in fact worsen the problem by implicitly shaming sexters whose privacy has been violated.

Though many people assume that teen sexting is always wrong and dangerous, the problematic effect of this assumption is that it becomes very difficult to see the distinctions between consensual sexting and the nonconsensual production or distribution of personal sexual images. This means that victims of such harm can be seen as equal participants and handed the same punishment (or an even greater one, such as in the Seattle case) as the people who deliberately violated their privacy. This book suggests that teens, and girls in particular, need protection from malicious peers and overzealous prosecutors, but to accomplish this it may also be necessary to recognize girls' agency and choices when they sext consensually. As Fine and McClelland (2006) explain, abstinence-only training may be counterproductive:

> Having skills merely to say no does not help young people make tough decisions, but instead simply drains decision-making from them and places them in the hands of more powerful others—the state, the media, advertisements, a partner, abuser, or predator. (p. 327)

The alternative is to understand young people's capacity for choice. It may be helpful to think about agency, for teen girls and for everyone, as always relative, constrained, and contextual. This book suggests that acknowledging girls' agency might help clarify the important distinction between willingly choosing to create and share an image of oneself and forwarding intimate images of other people without their permission to third parties.

Since the label "teen sexting" often does not differentiate between these behaviors, the most common and persistent way of dealing with sexting is to simply discourage the practice in any form. The message to sexters is that creating and sharing a private digital image is inherently risky. Yet, even the first survey about sexting found that most people understand the risks yet choose to trust the recipient of their private images ("Sex and Tech," 2008). Still, the simple logic of solving the problem at the source by preventing sexting is appealing, since sexting is indeed risky. It will continue to be risky even if all the legal and social changes this book suggests are implemented. And this risk makes it easy to blame sexters whose privacy has been violated. But how can a person who chose to trust someone bear more of the blame than the person who deliberately chose to harm her? While it may be useful to acknowledge and discuss risk, this discussion is problematic when it deflects responsibility from privacy violators.

Blaming those who are harmed by privacy violations also reflects larger cultural patterns in which women, and in particular, racialized, lower-income, queer, and trans women, are often constructed as deviant risk-takers and thus held responsible if they are sexually assaulted (e.g., Gotell, 2008). As feminist anti-rape advocates have argued for decades, no matter what risks a survivor of sexual assault may have taken, the perpetrator still bears all the culpability for harming and violating that person. Still, some observers assume that all mobile phone images should be considered public, and thus it is not possible to distinguish privacy violations from consensual sexting. However, as discussed in chapter 5, studies indicate that young people express relative clarity and consensus on the matter; most report that it is unacceptable for someone to forward an intimate sexual image that was intended to be private to a third party (Albury & Crawford, 2012; Hasinoff & Shepherd, 2014).

It is even easier to blame the consensual sexter who produced the image if the behavior is thought to be the result of some variety of individual pathology, which is often the assumption in legal, educational, and some scholarly discourses. Sexting is not usually framed as an explicit moral problem in the United States but is viewed instead as the result of personal biological or psychological weaknesses. Still-developing teen brains and teen hormone surges, self-esteem deficiencies, and susceptibility to sexualization in mass media are each thought to cause teen girls to sext. Much of the scholarly experimental literature on sexting is based on the assumption that there is something unusual and troubling about sexters. A number of studies examine correlations between sexting and other perceived risky or unsafe behaviors, such as alcohol consumption and unprotected sex, and the links to undesirable personality traits, such as impulsivity.[4] In a review article, Döring (2014) finds that 79 percent of the studies published on sexting emphasize the risks and link sexting to negative outcomes. The implicit question in a lot of the research on sexting seems to be: What kind of person would sext? And what exactly is wrong with this person?

This book takes a different view and assumes that, in most cases, teens and adults sext for simple and obvious reasons: because they enjoy it and because they trust the recipients of their images. As discussed in further detail in chapter 4, people of all ages, from teens to senior citizens, report that sexting can increase sexual communication and intimacy with a partner (especially in long-distance relationships), that it provides an outlet for sexual self-expression that can help people overcome inhibitions, and that many find it exciting, arousing, and fun. Indeed, an emerging body of research on sexting highlights the distinctions between consensual sexting and acts of harm that involve sexual images[5] and situates both the risks and benefits of sexting in their social context (Albury & Crawford, 2012; Albury et al., 2013; Cupples & Thompson, 2010; Karaian, 2012; Powell, 2010a, 2010b; Ringrose et al., 2012; Salter, Crofts, & Lee, 2013). Taken together, these studies suggest that consensual sexting is a normal, everyday part of some teenagers' and adults' romantic relationships and that the nonconsensual distribution of a private image can be a serious humiliation and violation. This work on sexting is consistent with the findings of a range of studies of mobile phones through the 2000s that offer a rich tradition of closely examining the role of the mobile phone in everyday life as a new tool for interpersonal communication that both reproduces existing social relations and encourages new forms of communication and new experiences of space and time (Fortunati, 2002; Goggin, 2006; Goggin & Hjorth, 2009; Gye, 2007; D.-H. Lee, 2009).

This book draws on feminist critiques of gender- and sexuality-based violence, queer critiques of the repression of nonnormative[6] sexual practices, and studies of the social construction of girlhood and adolescence in order to challenge the typical responses to sexting. The shift this book advocates is to frame sexting as an issue of consent and privacy. This is a significant departure from the usual discussions about sexting in academic, legal, media, and educational contexts, which often assume that sexters' personal pathologies are the cause and abstinence and criminalization are the solutions. Instead, this book positions sexting as a practice of personal sexual media production and use—consider sexting as the latest version of love letters, diary entries, suggestive Polaroid photographs, camcorder recordings, and phone sex. Consider as well that sexting is at once a sex act and a speech act. As with any other sex act, it is necessary to think about consent. And it is likewise important to consider privacy, which is a vital concern in many other kinds of speech acts that involve information production and distribution.

Sexting also demonstrates that current laws and norms of online privacy in the United States might be insufficient. Telling people to simply abstain from sexting because they can have no reasonable expectation of privacy reflects a problematic and increasingly common assumption that everything digital is public. This originates in both the early-internet-utopian idea that information should be free (Barlow, 1994) and the notion that privacy is dying out because of new media (Jeff Jarvis, 2011). It is perhaps no accident that these attitudes about information are convenient for media companies who seek to aggregate, distribute, and monetize users' personal information.

In critically analyzing the responses to sexting in the United States, this book also develops new ways of thinking about consent and privacy in digital media. By prioritizing consent in users' interactions with each other and with new media, the social, legal, and technological solutions this book proposes have broad implications for protecting privacy. To develop those ideas, this book relies on a range of new media scholars who raise interesting questions about the nature and value of participation and the importance of privacy and information ethics (Andrejevic, 2004; Barney, 2000, 2010; Nissenbaum, 2004, 2011; Solove, 2004). The problematic responses to sexting highlight issues of sexuality, gender, expression, and privacy and suggest that some of the existing models of new media production, participation, and distribution need to better account for consent.

Why is sexting illegal?

A key problem with teen sexting is that it can be legally classified as child pornography if the image is explicit enough and depicts a person under 18 years old. Advances in digital photography and distribution technologies have made it easy for many people to produce and distribute images of their sex acts. But child pornography laws make no exception for minors (people under 18 years old) who create sexually explicit images of themselves. Indeed, a number of teenagers in the United States involved in sexting have been charged with producing, possessing, and distributing child pornography (Pavia, 2011; Wolak, Finkelhor, & Mitchell, 2012a). In most U.S. states, two 17-year-olds can legally have sex, but if they create a digital image of their sex acts, even for their own use, this depiction can meet the legal definition of child pornography. This interesting contradiction emerges out of a long history of the regulation of teenage sexuality (Cocca, 2004; Odem, 1995) and concern about the harms and dangers of communications media in general and of sexual representations in particular (Heins, 2001; Levine, 2002). Moreover, it is illegal to investigate if there is, as the moral panic claims, a large "black market" for sexts on the internet—finding child pornography or even looking for it are illegal, even for a researcher. Thus, while this book is primarily concerned with the responses to teenagers' self-produced sexual images, the images themselves are not part of this research. The impossibility of viewing these images—for any researcher or journalist—means that the specifics of what they might contain involves considerable speculation.[7]

Though child pornography laws were designed to address adults who sexually exploit children, many forms of sexting can be technically illegal. It is particularly problematic that these laws make no distinction between consensual sexting and the nonconsensual production, distribution, or possession of private images. A teenager who chooses to send sexually explicit images to a peer is engaging in a very different activity than someone who distributes a private image with malicious intent or coerces another person to produce an explicit image; yet the law classifies all of these behaviors as felonies. U.S. federal laws began to specifically address child pornography in the late 1970s in response to a surge in public concern about child sexual abuse (Adler, 2001). As of this writing, there has been no specific Supreme Court decision on the constitutionality of prosecuting minors for child pornography offenses. Depictions involving minors are not protected speech under the First Amendment, and they do not need to meet the definition of obscenity that governs sexual depictions of adults (*New York v. Ferber*, 1982).[8] Because of this absolute prohibition on sexual images of minors, a prosecutor can use child pornography statutes against a teenager who creates, possesses, or distributes a sexually explicit image of herself.

Although a number of media reports imply that sexting images are always classified as child pornography, the laws governing which depictions actually qualify are complicated and subjective. U.S. federal law defines child pornography as a depiction of a person under 18 years old involved in "sexually explicit conduct."[9] While it is usually relatively clear if an image depicts a sex act, the law also considers "lascivious exhibition of the genitals or pubic area" as one type of such "explicit conduct."[10] One study found that nearly all sexting images their respondents described were not explicit enough to qualify as child pornography (Mitchell et al., 2012). At the same time, some prosecutors, judges, and nonspecialist attorneys interpret child pornography laws too broadly, leading many defendants to take a plea on suggestive images, such as topless photos, that would not technically qualify as child pornography (Richards & Calvert, 2009).

How can child pornography laws be used against the people they are intended to protect? One judge says to a prosecutor charging a minor with creating child pornography of herself: "It seems like the child here [is] . . . the victim, the perpetrator and the accomplice. I mean, does that make any sense? How does that make sense?" ("Temporary," 2009, p. 62). Indeed, this is possible because U.S. laws do not actually define a minimum age of consent or a minimum age for criminal responsibility.[11] Producing, distributing, or possessing child pornography is a crime, but the law includes no stipulation that the person must be at least 18 years old to be held responsible for it. Thus, while child pornography laws certainly imply that no one under 18 years old can consent to appearing in a sexually explicit picture, there is no specific age-based exemption, making it possible to hold minors legally responsible for an act to which they implicitly cannot consent. In a Florida case, a judge offers paradoxical logic for upholding the conviction of a teenage girl for sexting, explaining that she is "simply too young to make an intelligent decision about engaging in sexual conduct and memorializing it" (*A. H. v. State*, 2007, p. 239). According to this judge, and to the law, however, she is not too young to be held criminally responsible for her actions.

This book suggests that applying child pornography laws to teens who consensually use social media in their romantic and sexual relationships is a gross injustice. This harsh legal response to consensual sexting seems to occur with troubling frequency: According to one study, in 2009, an estimated 134 youth under 18 years old were arrested for consensually creating or sharing images "in the context of romantic relationships or for sexual attention-seeking" (Wolak, Finkelhor, & Mitchell, 2012c, p. 2). In the same year, an estimated 343 people under 18 years old were arrested for child pornography possession (Wolak, Finkelhor, & Mitchell, 2012b). According to these studies, child pornography possession and production arrests have significantly increased since 2000, and a proportion of that rise includes the increasing criminalization of minors.[12] These arrest numbers also do not include sexters who faced lesser legal consequences or who were punished at school or at home for consensual sexting.

Many youth studies scholars point out that legal structures impose a framework of normative sexual morality on young people, exerting a disproportionate amount of control on the sexual activity of girls in the name of protection, especially on low-income girls, girls of color, and queer girls (R. Alexander, 1995; Cocca, 2004; Devlin, 1998; Kunzel, 1993; Morton, 1993; Nathanson, 1991; Odem, 1995; Schlossman & Wallach, 1978). In discourses about sexting, observers tend to view the practice as inherently deviant and unsafe, thus demonizing a particular sex act rather than carefully examining abuses of power or trust and whether the alleged victim consented to the sexual activity or not. The criminalization of sexting limits teenagers' rights and can in effect criminalize many consensual sexual relationships between peers since intimate digital sexual communication is common. Further, these laws encourage victims of privacy violations or coerced sexting to blame themselves rather than the perpetrators.

Consider the following case. In Fall 2009, two young women in Oregon began dating. Antjuanece Brown was 19 years old and Jolene Jenkins was 16 when they met, and in the course of their relationship they exchanged some explicit text messages and suggestive photos. Jenkins's mother objected to her daughter dating a woman and so in the summer of the following year she took her daughter's cell phone and turned it over to local police. While the couple likely assumed their cell phone conversations were private, the prosecutor used the images and text messages they shared as evidence to press charges against Brown. She was originally charged with producing child pornography, which would have netted her six years in prison and mandatory sex offender registration. Ultimately Brown pleaded guilty to "luring a minor" and was in jail for more than a month. She lost her job at a call center because her workplace will not employ anyone with a felony conviction. At Brown's sentencing, her girlfriend, Jolene Jenkins, said: "I feel victimized by the state, not her" (Slovic, 2010). The disastrous and unjust results of this case illustrate the urgent need for legal and social reform to protect young people from the criminalization of their sexual practices. Brown's prosecution is likely not an isolated incident and may even be evidence of systematic bias in the criminal justice system, which has and continues to target queer people (D'Emilio, 1989; Spade, 2012; Sullivan, 1996) and people of color (M. Alexander, 2010; Davis, 2005) disproportionately—Brown and Jenkins are both African American.

This case garnered little national media attention. In fact, no national paper picked up the story. Instead, the top teen sexting stories of 2009 and 2010 were debates about new legislation in Vermont, Jessica Logan's suicide, the ACLU's victory against an overzealous prosecutor, and Philip Alpert, who was required to register as a sex offender because he forwarded his ex-girlfriend's nude photos to her friends, teachers, and family (Podlas, 2011). None of these cases involves people of color or queer youth and none directly addresses teen sexual rights— instead they are all framed either as legal debates or as evidence of the link between sexting and bullying. The fact that Brown's unjust conviction garnered so little attention is unsurprising. But it is important to note that the legal legacies that determine her fate emerge out of a set of mainstream discourses focused on the benevolent but misplaced desire to protect the supposedly inherent sexual innocence of white middle-class girls. This book unpacks the common sense assumptions underlying the problems with the responses to sexting in the United States and provides alternative ways of thinking about sexting that protect youth from harm and affirm their rights to self-expression.

Some judges, law enforcement officials, and media commentators believe that using child pornography laws against minors will help to protect them. These observers often assume that there is no such thing as safe sexting and that sexting usually has negative outcomes. Indeed, privacy violations can cause devastating harm, but, as this book explains, the rhetoric about the risks often exaggerates the actual danger and blames the consensual sexters for their failures to abstain from sexting. It may be more effective to focus on the most obvious, frequent, and direct forms of harm, which occur between peers (Englander, 2012; Ringrose et al., 2013). The challenge is that this is a problem with deep roots in gender and sexual norms and without simple, headline-friendly policy solutions.

The real problems with sexting are the same ones activists and researchers have been battling for decades on the issue of sexual violence: rape culture, victim-blaming, a discriminatory and counterproductive justice system, and systemic inequalities. Talking about sexting by panicking about deviant girls, predators, and pornographers is attractive because it sells papers and does not challenge mainstream views of gender and sexuality. Casting perpetrators as villains and monsters implicitly validates the dominant sex-gender system as basically sound and falsely locates harm and violence outside of everyday life and intimate relationships. Spade (2012) argues that the prison system reflects and exacerbates this problem, and he explains the importance of dismantling these assumptions: "If we deal with the complexity of how common violence is, and let go of a system built on a fantasy of monstrous strangers, we might actually begin to focus on how to prevent violence and heal from it" (p. 5). As chapter 5 suggests, steering violators away from prison cells and toward the retribution-based system of civil law might offer some practical ways to address harm between people who know or even love one another. At the same time, the larger project this book advocates is to focus on building and reinforcing norms of consent and privacy that work for and beyond new media.

It is unlikely that any of the systemic problems with gender- and sexuality-based violence will be solved, or even alleviated, by criminalizing sexting or advising abstinence. Many of the alternative solutions this book proposes follow from the observation that teen sexting, just like the adult variety, is not inherently deviant or pathological but that serious problems can occur with personal sexual images when there is a privacy violation, coercion, harassment, or transgression of consent and confidentiality. Unfortunately, the responses to sexting, especially from legislators, prosecutors, and youth educators, can make these problems worse by blaming and criminalizing sexters whose privacy has been violated.

The fear and promise of technology

Particularly in its early years, the internet seemed to offer the utopian demo-cratic promise that users and viewers could become producers instead of pas-sive audience members. Indeed, scholars point out that the internet is a place where young people can explore their identities and develop social and com-munication skills (boyd, 2008; H. Jenkins, 2006; Tynes, 2007). Henry Jenkins (2006) credits participatory cultures with providing youth with a long list of benefits: "opportunities for peer-to-peer learning, a changed attitude toward intellectual property, the diversification of cultural expression, the development of skills valued in the modern workplace, and a more empowered conception of citizenship" (p. 3). Celebrating youth media production that is newly vis-ible and potentially distributed to a far greater audience, these arguments often assume that such new practices of media production will help youth develop their critical faculties.

However, since mobile phones and the internet make producing and dis-tributing images extremely easy, they provide new venues for both sexual ex-pression between partners and for sexual harassment. Just as it is now easy to send a sexual partner a nude photo, it is also very easy for someone to send that photo to many other people. The data collection and surveillance capabilities of communication technologies also make both consensual teen sexuality and sexual harassment newly visible to adults and prosecutors, who sometimes view mobile phones and social network sites as the cause of sexist behaviors and sexual shaming.

Yet viewing technology as the root cause of sexting may not be the most accurate or productive position. When many communications and media tech-nologies were new, including the telegraph, telephone, radio, film, and TV, there was initially great optimism as well as considerable anxiety about their potential effects on society. Cassell and Cramer (2008) argue that these recur-ring moments of anxiety about new communication technologies often take on uniquely gendered dimensions, as the fear that girls will use these technologies in incorrect, frivolous, sexually inappropriate, and dangerous ways has repeated with the telegraph, telephone, and internet.[13] For example, Standage (1998) describes an 1886 popular periodical article entitled "The Dangers of Wired Love" (p. 136) that reports the story of a girl who pursued a relationship with a married man whom she met through the telegraph she operated in her father's store. Along with this recurring form of panic, in the U.S. imagination com-munications technologies also seem to offer great hope for the future and for democracy (Carey, 1989; Peters, 1999). This is especially true in discussions about youth and technology (Wartella & Jennings, 2000), each a symbol of the promise and anxiety of the future. As Thurlow (2007) explains, "On the one hand, young people are talked about as being somehow naturally technology inspired and literate, on the other hand, an image is promoted of young people being arch-consumers or tragic victims of technology" (p. 219). Indeed, the discussions about sexting are part of larger ongoing debates about new technologies, especially communications technologies, which tend to vacillate between extremes of fear and hope about their impact on society.

Sexting is perhaps so frightening and compelling precisely because of an expectation that new communications technologies should be inherently liberatory. Interaction, participation, and even active media consumption are often valorized as personally authentic actions that foster resistance to dominant ideologies. So if freedom for teenage girls is defined as freedom from sexuality, then the technology that enables sexting must look like a massive failure, and the blame for these dashed hopes for new media can fall on girls. Yet all media can be used for dangerous, damaging, silly, and frivolous things. Communications technologies structure, limit, and suggest certain uses, but do not determine them (Balsamo, 2011; Bijker, Hughes, & Pinch, 1987). Indeed, sexting seems to highlight the fact that new media does not automatically create the resistance to mass culture and meaningful democratic participation we hoped it would. As Barney (2010) and Andrejevic (2004) demonstrate, the celebration of participation in new media and the supposedly new active media user conceals the ways that participation can reinforce dominant political and economic structures.

Complicating agency

Though sexting provides new evidence of youth sexuality, this book illustrates the fact that observers still offer a range of excuses and explanations for teen girls' sexuality. Yet despite these excuses, girls are still blamed for sexting. As a result, girls seem to have agency in that their actions have an effect and they can be held responsible for them, but they also are constructed as lacking agency in that their choices are seen as inauthentic or not intentional. As I demonstrate in the chapters to come, people offer biological, psychological, and media-effects explanations for girls' sexual behavior. However, excuses for teen girls' sexuality typically adhere best to those with class, race, and other social privileges—the girls who are somewhat protected by a presumption of inherent innocence. Though such explanations for sexting are often sympathetic, they have a range of problematic side effects, especially since they can obscure the distinction between consensual sexting and malicious privacy violations and they imply that girls who create images should be the focus of educational and legal interventions.

Sexting is neither inherently liberating nor is it necessarily the result of coercion. The act of sharing an explicit photo of oneself can be done under extreme duress or with as much free will as any other choice. The problem with assuming that all girls who sext are passive victims is that it becomes difficult to recognize or understand girls' choices. While all people make choices within contexts they did not create, the dominant discourses about girls tend to entirely erase their capacity for agency in sexual decisions. This erasure of sexual agency appears to be especially prevalent in discourses about sexting (Angelides, 2013). This book suggests that recognizing girls' choices is a good way to avoid victim-blaming and to separate consensual sexting from acts that cause harm. In practical terms, this means that consensual sexting would never be criminalized and that educational interventions would focus on harassment and privacy violations rather than on the girls who create sexual images of themselves. Pushing past the attractively simple explanations that sexualization in media, or raging hormones, or low self-esteem causes sexting opens up spaces for thinking about the complexity of girls' agency.

The alternative explanations people tend to offer for sexting fit with dominant ideas that girls' sexual agency primarily consists of their refusal of male advances. It would disrupt such norms to offer a simpler explanation for why some girls might sext, such as, "because they enjoy it." Girls' active sexuality is often assumed to indicate some kind of deviant pathology or victimization by peers or mass culture, while teen boys' sexual interests and behaviors are often expected and tolerated. Using nonsexual explanations for sexting girls allows observers to express sympathy for those affected and criticize their behavior at the same time. Tolman says that in her decades of research she has often heard girls give excuses and apologies for their sexuality. She calls these "cover stories," which she describes as

> sanctioned ways that girls can speak about their sexual experiences, in which they are not blameworthy or even active participants. By saying "it just happened" or by being drunk, they have recourse from emotional, social and in some cases physical repercussions within a system that denies them their sexuality. (Tolman, 1999)

In discussions about sexting, adults also use a staggering variety of such "cover stories" to account for young female sexual behaviors without giving them any agency or responsibility for their sexuality. This is useful when it can garner sympathy and even leniency from a harsh criminal justice system, but there are other problematic implications.

Whether girls' supposed deficiencies in sexual agency are sympathetically lamented or condemned as pathological relates to assumptions about race, class, and sexuality. For privileged teenage girls, a perceived lack of sexual agency can help to redeem their innocence by shifting the blame for such sexual activities as sexting onto media sexualization, male pressure, and biology. Yet not all girls enjoy the privilege of inherent innocence. For example, the teenage pregnancies of low-income girls and girls of color are often characterized as irresponsible and careless while more privileged girls' pregnancies might be seen as accidental or unintentional (Luker, 1996; Tapia, 2005). Like privileged girls, structurally disadvantaged girls are also viewed as lacking agency, but in contrast, the explanations for their transgressions are less often admissible as excuses.

One of the key problems is that the focus on girls' lack of agency leads to policy and educational interventions that assume that girls—not men and boys—need to be controlled and managed and should undertake projects of personal improvement and change. Viewing girls' deficiencies in resisting sexualization and peer pressure as the problem usually leads to solutions that aim to increase teen girls' personal agency, which supposedly will prevent them from being victimized or making risky choices. The goal is to help girls strengthen their ability to voluntarily refuse and consent to sex. Yet, often this type of advice reinscribes long-standing moral judgments about sexuality under the pretext that girls with sexual agency will make the choice to avoid sexual activity outside committed long-term relationships.

There is a common assumption that girls are susceptible to mass culture and that this is a flaw or weakness to be overcome. Some scholarship in girls studies attempts to rectify the popular perception of this passivity by uncovering evidence of girls' agency. Driscoll (2008) argues that this kind of contemporary feminist girls studies became especially common in the early 1990s. She explains that in this mode of girls studies, "every indication of the conformity for which girls had become famous was mined for signs of agency" (p. 21). She critiques this part of the field for focusing on "evaluations of agency and conformity . . . when [these issues] have been abandoned as counterproductive in studies of women" (Driscoll, 2002, p. 169). Many scholars who study girls through audience research and ethnographic work argue that girls' voices need to be heard and prioritized. This research serves laudable goals and can offer valuable counterarguments to accusations that women and girls are passive. Yet by idealizing resistance, such studies sometimes view what counts as agency in a limited way. That is, they respond to the charge that girls are passive by arguing, "No, they are agents." The alternative is to answer these accusations by changing the terms of the question, which requires recognizing the continuities between passivity and agency and the impossibility of defining either without relying on normative expectations.

In order to develop new ways of thinking about sexting, it is necessary to reframe agency as relative and contextual for all people. As Abu-Lughod (2002) explains, agency must always be understood in context, as a social relation rather than as an absolute fact. She asks: "What does freedom mean if we accept the fundamental premise that humans are social beings, always raised in certain social and historical contexts and belonging to particular communities that shape their desires and understandings of the world?" (Abu-Lughod, 2002, p. 786). Adolescent girls, like all people, make choices to negotiate with social norms, institutions, and structures that they did not create. This begs the question: Why do discourses produce adolescent girls as lacking agency? What are the implications of assuming that girls lack sexual agency? How do these constructions of agency map onto race, class, gender, and age? How do they reinforce structural inequalities? Instead of uncovering an idealized agency in girls, a central task of this book is to examine the cultural and political effect of constructions of girls' agency and to develop alternative understandings of it.

Common sense

The fact that child pornography laws are vague enough and broad enough to use against sexting teenagers amplifies the panic about sexting: The label "child pornography" makes sexting seem more dangerous and deviant while the law allows prosecutors to pursue these cases, adding to the public discussion of the issue.[14] Sexting is a moral panic in Cohen's (2002) sense, since concern is exaggerated and focused on the wrong object. The target for the sexting panic is white middle-class teenage girls and their sexual choices[15] rather than the more pressing issue about sexuality: the pervasive and continuing problems of sexual violence and harassment, which I discuss in more detail throughout this book. Though there is an actual behavior to which the panic about sexting refers, the way that behavior is understood shapes the reactions to it. This book suggests that many mass media and policy reactions have so far exacerbated the problems and failed to effectively protect girls—or anyone—from sexual coercion or privacy violations. Thus, it is crucial to interrogate the concepts and assumptions that characterize mainstream understandings of sexting and underlie the problematic legal and policy responses to sexting.

To investigate these issues, I take a cultural studies approach to digital media by focusing on the construction of meaning about new technologies (Balsamo, 2011; Slack & Wise, 2005). Since the main problem with sexting is how legal authorities, youth educators, and policymakers are responding to it, I look to texts produced by these people to understand their assumptions about sexting. I analyze published texts because they offer a particular kind of edited, carefully worded common sense discourse. A press release or a newspaper article better represents the common sense assumptions of the organization that produced it than an interview with an individual, who might express personal opinions. Though fiction and nonfiction mass media alike draw on and produce common sense, follow generic conventions, and are institutionally produced, only nonfiction media see themselves as factual, objective, and true. Looking across a variety of texts, I select particular statements that are legitimated by rhetorics and practices of scientific truth, governmental authority, journalistic objectivity, and rational thought. A moral panic like sexting also provides copious examples of extreme and exaggerated discourse that is nevertheless positioned as common sense. These taken-for-granted ideas structure the way authorities think about the risks of sexting and how they respond to it, which can include ignoring privacy violators, prosecuting their victims, passing misguided laws, and expelling youth from school for their perceived transgressions. An analysis of common sense illuminates the roots of the problems with the responses to sexting in policy and legal contexts. (See appendix 2 for further discussion of methodology.)

Common sense is my object because I see it as the key agent in this story about the responses to sexting. It is a particular textual form that permits an analysis of the connections between nonfiction mass media and government.[16] Journalists, commentators, talk show hosts, and political actors create and contest common sense by drawing on preexisting assumptions and by working to produce their particular position as rational and logical. Common sense is the prevailing set of facts and assumptions that are by definition (at least temporarily) authorized and agreed-upon through the consensus that these organizations and institutions produce in talking to and about one another. It is not a fixed way of seeing the world, but a category of knowledge that is historically contingent, malleable, and constantly produced, reproduced, and contested. My model of common sense builds on Cook's study of the interactions between news and policy and the implications of that relationship. Cook (2005) argues: "Not only is the news a 'coproduction' of the news media and government, but policy today is likewise the result of collaboration and conflict among newspersons, officials, and other political actors" (p. 3). The implications of this intimate connection between news and the state are profound: "News values become political values, not only within the news media but within government as well" (Cook, 2005, p. 140). I focus especially on news because it is often the outcome of a conversation and negotiation between institutions, including journalism itself, other nonfiction mass media, the branches of government, and a range of organizations.

While common sense typically aligns with dominant interests, it is a shared understanding that emerges through the struggle between institutions as they speak to and about one another. This shared set of assumptions then in turn dictates what these institutions can say and still be recognized as reasonable and legitimate. Because power is dispersed and negotiated among a network of interrelated groups of interests and actors (Foucault, 1980), all groups must draw on common sense even as they attempt to change it—otherwise they will not be heard or recognized as a legitimate part of the debate. Understanding the common sense assumptions that adhere to any social issue is a prerequisite for changing how we think about it.

This book draws on common sense while trying to change it at the same time. The challenge is to speak in multiple registers that do not compromise each other. The first that I offer is to shift the protectionist discourses by arguing that instead of protecting girls from themselves, as the dominant response to sexting suggests, all teens need protection from the state's criminalizing overreach and from privacy violators. When the problem is framed in this way, better solutions can emerge to protect everyone from harassment and privacy violations. With this, I reproduce a common sense argument that girls are vulnerable and in need of protection. At the same time, the second, less commonsensical intervention this book offers is the contention that teen girls have sexual agency, which, as discussed earlier, is as contextual and relational as it is for adults. As such, I maintain that girls have the right to view and create sexual media. While these two positions are complementary, readers need not follow me all the way to rethinking girls' sexual agency to understand and support the protectionist arguments and the legal and educational reforms that I suggest. My study of common sense is fundamentally in service of changing it, and to that end this book offers a range of alternative ways of thinking about mediated sexuality, privacy, and consent in the chapters that follow.

Chapters

Part I has three chapters that each illustrate a problematic way that media, legislators, legal officials, and youth educators often think about sexting: as a criminal problem (chapter 1), a biological problem (chapter 2), and as a psychological problem (chapter 3).

Chapter 1 examines the problems with folding sexting into the criminal justice system and argues that consensual sexting should be decriminalized. This chapter examines the consensus in two unique cases that were sympathetic to teenage sexters but stopped short of arguing for their right to sext. In the first, the American Civil Liberties Union supported three girls who were threatened with child pornography charges by an overzealous prosecutor. Instead of making a freedom of expression claim, existing child pornography laws compelled the ACLU lawyers to argue instead that the images were nonsexual and thus should not be subject to prosecution. The second case is the development of Vermont's sexting legislation in 2009. Though legislators initially proposed a relatively sensible decriminalization bill to prevent teens from being charged with child pornography offenses, after national outrage the state instead passed a misdemeanor bill that criminalized a wider range of images than child pornography laws previously covered. Though the decriminalization advocates were careful to state that they did not support or condone sexting, their proposal was swiftly defeated. The limited terms of sympathy for consensually sexting girls in the first case and the results of legislative reform in Vermont each sets a disturbing precedent at the national level that teen sexting would be prohibited. Many states have adopted similar misdemeanor laws that offer prosecutors the option of using a lesser charge than child pornography against sexters but often include more images in their purview and do not address privacy violations at all. In short, since 2009, teen sexting has become more illegal in many states, and there are still few effective ways to address coercion, harassment, or privacy violations that do not shame or criminalize consensual sexters.

This chapter critiques the consensus that sexting must be criminalized and suggests an alternative legal framework. One of the key problems is the uneven application of the law. Since sexting is a relatively common behavior and decades of research have demonstrated systemic racism and homophobia in the justice system, both new sexting misdemeanors and existing child pornography laws are likely being disproportionately applied to queer youth, lower-income youth, and youth of color. Laws against sexting are particularly troubling because they expand parents' and schools' control over adolescents' sexual choices. While the First Amendment and some recent decisions about child pornography online could provide a potential constitutional defense for teens' right to sext, decriminalizing sexting on free speech grounds is an unpopular position. Based on the consensus in the debate about sexting, I argue that the most practical way to decriminalize sexting may be to regulate consensual sexting like other teen sex acts by using age-spans that account for consensual sexual practices between peers. As a consensual, intimate practice, it makes sense to think about teen sexting like any other sex act. Though sexting is also a speech act, this matters much more in privacy violations, which chapter 5 discusses in greater detail.

Chapter 2 questions the popular explanation that sexting is the result of teenage hormones and still-developing brain structures dangerously alchemizing with new technologies. Some observers are concerned that teens are biologically incapable of using the internet and mobile phones rationally and responsibly. Particularly since the early 2000s, teen misbehavior has been attributed to their brains. New MRI studies show structural differences in teens' brains and point to evidence that interacting with digital media alters teens' developing brain structures. Yet, critics argue that the brain changes constantly in response to all stimuli and that the observed differences between teenage and adult brains could just as easily be the result of the social constraints on adolescents. Detractors from the biological model of adolescence insist that the differences between teen and adult behavior are primarily socially constructed, since most teenagers have few legal rights or economic responsibilities.

Like the desexualization of sexting discussed in the previous chapter, blaming the practice on teens' brains and hormones can indeed achieve short-term goals by encouraging authorities to be sympathetic rather than punitive. But this type of sympathy is dangerous because it reaffirms the common assumption that teens have no genuine sexual agency and thus do not deserve the right to sexual expression. Perhaps even more troubling, these biological narratives can often serve in a backhanded way to blame the victims of privacy violations and harassment. Instead of discussing privacy violators and systemic problems of gender- and sexuality-based violence, narratives of irrational teen brains causing risky technology use can shift all the attention and condemnation back onto the victim as a risk-taker.

A girl's role in this dominant biological model is to work against the sexual desires that supposedly originate in the chaos of her physiology. The discourse of sexual development acknowledges adolescent female sexuality but maintains that this sexuality needs protection, control, and management. As early work in queer theory made clear, sexuality is inseparable from discourse, culture, and subjectivity. While this position is still controversial outside the field, it is even less common in relation to youth sexuality. For young people, assumptions about the biology of sexuality are particularly enduring. Complicating the biological determinism in ideas about teens' mental capacity and sexuality means abandoning some of the easiest ways to gain sympathy for young people who transgress. Yet, it may be the only way to adequately recognize young people's choices and grant them the rights they deserve.

Chapter 3 examines the construction of sexting as a symptom of low self-esteem and the subsequent advice that mass media and public service announcements offer girls. A range of nationally distributed U.S. public service announcements (PSAs) as well as informal advice to girls in newspaper coverage of sexting implores teenage girls to raise their self-esteem and "think before you post" in order to prevent them from making supposedly risky sexual decisions online. This advice to girls reconfigures existing discourses of "girl power" by counseling sexual self-control as a strategy for achieving and demonstrating high self-esteem. While this might seem like sound advice, it unfairly holds girls responsible for preventing harassment. Further, as with the other excuses for girls' sexuality, white, middle-class, heterosexual girls' sexuality is more likely to be seen as the result of low self-esteem while less privileged girls may be seen as pathologically deviant—though all girls are viewed as in need of more self-esteem.

Discourses of self-esteem have been dominant in girl-centered programming since the late 1990s. Yet, critics argue that low self-esteem is a symptom rather than a cause of the many social issues it is blamed for. Nonetheless, low self-esteem is often viewed as a problem that can and should be solved—in and of itself and independent of social context—through girl-empowerment strategies that primarily consist of self-discipline. The postfeminist, postrace logic that underlies the focus on self-esteem is that our structural problems and inequalities have been solved, so now the task of social justice falls to individuals, who simply need to adjust their attitudes to take advantage of the equal playing field they have been given. Like the discourses of biology, shifting the conversation to some quality of the sexter (in this case her low self-esteem), allows privacy violators to escape blame. Moreover, despite the common sense logic of the idea that girls who sext must be suffering from low self-esteem, there is little compelling evidence that high self-esteem actually leads to more cautious choices. In most of the mainstream educational materials about online safety and sexting, girls are the primary target of attention and intervention. Like the victim-blaming rhetoric of rape myths that still persist despite decades of feminist intervention, online safety advice for girls repeats the same victim-blaming mythology.

Part II continues the critique of the dominant responses to sexting, complicating the imagined connections to sexualization in media and disputing the common ideas that privacy is dead and sexts will always be distributed. This second half of the book also offers new ways of thinking about sexting that considers the practice, in chapter 4, as media production and, in chapter 5, as private intimate communication.

Chapter 4 discusses the tension between the idea that participatory new media practices typically produce positive, democratic effects and the assumption that sexualization creates a problematic type of new media practice—sexting. Drawing on postcolonial feminist scholars who question the normative definitions of agency, I argue that the complexities of sexting suggest that resistance and participation might be overvalued ways of interacting with mass culture.

Dominant models of adolescent sexuality in scholarly and popular contexts often maintain that media can have only a negative impact on girls' sexuality. As such, consensual sexual practices that are mediated by mobile phones or the internet are assumed to be evidence of sexual deviance or of victimization by either another person or by sexualization in mass media. Sexualization has been a common explanation for many gendered social problems since the mid-2000s, though a range of critics point out that these popular and state-sponsored discourses often oversimplify media effects and rely on a politics of respectability that often demonizes working-class femininities. Another problem is that the solutions to sexualization that are typically offered are that girls (rather than men and boys) need to gain more agency to resist the supposedly controlling influence of mass culture. Discourses criticizing girls for sexting sometimes blame them for contributing to the problem of sexualization and, as a result, for broadly promoting the sexual exploitation of children. This chapter interrogates the stakes of pathologizing conformity to mass culture and suggests that the supposedly deficient agency of girls who create sexual photographs of themselves should not be a primary site for intervention.

This chapter maintains that it could be useful to think about sexting as media production but at the same time contests the common assumption that media participation is inherently good. Thinking about sexting as a form of media production, which has a basically positive connotation for youth, suggests the need to consider the potential benefits of sexting, such as intimacy and interpersonal communication, alongside the well-known risks. "Media production" also references discussions about ownership and authorship in social media environments, which helps to separate consensual practices from malicious privacy violations and harassment. If legislators and legal authorities thought of consensual sexting as a creative form of self-expression, they might shift their focus away from criminalizing teens who produce sexts and instead concentrate on developing legal structures to protect adolescents (and adults) from the distribution of their private images. If youth educators saw sexting as a form of media production, they could center their efforts on discouraging unauthorized image sharing and talking to youth about online privacy and sexual discrimination.

Chapter 5 argues that sexting illustrates the need for better policies and a more robust conversation about social norms of privacy online. Many people believe that sexting must be prohibited because of the myth that private images will always be distributed. As Nissenbaum (2011) argues, it is important to find ways to transfer and modify existing offline privacy practices to online interactions. That is, while most mobile phone users typically do not violate the privacy of personal sexual images, many laws, media discourses, and educational interventions assume that privacy is impossible. Indeed a troubling notion that all digital information is public seems to be emerging. While the idea that freeing information from all constraints and regulations seems to support individual freedom, the state and corporations stand to gain the most from the free circulation of personal information.

By considering sexting as a form of intimate communication, it is clear that current models of privacy and information flows online do not adequately account for consent. Building on feminist theories of sexual consent and pushing back against the view that all information should be free, I propose a framework for privacy that requires explicit consent for the circulation of any private information. Thinking about consent in the circulation of media leads to a range of alternative responses to privacy violations. If legislators and legal authorities thought more about consent, they would not criminalize teens who produce sexts and could instead focus on developing legal structures to protect adolescents (and adults) from the distribution of their private images. If educators considered consent in social media, they could concentrate their efforts on discouraging unauthorized image-sharing and talking to youth about online privacy and sexual harassment.

Though copyright is relatively well protected, my model of explicit consent responds to the issue that the circulation of information can create harms that are not merely financial. Developing better ways of protecting information for reasons other than commercial gain would have wide implications not only for sexting but for restricting how media companies collect and use personal information, offering user-controlled privacy protections on digital devices, and reforming privacy laws to better protect individuals. There is a need to set limits on the free circulation of personal information that are attuned to power—currently controlling the flow of information in the service of profit and crime prevention are the only reasons well supported by law and policy. This chapter contends that privacy should be seen as context-dependent, not technology- or format-dependent.

This book offers a resource for people who care about protecting teenagers from gender- and sexuality-based victimization (whether from peers, exploitative adults, or the justice system), about upholding young people's rights to self-expression, and about broader issues of privacy and consent in new media. Specifically, it details an alternative version of common sense that might one day come to replace the current assumptions that are at the root of the problems with the responses to sexting. To that end, this book offers models of social media production and participation that can better account for privacy and consent. Integrating sexting into broader debates about new media both pushes the limits of these debates and sheds light on sexting by asking that it be viewed as a new media practice rather than a moral crisis, a biological or psychological problem, or a crime. Though no doubt the next panic about youth, technology, and sexuality will repeat many of the same problems while seeming to be completely new and different, this book offers an archive of some of the pitfalls of this kind of moral panic as well as a way out through a critique of common sense.

PART I

Typical responses to sexting

CHAPTER 1

The criminalization consensus and the right to sext

Freedom of expression and access to information have been particularly idealized since the early internet. Yet the discussion of young people's information rights regarding their access to or creation of sexual media is virtually nonexistent. That minors should be protected from seeing representations of sexuality is so deeply embedded in common sense that the harmful effects of these prohibitions are rarely discussed (Levine, 2002). Despite the restrictions, many youth access sexual content online (Wolak, Mitchell, & Finkelhor, 2007) and some break laws in order to create and share sexual images (Mitchell et al., 2012). This book argues that granting young people the right to consensually see, create, and distribute sexual media may be the most effective way to protect them from harm.

By examining and critiquing the consensus that teens should have no right to sext, in this chapter I argue for the decriminalization of consensual teen sexting. The first half of this chapter covers two cases at the beginning of the moral panic about sexting in 2009. In these two debates, shared assumptions on both sides illustrate that, in the mainstream discussion about teen sexuality and digital media, nearly everyone agrees that teenagers should not be sexting and should have no right to do so.

The second half of the chapter outlines arguments for why adolescents should have the legal right to sext. While this position may be unpopular, it could help address some of the problems with criminalization. Allowing teens to sext could accomplish three things: (1) shielding youth from discriminatory prosecutions for consensual behavior; (2) enabling youth to seek recourse against privacy violators without incriminating themselves; and (3) confirming that young people are entitled to free expression. Despite these compelling reasons, it is unlikely that arguments for adolescents' right to sexual self-expression will be positively received in mainstream legal, media, and educational contexts. It may be more practical to think about regulating consensual sexting as a sex act (rather than a speech act), using the same age-span exemptions that exist in most statutory rape laws. This solution is imperfect, but it highlights the intimate relational context of consensual sexting and could also solve many of the problems with current sexting prohibitions.[1]

The consensus

A consensus is emerging in U.S. mass media that the criminal justice system should deal with sexting.[2] For example, well-known internet law expert and on-line safety advocate Perry Aftab argues: "The laws are either too hot or too cold and we need to make sure we find one that is just right" (Marks, 2009). Many commentators condemn sexting and insist that the teens involved should be punished—indeed, the following chapters include quotations from a number of these people. However, in this chapter I analyze two cases in which people in national mainstream media outlets defend sexting teenagers. I chose these cases because they are unique in this respect. They allow for an analysis of the outer limits of the dominant discourse about sexting, since in both cases even teen sexters' strongest supporters stop far short of supporting their right to sext.

The first case involves three teenage girls who, with the help of the Pennsylvania American Civil Liberties Union (ACLU), successfully prevented an overzealous prosecutor from punishing them for sexting. Because of existing child pornography laws, the ACLU has to defend the girls by dodging around the fundamental issue of youth rights to sexual self-expression.[3] Instead, their strategy is to reiterate the common sense position that sexting is "foolish" and "wrong." The second case is the development of new sexting legislation in Vermont, where legislators originally proposed to decriminalize some forms of sexting. After national pressure they passed a new misdemeanor law that criminalizes a broader range of sexting practices. As one of the first such laws, Vermont's became a model for other states to follow. The consensus that teens should not have the right to sext is so broad that even though the lawmakers who originally advocated decriminalization were clear that their reform did not condone sexting, they still had to abandon their proposal.

In both the Pennsylvania case and the Vermont debate, both sides agree that teens should not have the right to sext. While the ACLU was compelled to avoid addressing the right to sext in order to make the best case for its clients, Vermont legislators could have theoretically taken any approach to argue for legal reform. Yet, the social limits on the discourse about teen sexuality and technology are such that Vermont legislators are also bound by unspoken, taken-for-granted restrictions on the range of ideas and political positions that mainstream news and politics considers to be part of a valid and reasonable debate. Hallin (1986) describes this as the "sphere of legitimate controversy." As it turns out, the debate about what the criminal penalties for sexting should be (a misdemeanor or a felony) constitutes two sides of a "legitimate controversy." The assertion that consensual sexting should not be a crime at all is absent in mainstream discourses and thus is located, in Hallin's terms, in the "sphere of deviance." In these two cases, in which teen sexters enjoy some of the most sympathetic support of any mainstream media coverage of sexting, the right to sext is still so unthinkable that it is excluded from the discussion entirely.

THE LIMITS OF SYMPATHY
IN *MILLER V. SKUMANICK*

In early 2009, parents of nearly twenty students at a high school in Tunkhannock, Pennsylvania, received a letter from district attorney George Skumanick that opened with this statement: "[Your child] has been identified in a police investigation involving the possession and/or dissemination of child pornography" (Searcey, 2009b). Skumanick explained that school officials had found sexually explicit photos on some of the students' cell phones, and those appearing in or possessing the photos could face child pornography charges unless they agreed to complete an education program and serve six months of probation, including random drug testing (Munley, 2009; Walczak, Burch, & Kreimer, 2009; Zetter, 2009).

Most of the students agreed to a version of this deal, while three students and their parents sought the help of the Pennsylvania American Civil Liberties Union (ACLU) to resist Skumanick's demands. In March 2009, ACLU attorneys obtained a restraining order preventing the filing of child pornography charges.[4] In a press release, the ACLU describes the images: "One [photograph] shows Marissa Miller and Grace Kelly from the waist up wearing white bras. The other depicts Nancy Doe (a pseudonym) . . . standing outside a shower with a bath towel wrapped around her body beneath her breasts" (2009). The ACLU argued that the photos did not meet the definition of child pornography and there was no evidence that the girls disseminated the photos.

The sympathy for sexting girls in this case is contingent on assertions that the photos were not intended to be sexual and on the notion that teenagers sext because they are innately irresponsible. For example, the lead ACLU attorney routinely refers to the girls as "careless," "irrational," and "foolish" in interviews with the press. These insults garner compassion and leniency, as the Miller case is one of the few in which mainstream media view girls who sext in a sympathetic light. The girls' supporters, however, still cannot defend their right to freedom of expression. Instead, the ACLU won the case by arguing that forcing the girls to attend Skumanick's education program would violate their parents' right to control the upbringing of their children and the girls' right to freedom from compelled speech (*Miller v. Skumanick*, 2009; Walczak, Rose, & Burch, 2010). While the ACLU's rhetoric is overwhelmingly sympathetic to the girls, its exclusive focus on desexualization and innocence—that the girls took the photos for "fun" and were topless only because of the summer heat—precludes a larger discussion about teenagers' right to freedom of expression.

The Miller case[5] offers the opportunity to examine explanations for sexting in a specific, well-documented case. Both the ACLU and Skumanick agree that adolescents are not entitled to the same rights as adults.[6] The only major disagreements between the two sides are whether to monitor, control, and guide adolescent sexuality through the legal system or through parental and school-based instruction, and whether the photos in question actually qualify as child pornography. The similar assumptions on both sides illustrate the limits on the discussion about teen expression and sexual rights in mainstream media and legal discourses about these issues.

DESEXUALIZING SEXTING The unprecedented victory for the girls in the Miller case is dependent on their ability to prove that the images they created were not intended to be "sexual." In the press and in the courtroom, the girls' supporters refer to hot weather, the context of a girls-only sleepover, and the types of bras the girls wore to desexualize their images and reclassify them as naive and innocent. Removing sexual agency from sexting may work to garner sympathy for some girls, but this rhetorical strategy ultimately reaffirms restrictions on girls' rights and freedom.

Without a constitutional challenge to child pornography laws, which make no exception for self-produced images, the ACLU cannot effectively argue for the girls' right to freedom of expression. Instead, the ACLU chooses the best strategy to win the case. ACLU attorneys dispute the prosecutor's claim that the photos qualify as child pornography, arguing that since the photos of the teens were "harmless," "fun," and "not sexual," they do not qualify as child pornography under even the vaguest part of Pennsylvania law. This law prohibits "nudity if such nudity is depicted for the purpose of sexual stimulation or gratification of any person who might view such depiction" (18 PS § 6312) and thus could potentially apply to a wide range of sexting images. Pennsylvania child pornography law is specific enough that photos of girls in bras would likely not qualify as "nudity," though the photo of Nancy Doe's breasts could. However, the ACLU reports that at the initial meeting with parents, Skumanick (2009) informed them that he "has the authority to prosecute girls photographed in underwear . . . or even in a bikini on the beach, because the photos are 'provocative.'" Furthermore, as Skumanick says to the press, he could prosecute all the photos on the lesser and even vaguer charge of "open lewdness" (Zetter, 2009).

As such, the rhetoric that desexualizes the girls' images is crucial. It is precisely the subjective determination of whether a photo is provocative or lewd that can distinguish a legal photo of a topless female minor from an illegal one. The ACLU thus must maintain that the images in question are not intended to express sexuality so they are less likely to qualify as child pornography. The ACLU attorneys defend the topless photo of one of the girls by arguing that it is "an innocent artistic image of a minor in a state of simple partial nudity, not a sexually provocative image intended to titillate" (Walczak et al., 2009, p. 29). This strategy is indeed successful, as the federal circuit courts handling this case agree that even the topless photo would likely not be found to qualify as child pornography at trial (Ambro, Chagares, & Stapleton, 2010; Munley, 2009). However, when the ACLU attorneys make these arguments, they also reaffirm that adolescents do not deserve the same right to freedom of expression as adults. The ACLU is not challenging the constitutionality of Pennsylvania's child pornography statute, but instead argues that it has simply been misapplied to these girls' "innocent" images (Walczak et al., 2009, p. 44).

Another way that sexting is desexualized in this case is through rhetoric that it is merely a popular teen fad. In his decision in the Miller case, the judge comments: "At issue in this case is the practice of 'sexting,' which has become popular among teenagers in recent years" (Munley, 2009, p. 1). He thus suggests that Skumanick may be overreacting to the latest teen trend, a relatively harmless activity. The judge's comments imply that teens' actions are neither serious nor intentionally criminal, since they are just following a fad established by their peers. Skumanick disagrees and explicitly refutes the judge's and the ACLU's argument that sexting is merely a "trend," commenting on the case, "You can't call committing a crime fun or a prank. If you do that, you can rob a bank because you think it's fun" (Feyerick & Steffen, 2009). Since child pornography laws are so vague, asserting that sexting is "trendy," "fun," "innocent," "artistic," and "not intended to titillate" serves to desexualize sexting and help win the girls' case.

A number of news stories that appear generally sympathetic to the teens in the Miller case stress specific details about the conditions of the photos' production to convey the teens' innocence. One narrative that appears a number of times is that the girls removed their shirts because of the summer heat, and another portrays the incident as "just girls having fun." An Associated Press story that was also picked up by ABC News positions the photos as nonsexual:

> One summer night in 2007, a pair of 13-year-old northeastern Pennsylvania girls decided to strip down to their skivvies to beat the heat. As Marissa Miller talked on the phone and Grace Kelly flashed a peace sign, a third girl took a candid shot of the teens in their white bras. It was harmless, innocent fun, the teens say. (Rubinkam, 2009)

A CNN story also draws on heteronormative assumptions about girls' sleepover parties to de-eroticize this homosocial space, providing Marissa Miller's argument that the photo was taken in "fun," not to be sexual: "[Miller] was 12 when she and a friend snapped themselves wearing training bras. 'I wasn't trying to be sexual. . . . I was having fun with my friends at a sleepover, taking pictures, dancing to music'" (Feyerick & Steffen, 2009). An ACLU lawyer representing the girls repeats the same sentiment in a TV news interview, that it was innocent and that the exposed underwear was due only to hot weather (Galanos, 2009). These narratives present the girls wearing only bras as incidental and "fun" rather than as a planned intention to attract (male) sexual attention.

Describing the girls' bras as "training bras" also positions them as prior to the onset of sexuality and as a strong piece of evidence that the photo was "fun" rather than sexual, as if the two were mutually exclusive. The AP story reports Marissa saying: "It was a first-ever bra that your parents buy you, an old grandma bra" (Rubinkam, 2009), and a *Wall Street Journal* story quotes her explaining, "It was like an old grandma bra. Nothing skimpy" (Searcey, 2009b). These comments draw on assumptions about the temporality of female sexuality, which is presumed to exist neither while parents still control the purchase of training bras nor after a certain age at which a woman would presumably become an asexual grandmother. The comments about the type of bra, the summer heat, and the sleepover deploy assumptions about female sexuality to argue that the teenage girls did not intend to provoke or sexually stimulate a hypothetical viewer of the photos. Such assumptions seem to work in securing the injunction from the federal judge as well as public sympathy.

I make no claim here about the actual intent of the photos. The point is that arguing that they are nonsexual is the only option for the girls' supporters.

One of the few arguments in support of the girls that can acknowledge sexuality does so by folding sexting into a normative framework of adolescent sexual development. An amicus brief for the case by the Juvenile Law Center references "the well-recognized adolescent need for sexual exploration" in combination with technology to explain why teens are sexting (Levick & Shah, 2009, p. 6). The Center argues that sexting is an innocent "expression of normal adolescent sexual exploration" rather than for the purpose of "sexual gratification," which would be illegal (Levick & Shah, 2009, p. 20). These kinds of comments emerge from a legal and social context in which adolescents do not have the capacity or the right to pursue sexual pleasure. Instead, as chapter 2 discusses, they are thought to need adult intervention to ensure that they properly fulfill their developmental needs through limited sexual "exploration." The underlying goal of such exploration is not sexual pleasure, but to fulfill the scientifically sanctioned aim of becoming a sexually healthy adult. While arguments like these can affirm some forms of adolescent sexuality, they still do not affirm teens' sexual autonomy and privacy.

ABANDONING FREEDOM OF EXPRESSION The ACLU's strategy of desexualizing sexting and clarifying that it does not condone it mobilizes both public and judicial sympathies. However, to do this the ACLU has to put itself in the strange position of seeking to protect some legal rights for teens while simultaneously reproducing the broader popular discourse that dictates that since teens are inherently inferior, irresponsible, and immature, they do not deserve the same rights as adults. The ACLU contends that forcing the girls to attend Skumanick's educational program infringes on their freedom from compelled speech and on their parents' freedom from excessive state intrusion in the upbringing of their children. Yet, the ACLU's public statements also deploy some common sense arguments that position teens as unworthy of basic rights. The ACLU argues that sexting teens should not be prosecuted because they are too immature and foolish to be held accountable for their actions. This rhetoric helps desexualize the photos, but it is at odds with the idea that teens have other rights; for example, if they are so irrational and out of control, why should they have freedom from compelled speech? While the ACLU is known for its defenses of freedom of expression rights, it can best represent these clients by choosing a strategy that reproduces the dominant discourses that sexting is fundamentally dangerous, wrong, immature, and foolish rather than trying to protect their free speech rights.[7]

The ACLU's strategy of arguing that sexting teens are irresponsible and thoughtless means that the right to sext is off the table in this discussion. The ACLU wins its case with the best legal tactic it can, but in doing this, it produces the girls as subjects who do not want or need the right to express themselves sexually. In a TV news interview (figure 1), the host asks the lead ACLU attorney in the Miller case, Witold Walczak: "You're not saying—I want to be clear about this—that kids have the right to sext," to which Walczak replies that he agrees "absolutely" that teens do not have the "right to sext" (Galanos, 2009). Though the tagline of the news program asks, "Is 'sexting' a first amendment right?" the answer in the segment is a clear "no." Even the ACLU attorneys, the most vociferous defenders of First Amendment rights, are not arguing that sexting could be considered a protected form of speech for this case.[8] Walczak continues in the interview: "Anytime you take a digitized image of yourself in an embarrassing or compromised position, you're asking for trouble" (Galanos, 2009). Walczak is not only agreeing that teens do not have the "right to sext" and that nothing but "trouble" can ever come of it, he is also implying that girls should modify their behavior accordingly.

In many of the ACLU's public statements about the case, attorneys argue that the teens should not face felony charges because they are "immature" and "foolish." In the ACLU press release, which was widely used in newspaper articles about the case, Walczak (2009) calls the girls "irresponsible and careless," and news articles quote Walczak saying that sexting is "stupid, careless, naive, poor judgment—all of the things that teenagers are" (Marks, 2009) and that "teens are stupid and impulsive and clueless" (Zetter, 2009). Attempting to garner sympathy for young sexters, Walczak insists with these statements that teenagers should not be held legally accountable for their actions because they have no criminal intent and in fact barely have the ability to control or judge their own actions. Though ignorance of the law is not a legal defense, in this case it may be a publicly compelling one. This presumed ignorance of the law and of sexuality in general is especially important for the ACLU's argument that Miller and her friends accidentally created innocent photos that are now being misinterpreted as provocative.

The ACLU and media commentators who oppose felony prosecutions maintain that adolescents' ignorance and carelessness dictate that they need to be taught about the dangers of sexting. In a widely reproduced ACLU press release, Walczak argues that instead of charging youth with producing child pornography, they should be educated about the dangers and consequences of sexting (2009). In a Reuters story, Walczak says: "This country needs to have a discussion about whether prosecuting minors as child pornographers

FIGURE 1. Mike Galanos says, "It's not right, girls"
(CNN, March 30, 2009). Source: CNN

for merely being impulsive and naive is the appropriate way to address the serious consequences that can result from sexting" (Hurdle, 2009). These comments stress that while prosecution may be too harsh for teens who are "merely impulsive," they still need adults to inform them about the consequences of sexting. This might seem like common sense, but in fact surveys indicate that adolescents are aware of the potential risks of sexting ("Sex and Tech," 2008) but may choose to sext anyway because of the potential benefits. Statements about the need to instruct foolish youth on these risks also reproduce damaging assumptions about teenage carelessness and irrationality. Though here they are deployed to garner compassion, the same set of ideas underlies the commonly accepted logic that adolescent sexuality, particularly for girls, needs to be carefully controlled and harshly punished.

FELONY OR MISDEMEANOR?
DECRIMINALIZATION DEBATES IN VERMONT

Many states that have pursued legal reform have developed new misdemeanor crimes specific to minors who produce, possess, and/or distribute nude or sexually explicit digital images (Greenberg, 2011). By maintaining that sexting should be at the very least a misdemeanor offense, U.S. state laws reflect the dominant idea that teenagers should not have the right to sext. These new laws are particularly problematic because many of them target minors who trans-

33

mit images of themselves rather than a person who has maliciously forwarded such an image without permission. News commentators, legislators, and law enforcement officials seem to universally praise new laws like Vermont's that classify sexting as a misdemeanor offense because of the expectation that this will protect youth from overly harsh child pornography convictions and from the harms of sexting. Unfortunately laws like this one do neither.

After intense pressure and national media attention, Vermont legislators abandoned a bill exempting teens from child pornography charges and instead passed a new law criminalizing sexting as a misdemeanor. The result is that most young people in Vermont can still be subject to child pornography convictions, but prosecutors now also have the option to charge minors with distributing "indecent" depictions of themselves or possessing such images (Vt. Stat., 2009). The national backlash to Vermont's initial proposal to decriminalize sexting among teens may have served as a warning for other states considering similar reforms and a lesson that misdemeanor penalties for sexting would instead be more readily approved.[9] Vermont's child pornography laws apply only to images of people under 16 years old that depict sexual conduct or the lewd exhibition of genitals. The new sexting law covers images of any person under 18, criminalizing depictions that are merely "indecent," including nudity. Sexting laws like this significantly expand the range of images that are illegal, and may pose an unconstitutional restriction on minors' freedom of expression rights (Podlas, 2011; Walters, 2010).

While Vermont legislators and news commentators may disagree about the specifics, they clearly agree on two things in the debate about sexting: (1) sexting is wrong and (2) felony child pornography convictions are too severe as a punishment. Indeed, from the earliest media coverage, supporters of the Senate's original decriminalization bill maintain that sexting is wrong. Though they explain that their intent is to avoid putting adolescents who sext consensually on public sex offender registries, they often add comments specifying that they nonetheless do not condone sexting. Democratic senator Richard Sears, a key supporter of decriminalization, asserts that sexting is "wrong" (Silverman, 2009), "poor behavior" (Gram, 2009), and "ill-advised" (Sears & Mullin, 2009). He clarifies that the bill is "in no way condoning" the practice (Sears & Mullin, 2009). Another supporter of decriminalization even calls teen sexting "a perverted, albeit new, form of courtship" (Silverman, 2009). It seems that the logic that sexting teens should not be convicted of child pornography offenses and listed on sex offender registries does not stand on its own as a justification for decriminalization. Supporters know there is a significant danger that their position may be construed as promoting sexting, so they are careful to assert that teen sexting is "wrong" or even "perverted" alongside their comments about the need to eliminate the draconian penalties that could be applied to sexters.

Though the consensus in news media and among legal scholars is that child pornography charges and sex offender registration are inappropriate penalties for sexting (Podlas, 2011), the decriminalization bill is still widely criticized for going too far in completely legalizing sexting. Some news commentators and observers are incredulous that the Senate would even consider legalizing sexting. A CNN news host asks, "Would you believe one state is thinking about changing laws to actually make [sexting] legal?" (C. Brown, 2009). Letters to the Editor in local Vermont papers also call the proposal "moronic" (Gantt, 2009) and express displeasure at a legislature that had recently legalized same-sex marriage and would now potentially legalize child pornography for teens (Fitzgerald, 2009). A number of callers to the Fox news show *The O'Reilly Factor* who are opposed to decriminalization comment that the legislature is "out of control" and that the proposal is "madness" and "crazy" (O'Reilly, 2009).

Even those who support making sexting a misdemeanor rather than decriminalizing it still provide the caveat that reducing the penalties for some forms of sexting does not mean that they support the practice. Nearly a month after the new misdemeanor law passed, a *USA Today* editorial praised Vermont, recommending that other state legislatures follow its lead (O'Brien, 2009). However, the editorial refers to sexting as "disturbing" and "stupid" and concludes, "Without question, sexting is crude, deplorable and juvenile. But it's up to adults to ensure that the punishment fits the offense" (O'Brien, 2009). Comments like these reflect prevailing assumptions that teen sexting is wrong and sexters must be punished in some way but that child pornography convictions are too harsh.

Problems with punishment

The emerging use of child pornography and sexting laws to intervene in the sexual lives of teenagers potentially extends many U.S. parents' legal control over their children's sexual relationships until they turn 18. Common social media practices such as emailing, texting, and sending pictures to romantic and sexual partners creates a record of private behaviors. These technologies create new forms of evidence that law enforcement can use to prosecute sexual assault. However, since a variety of consensual sexual behaviors between minors are illegal, adults can also use these social media artifacts to monitor and control young people's sexuality. In the previously mentioned Jenkins-Brown case, it was the photo Jenkins's mother found on her daughter's phone that allowed prosecutors to pursue charges against the teen's 19-year-old girlfriend. Social media use creates readily available evidence and facilitates amplified scrutiny of teen sexual behavior.

Parents, schools, and law enforcement are rarely criticized for their techniques of monitoring youth sexuality through digital media. Instead, many mainstream discourses of online safety advise parents that installing applications for filtering and monitoring their children's computer and cell phone use is a necessary practice of responsible parenting (Shade, 2011). The use of digital media as sexual surveillance technologies requires more attention.[10] This is particularly important since misdemeanor laws like Vermont's newly criminalize a broad range of images, which radically increases parents' and schools' abilities to use the criminal justice system to control teenagers' sexual choices.

The use of child pornography laws against teens is part of a larger set of problems with the justice system and specifically with how this institution deals with youth. While juvenile justice is intended to rehabilitate youth and protect them from harsh criminal penalties, critics charge that this increasingly privatized system is providing more punishment than treatment (R. Epstein, 2007a; Levesque, 2000). Parents and courts have expansive powers to commit youth to secure treatment facilities indefinitely with only the authorization of a physician (Feld, 1991; Kupfner, 2001), and youth do not have the same legal procedural rights as adults, such as a trial by jury (Levesque, 2000). All of this matters even more for racialized, queer, female, and low-income youth, who are punished more harshly than their more privileged counterparts for minor crimes such as violating parole or breaking curfew.[11]

There are three key problems with the criminalization of consensual sexting: the uneven application of the law, punitive and unfair education programs, and the silencing of victims whose privacy has been violated. I take up each of these problems in turn.

PROSECUTORIAL DISCRIMINATION

The criminalization of sexting will probably have a disproportionate impact on queer, racialized, and low-income youth. While no data have yet emerged to confirm this, it is likely that sexting laws will be applied in the same discriminatory ways as other laws (M. Alexander, 2010; Davis, 2003; Stanley & Smith, 2011), particularly those related to sex crimes (e.g., Filler, 2004; Sullivan, 1996). When a common behavior like sexting is subject to harsh punishment, authorities decide whom to investigate and whom to prosecute, and these decisions are not always fair. If an image is explicit enough to qualify as child pornography (or if it merely depicts nudity in a state like Vermont), a prosecutor who is alerted by a parent or school about it can choose to charge the minors involved. The *USA Today* editorial praising Vermont's misdemeanor laws suggests, "Prosecutors ought to focus on egregious cases of redistribution of lewd images by third parties, particularly if there is intent to inflict harm or emotional distress" (O'Brien, 2009). However, legal officials are often expected to address and solve the problem of sexting in their communities (Barry, 2010). Prosecutors facing reelection are even less likely to make the unpopular choice of protecting adolescents' sexual autonomy and privacy (Pavia, 2011). It is dangerous to leave existing child pornography laws unchanged and assume that prosecutors will avoid using such laws, particularly against youth who are racialized, queer, or from low-income families.

Parents can also be a source of discrimination in their exercise of legal control over their adolescents' sexuality. Statutory rape convictions are not secured through proof of coercion but through the legal definition of sex between the two parties as inherently nonconsensual. Sometimes young victims of sexual assault are well served by statutory rape laws, since consent to the victimizing sexual act in question is legally defined as impossible and thus convictions are far easier to obtain than for rape. However, as I discuss further in chapter 5, when minors engaging in such illegal relationships do so voluntarily, age can be an insufficient proxy for a nuanced evaluation of consent. In those cases, it is often up to parents to decide whether older partners should be prosecuted (Kimpel, 2010). That is, parents have the choice to provide their permission for a marriage (if the couple can marry in that jurisdiction), to report the older party for statutory rape, or do nothing. One researcher critiques the uneven and unfair enforcement of statutory rape laws: "In many cases, they are enforced largely by how angry the parents of the younger party are" (Gramlich, 2007). Some states have turned to statutory rape laws to attempt to reduce teenage pregnancy rates, but many researchers suggest that such policies are excessively applied to the older partners of low-income and nonwhite young women (Cocca, 2002; Hollenberg, 1999; Oliveri, 2000; Tapia, 2005). Like statutory rape law, which is rarely enforced (Oberman, 2000), the vast majority of teen sexting violations of child pornography law are likely never prosecuted (Wolak et al., 2012a) or even discovered (Englander, 2012).[12] Given that statutory rape laws are disproportionately applied to relationships parents disapprove of because of sexual orientation, race, and class (Cocca, 2004), it is likely that the same biases will apply in the use of laws that criminalize sexting.

Though boys create sexual images of themselves as well (in some surveys at the same rate as girls), much of the attention to sexting is directed at teenage girls who take photos of themselves. As Ringrose and her coauthors (2013) explain, discourses about the risks of sexting often "[construct] girls' sexuality as a particular problem to be surveilled and regulated" (p. 307). Laws like Vermont's that prohibit the creation of sexts are problematic because girls may be disproportionately punished for sexting (Bailey & Hanna, 2011). Such negative consequences can be meted out by peers, parents, school officials, and legal authorities. The double standard in which sexually active teenage boys are often praised or tolerated while girls are criticized and shamed for engaging in the same activities (e.g., Tolman, 2005) is often reinforced in the responses to sexting (Ringrose et al., 2013). That is, girls who sext can face slut-shaming while peers celebrate the same behavior in boys (Ringrose et al., 2013). Adult educators and legal authorities who (perhaps unwittingly) subscribe to the sexual double standard are likely to punish girls who sext consensually while ignoring boys who violate privacy. Punishing everyone equally is also unfair, since engaging in consensual sexting is very different from committing privacy violations or harassing peers. This has indeed been the response in a number of instances,[13] but further research is needed to confirm the frequency of such gender-biased responses to sexting among legal and educational officials.

I suspect that criminalizing sexting will also disproportionately affect non-heterosexual and gender nonconforming youth. The sexual activities of queer youth are often scrutinized more thoroughly and punished more severely than their heterosexual and gender-normative counterparts in school and in the criminal justice system (Allender, 2009; Himmelstein & Brückner, 2011; Stanley & Smith, 2011).[14] This discrimination is even written into the law in some states where close-in-age exceptions to statutory rape do not apply to oral or anal sex (Curtis & Gilreath, 2008; Higdon, 2008). Since any minor's relationship that violates local age-of-consent laws or that involves explicit pictures can be reported to police by a disapproving family member, parents' and prosecutors' opinions of what constitutes acceptable teenage sexuality determine who is charged with these kinds of crimes. Homophobic parents of queer youth are especially likely to pursue legal charges for consensual sex between similarly aged teens (Sutherland, 2003). Legal scholar Anne Coughlin worries that prosecuting juveniles for producing child pornography of themselves will be discriminatory: "The idea that [teens who are sexting] are troubled kids having sex, that's going to be determined by prosecutors, and I fear that the targets would be gay youth" (K. Reitz, 2008). For example, in one study of sexting-related cases brought to the attention of law enforcement, researchers recounted this incident:

> Parents called the police when they discovered their son, 16, had received a video of a 17-year-old boy masturbating. Their son was gay and in a relationship with the other boy. His parents were upset about his sexual orientation.

The 17-year-old was put on probation and required to write an essay about what he had done. (Wolak et al., 2012a, p. 8)

Furthermore, one study on people's attitudes about requiring sexters to register as sex offenders found that people were significantly more likely to recommend this punishment for gay and lesbian youth than for heterosexuals (Comartin, Kernsmith, & Kernsmith, 2013). I expect that future research will confirm that criminalizing sexting reproduces the historical (e.g., Chauncey, 1993; D'Emilio, 1989; Lancaster, 2011; Rubin, 1993) and continuing (e.g., Himmelstein & Brückner, 2011; Stanley & Smith, 2011) problem of the criminal justice system targeting gay, lesbian, and trans people.

Criminalizing sexting may also have an excessive impact on low-income youth, who are also disproportionately monitored and punished by the state. Since private counseling services are largely inaccessible to low-income families, these families tend to rely on or allow public justice systems to discipline and control their children, especially their daughters (Chesney-Lind & Irwin, 2008; Dohrn, 2004; Odem, 1995). Officials are more likely to waive or reduce criminal charges for middle- and upper-class youth, whom they assume are supported by parents who have the resources and ability to address their children's problems. For example, in an Ohio case, a prosecutor singled out a girl in the foster care system for sexting. A state public defender commenting on this case on a TV news segment criticized the prosecutor for misusing child pornography law and for choosing "an economically disadvantaged person to make an example of" ("Teen Faces," 2008). Given the existing patterns in the policing of girls' transgressions, sexting laws may be applied more often to low-income youth, but further study is needed to verify this suspicion.

The evidence from studies of other types of crimes strongly suggests that the criminalization of sexting will have a disproportionate effect on girls, youth of color, queer youth, and low-income youth. Youth with more access to resources and to white, heterosexual, and male privilege will likely be better able to avoid the criminal justice system or to secure more lenient treatment. Social media offers parents and prosecutors new and powerful ways to determine the boundaries of acceptable teenage sexuality. Both the nature of these boundaries and their uneven enforcement are inextricable from deeply held assumptions about social class, gender, race, and sexual orientation.

SENTENCED TO EDUCATION

The idea of offering educational diversion programs instead of criminal punishment for sexting might seem like a positive development. However, such programs can serve as an alternative way of blaming victims of privacy violations and punishing participants in consensual sexting. While misdemeanor convictions and mandatory diversion programs for sexting are mild penalties compared to child pornography felony convictions, entering the criminal justice system in any way can have serious and long-lasting consequences, particularly for youth without access to private legal resources (Levick & Moon, 2010).

In the Miller case, Skumanick argues that he is "helping" the teens by giving them probation and the "opportunity" to take a class instead of facing felony charges (Zetter, 2009). He says, "We thought we were being progressive" (Searcey, 2009b), and explains, "If we were just out to be nasty about this, we would have just charged everybody" (Rubinkam, 2009). However, Skumanick's deal required that the students complete a punitive probation term and a course that shamed the girls for their behavior. One of the assignments in Skumanick's course asks all the students to write a report explaining: "What you did. Why it was wrong. Did you create a victim? If so, who? How did what you did affect the victim? The school? The community?" (S. Mullen, personal communication, March 27, 2009). By conflating consensual sexting with the violation of privacy, this assignment assumes that all sexting, consensual or not, is equally damaging and wrong.[15]

A few states have taken a similar approach by requiring some accused sexters to attend educational programs. In 2011, New York, New Jersey, and Texas added nearly the same requirements for sexting prevention programs into their respective state statutes (Greenberg, 2011). Texas mandates that schools provide the program to all students, while the other two states offer the program as an alternative to other criminal penalties for some types of sexting between youth of specified ages. The Texas statute requires that these programs inform youth about the negative legal, social, and emotional consequences of sexting. The goal is to prevent all sexting, whether it is consensual or harmful. The Texas School Safety program, designed to meet the statute's requirements, notes that the negative consequences of sexting could include: "Others may think of you as 'easy' or sexually active" and "Others may be embarrassed to be seen with you" ("Before," 2012). Though the program materials note that forwarding a private image is a form of harassment and bullying, the dominant message is that people who choose to create sexual images of themselves are responsible for the shame, humiliation, embarrassment, and victimization that could follow.

Skumanick's curriculum and the types of education programs embedded in new laws powerfully illustrate the mainstream consensus that all youth who participate in sexting—whether their actions were consensual or harmful—are equally guilty. The educational alternatives I advocate, which I describe in more detail in later chapters, is for schools to reduce digital privacy violations by working with students to develop programs that promote consent in sexting and combat gender- and sexuality-related harassment.

SILENCING VICTIMS

Though it may sound counterintuitive, affirming teens' right to sext helps protect them from privacy violations. The problem with viewing sexting as simply deviant and criminal for everyone involved is that it makes the malicious distribution of private images seem like a normal and inevitable part of sexting (Slane, 2010). If the typical sexting scenario is instead viewed as the consensual exchange of images, then it is obvious that sexting is not inherently harmful, but that the malicious distribution of private images certainly is. In order to accurately recognize harmful, malicious behaviors, it is necessary to first recognize and acknowledge teenagers' right to engage in consensual sexting. If teens have the right to consensually create sexts, then they also have the right to demand respect for their privacy, even if they distribute these images selectively.

While many legal and educational commentators believe they are protecting youth from victimization by criminalizing sexting, they are actually exacerbating the problem. Even in cases of malicious privacy violations, child pornography charges are still a disproportionately harsh penalty. This means that most prosecutors will be reluctant to actually convict on this charge, and other laws do not adequately address the issue. Under Vermont's new misdemeanor law, any minor who coerces another minor to create an explicit image or who forwards a private image of someone to other people can still be potentially charged only with distributing child pornography or possibly with other laws such as voyeurism, lewd and lascivious conduct, luring, and obscenity. As such, this new law offers no new solutions for addressing privacy violations. The existing options remain unchanged: Use an unreasonably harsh felony charge, apply other laws that are not a good fit with the offense, or ignore harassment and privacy violations altogether.

In fact, Vermont's new law applies primarily to consensual sexting. It covers only minors who transmit depictions of themselves to one or more other people and the possession of such self-produced images.[16] This means that teenagers in Vermont who suffer from privacy violations have even fewer options for recourse against privacy violators than they did before. Informing authorities about the incident makes victims of privacy violations vulnerable not only to harsh judgment and punishment but potentially to criminal charges (Bailey & Hanna, 2011; Slane, 2010). While this was still a risk when child pornography laws were the only option for charging sexters, it is even more of a danger with new misdemeanor laws because they criminalize a broader range of images and because prosecutors may be more likely to actually use these laws since they carry milder penalties.

An image has to be legal to produce and possess before young people can hope to demand their right to having such images kept private. One of the ways that privacy violators avoid blame is because of the problematic consensus that all people involved in sexting—regardless of whether their behavior was consensual or harmful—are equally guilty of wrongdoing. While further legal reforms are needed to protect online privacy (for youth and adults), allowing teens the right to sext is the first step to clarifying that people who receive these images have no right to distribute them further without permission.

Sexual expression rights

By making teen sex impossible to legally represent, current laws restrict youth sexual rights (Albury, Funnell, & Noonan, 2010). Laws like Vermont's go further by criminalizing the creation and possession of self-produced electronic indecent images, which were not previously illegal. A handful of legal scholars suggest that these kinds of laws might unconstitutionally limit adolescents' rights (Haynes, 2012; Humbach, 2010; Nunziato, 2012; O'Connor, 2010; Stuart, 2010; Sweeny, 2011; Wastler, 2010). Yet, this position is unpopular. Even supporters of the Vermont senate's original proposal to decriminalize sexting explicitly position it as a way to protect teens from harsh child pornography prosecutions rather than to affirm their rights. These supporters in fact stridently oppose teens' rights to engage in consensual sexting, declaring that sexting is "wrong" and even "perverted."

Since there is very little support for upholding minors' expression rights, especially when they involve sexuality, I suggest that consensual sexting might reasonably be regulated as a type of sex act instead. Because there is no harm to the participants in consensual sexting, it makes sense to think about it as private sexual conduct. As argued in chapter 4, banning all such images categorically on the basis that adult abusers could use them to harm a child is a claim without sufficient evidence and is unfair to consensual teen sexters. It is possible that sexting only needs to be seen as a speech act when it involves privacy violation—in these cases the harm can be described with existing concepts of harmful speech, such as breech of privacy or confidentiality, libel, slander, and defamation. The remainder of this chapter examines the problems with regulating sexting as a speech act (since child pornography laws carve out a large exception to First Amendment rights) and suggests that legislators should regulate sexting as a sex act instead.

THE LIMITS ON MINORS' FREEDOM OF EXPRESSION

Despite strong freedom of expression protections in the United States, minors lack the privileges that adults enjoy. The First Amendment is often understood to protect the free flow of ideas in the public sphere in order to facilitate democratic self-governance. But in addition to enabling citizens to be informed voters, the Supreme Court has also established that this amendment protects the deeper principle of the right to "self-exploration, self-expression, and self-definition" (Nunziato, 2012, p. 77). In a successful class action challenging prisoner mail censorship, the Supreme Court decided, "The First Amendment serves not only the needs of the polity, but also those of the human spirit—a spirit that demands self-expression. Such expression is an integral part of the development of ideas and a sense of identity" (*Procunier v. Martinez*, 1974, p. 427). While this right is meant to apply to everyone, minors do not enjoy the same degree of freedom as adults. For example, school officials can restrict speech that is lewd or disruptive if it occurs on school grounds.[17] In a 1986 decision, the Court argued that a student's vulgar sexual statements at an assembly did not constitute a political message and that a school can prohibit some forms of expression to teach students "the boundaries of socially appropriate behavior" (*Bethel school dist. v. Fraser*, 1986, p. 681). While this decision was based on a student's public speech at an assembly, the case sets a broad precedent that school officials can arbitrate what constitutes appropriate speech.[18] In schools, preventing disruptions and reinforcing social norms are defined as more important than the needs of the human spirit for self-expression.

Though many sexting images are created and shared off school grounds, they might easily also be possessed, viewed, or shared on school property as well, even if the image is privately shared between two people. Schools may also have strict cell phone use policies as well as the power to seize and search cell phones. Thus, schools have broad powers to police sexting without even resorting to criminal law. For example, the girls in the Seattle case I mentioned previously can be suspended for sexting if schools decide that they caused a disruption, and they can be dismissed from the cheerleading squad if they are found to violate the athletic code of conduct (Blanchard, 2008). Recall that the Seattle school did not consider the boys, who distributed these private photos without permission, to be causing a disruption or violating the athletic code. A potential complication is that in many jurisdictions school officials are bound by law to report suspected child exploitation (Findholt & Robrecht, 2002). In sexting cases, these reporting requirements can mean that school officials who learn of sexting among students can be technically required to report them to police if the images are explicit enough to qualify as child pornography.

Child pornography laws are just one of a number of legal structures that define youth sexuality as inherently illegitimate and nonconsensual. Levine (2002) explains that although the harm to minors of viewing sexual materials is not physical or measurable, "The moral wisdom of shielding minors from sexy materials is seen as self-evident" (p. 13). While the landmark Supreme Court decision in *Lawrence v. Texas* affirmed that it is unconstitutional to criminalize private consensual sex acts between consenting adults (*Lawrence v. Texas*, 2003), private youth sexual conduct has no such protection (Allender, 2009). There are a variety of restrictions related to minors viewing, creating, or possessing sexual content, including a number of internet-specific laws that have been passed, declared unconstitutional, tweaked, and passed again since 1995 (Gehman, 2006; Levine, 2002; Marwick, 2008). The development of Vermont's legislation is an example of the difficulty of affirming youth sexual rights and the ease of restricting them even further.

Laws about sexuality and sexual representations are wide-ranging and subjectively applied. Even the legal definition of obscenity is subjective, as it requires a jury to reflect on "community standards" to determine what counts as obscene. Since material qualifies as obscene only if an "average person, applying contemporary community standards" would find that the work "appeals to the prurient interest" (*Miller v. State of California*, 1973), many jurors inevitably rely on their assumptions about sexuality to determine what constitutes "prurience," who counts as "average," and what the "community standards" are. A Supreme Court decision clarified that this does not include material that "provok[es] only normal, healthy sexual desires," maintaining that material is obscene if it appeals to "a shameful or morbid interest in nudity, sex, or excretion" (*Brockett v. Spokane Arcades Inc.*, 1985, p. 498). Since this definition still leaves it up to juries to decide what is "healthy," they may find, for example, that images of homosexual sex are obscene while similarly explicit images of heterosexual sex are not (Glazer, 2008). Likewise, in an obscenity case, a jury of adults would decide whether images of adolescent sex acts are normal and healthy or if they are "shameful or morbid" (Humbach, 2009). Since most adults view adolescent sexuality as negative and harmful (Cocca, 2004), teens' sexual images could be prosecuted as "obscenity," even if they did not qualify as child pornography (Humbach, 2009).

POTENTIAL PROTECTIONS FOR SEXTING

Teen sexting images that are explicit enough to qualify as child pornography are difficult to defend in court given current laws. Yet some legal scholars suggest that even explicit images might conceivably be constitutionally protected if they are not linked to sexual exploitation, though the U.S. Supreme Court has yet to rule on this issue directly. A decision striking down a law banning virtual child pornography (in which no actual children are involved or depicted) explained that it is unconstitutional to prohibit images that are not the product of sexual abuse or proximately linked to it (*Ashcroft v. Free Speech Coalition*, 2002). Some legal scholars argue that this ruling suggests that minors should be protected from child pornography prosecutions, since many forms of consensual sexting do not depict any illegal sexual acts (Humbach, 2010; Nunziato, 2012; Wastler, 2010; Weins & Hiestand, 2009). They explain that since sexting does not document child abuse, nor is it demonstrably linked to it, this Court decision could theoretically be interpreted to mean that consensual sexting among teens should be decriminalized as long as the sex acts the images depict are legal.[19] This anticensorship position conceives of sexting principally as a speech act by drawing on the history of legal thought about freedom of expression and child pornography to argue that teens should have the right to freely express themselves sexually.

This legal reform would also mean that adults could possess sexual images of minors as long as they were self-produced, willingly shared, and depicted no illegal sex acts. Wastler (2010) describes this as an "unsettling consequence" but maintains that any obstacles this may create for the detection and prosecution of sexual assault perpetrators does not justify the restrictions on minors' sexual self-expression (p. 700). She also notes that any potential that such images could encourage adults to commit sexual assault against minors also does not warrant banning them (Wastler, 2010)—a point I elaborate in more detail in chapter 4. In the ruling on virtual child pornography the Court stated, "The mere tendency of speech to encourage unlawful acts is not a sufficient reason for banning it" (*Ashcroft v. Free Speech Coalition*, 2002, p. 253). While I sympathize with these anticensorship arguments, they will likely fail to gain mainstream acceptance given the deadlocked discourse in which it is impossible to support a teen's rights to sexual self-expression.

REGULATING SEXTING AS A SEX ACT

An alternative way of looking at sexting that might be more palatable to legislators and news commentators would be to think of sexting not primarily as a speech act but as a sex act, and to regulate it as such. Given that young people already have more rights to engage in sex with their peers than they do to view or create sexual images, thinking of sexting as a sex act instead of a speech act might garner youth more sexual freedoms. Since viewing sexting as a sex act can draw on a preexisting set of laws that decriminalize some sex acts among teens, it could be more readily accepted than freedom-of-speech–based arguments.

If consensual sexting is regulated as a sex act, child pornography laws could be modified to include the same kind of age-span provisions as statutory rape laws, eliminating the inconsistency that teens may engage in some sex acts legally as long as they do not photograph them (Geyer, 2009; Sacco et al., 2010; Sherman, 2011; Sweeny, 2011). As Tallon and her coauthors (Tallon, Choi, Keeley, et al., 2012) advocate in Australia, age-span exceptions should be added to child pornography laws to bring them in line with statutory rape laws. While age-of-consent laws vary by state, they provide an existing legal framework that decriminalizes sexual activity between consenting, similarly aged peers. For example, child pornography laws could be reformed to exempt young people four years apart or less.[20] Such a reform would not interfere with prosecutions of adults outside this narrow age-span but could protect some youth from unfair prosecutions. Age-spans for child pornography would also need creative definitions so that, for example, a 15-year-old who could legally possess an explicit photo of herself does not commit a felony if she keeps the photo past age 20. While there are many legal nuances to iron out, adding simple age-span exceptions to child pornography laws could help alleviate some of the problems of discriminatory prosecutions, some of the barriers to reporting privacy violations, and some of the disruptions to adolescents' First Amendment rights. However, any legal reform would be only one small technical part of a much larger goal to lessen the discriminatory and unnecessary institutional and social prohibitions on adolescent sexuality.

In addition to viewing consensual sexting as a sex act, non-consensual sexual image distribution or creation can also be regulated like sexual assault. One example is found in North Dakota, where legislators created an age-neutral misdemeanor offense in 2009 for distributing or publishing "sexually expressive" images that are created surreptitiously or without consent, intended to cause "emotional harm or humiliation," or distributed after notice has been given by the people depicted or their legal guardians that they do not consent to distribution ("North Dakota century code," 2009). The implication is that sexting is legal (for adults) when it is consensual, and like rape, lack of consent to a sex act defines it as sexual assault. A sexting inquiry from the Victoria Parliament in Australia recommends a similar type of law making it an offense to distribute "intimate" images without the consent of the people depicted but cautions it should not be classified as a sexual offense, which would add people to the already bloated sex offender registry (Newton-Brown et al., 2013). However, given the significant problems in the prison system, especially with racial and sexual discrimination (M. Alexander, 2010; Davis, 2003; Stanley & Smith, 2011), creating new criminal laws to address the harm of privacy violations is dangerous. Since other information-related harms (libel, slander, breech of confidentiality, publication of private facts, etc.) are in the domain of civil law, a better way to deal with privacy violations might be to use lawsuits as well, which I discuss further in chapter 5. While I argue that consensual sexting should be regulated like a sex act, sharing personal sexual images without permission might be best understood as a speech act, since the key harm in this scenario is the violation of privacy. Whether sexting is understood and regulated as a speech act or a sex act—and indeed it is actually both—the existing laws that criminalize consensual sexting appear to be unfairly applied and ineffective in addressing harm.

Conclusion

In mainstream discourse, as the Miller case and the legislation in Vermont demonstrate, there is a clear consensus that sexting is always dangerous and wrong and must be prohibited in some way. There is so little room for debate on this point that Vermont's sensible initial decriminalization bill was quickly taken off the table in response to a national backlash. Likewise, the ACLU, normally a strident defender of freedom of expression rights, has to appear to agree with pundits and prosecutors that teens should have no right to sext. Given the range of laws criminalizing youth sexual behavior and the new forms of evidence that social media use can leave behind, decriminalizing consensual teen sexting may be the only way to protect youth. It is unlikely that legally prohibiting sexting will significantly reduce the rate of either consensual sexting or harm. This is because harassment, coercion, and privacy violations reflect problems that are much larger than cell phone cameras or teen sexuality and require significant changes in the attitudes and policies that underlie gender- and sexuality-based violence (Ringrose et al., 2012).

Adding age-span exceptions to child pornography laws is a simple solution that would protect many young sexters from prosecution. Current laws enable digital media to seamlessly function as sexual surveillance technologies that may excessively impact girls and queer youth. Affirming that teens have the right to sext would help alleviate part of this problem and would also allow youth the option to report privacy violations without fear of prosecution for their consensual participation in sexting.

The urge to protect adolescents from their own mistakes runs through many of the discourses this chapter examines. For many, prohibiting sexting appears to shield teens from its dangers and supposedly prevents them from committing an error that could have terrible life consequences. The next chapter looks more deeply at the dominant ideas about adolescents that support the belief that teens need to be strictly monitored and guided in order to develop into normal adults.

CHAPTER 2

Beyond teenage biology

Adolescents are often described as irrational, impulsive, out of control, and even crazy or stupid. This pejorative characterization is usually attributed to teen physiology: raging hormones, still-developing brains, and an innate orientation to peers. Such explanations are typically seen as obvious, rational, and uncontroversial. Yet, a growing number of researchers are questioning the dominance of biological models of youth behavior (R. Epstein, 2007a; Lesko, 2001; Levesque, 2000; Males, 1996, 1999; Walkerdine, 1984). As Thurlow (2007) points out, the homogenization and biological determinism that is common in mainstream media (and some scientific studies) about teenagers would not be tolerated for most other categories of social identity.

This chapter examines the implications of the dominant discourse about the unruly biology of adolescence. While many people believe that teen hormones and immature brains offer scientific and objective explanations for adolescent behavior, such beliefs are problematic. That is, using teen biology as a sympathetic explanation for sexting can divert attention from malicious privacy violators. With the focus and blame placed squarely on victims, their physiological flaws and inadequacies become the nexus of the argument instead of the harm that was done to them. This chapter complicates biology-based assumptions about teens' irrational brains, raging hormones, and fixed trajectory through sexual development as explanations for sexting.

Biological explanations for social differences and inequalities have been common throughout the past century. Fortunately, the scientific racism that explicitly links mental capacity and personality to race is beginning to recede from contemporary culture. Still, gendered social differences and sexual behaviors are often seen as largely biologically determined, despite the critical interventions of feminism and queer theory. Many feminist science studies scholars demonstrate that scientific knowledge is not neutral but instead reflects culturally pervasive assumptions about gender.[1] Haraway (1991) explains, "Sciences act as legitimating meta-languages that produce homologies between social and symbolic systems . . . science is our myth" (p. 42). Indeed, there is an ongoing dialogue between common sense and scientific knowledge.[2] For example, many scientific studies reflect and reinforce the assumption that women are inherently inferior to men (Birke, 1986; Fausto-Sterling, 1985; Haraway, 1989; Marchessault & Sawchuk, 2000; Treichler, Cartwright, & Penley, 1998) and that queer sexual practices are deviant (Hoad, 2000; Kitzinger, 2006; Somerville, 2000; Terry, 1999). Feminist science studies like these are part of a broader project of shifting the location of gender and sexuality from within the body to culture and social structures (Butler, 1990; Foucault, 1990).

Like race, gender, and sexuality, adolescence is a category of social identity that is overdetermined by unquestioned biological narratives. Many studies and popular media discourses presume that adolescents' sexuality is written in their physiology and biochemistry. Teenage sexuality is typically viewed as determined by biological forces and rarely as authentic, complex, and heterogeneous as the sexual practices of adults. Narratives about the supposedly unique teenage brain powerfully combine with fears about the potential impacts of new media on vulnerable (young) people. The homogenizing assumptions that teenagers are controlled by their raging hormones and that they are peer-oriented and sex-crazed work together to provide common sense scientific explanations for sexting and teen sexuality.

Though these sympathetic excuses for sexting seem to apply most easily to white, economically advantaged, heterosexual girls, the rhetoric of biology can lead to problematic laws and policies that affect all girls. The idea that innocent girls need to be protected from themselves—from their innately irrational brains and the overwhelming biological forces of their sexuality—can reinforce policies promoting abstinence and the criminalization of sexting. The idea that young people are biologically and innately mentally incapable, and therefore not culpable, ensures that they cannot be granted any of the sexual expression rights that were discussed in chapter 1. Moreover, Meiners (2011) points out that biological ideas about young people's innocence in criminal justice contexts might also reinforce the basic logic of mass incarceration, asking: "If juveniles are protected because of immature brain development, does this make the rest of us culpable?" (p. 556).

This chapter focuses on hormones and brain structures because these biology-based explanations for teen sexting are common in the media coverage of the practice.[3] Angelides (2013) finds in a study of responses to sexting in the U.K.: "Trading in popular, long-standing narratives of teenagers as foolish, rash, hormone-driven, and psychologically and emotionally immature, teenage sexters are represented as lacking the wherewithal both to engage in the practice maturely and to deal with any unforeseen consequences" (p. 682). Before turning to sexting, it is first necessary to look at some of the dominant narratives about the biology of adolescence evident in magazines, such as *Time,* and television programs, like *Frontline,* as well as critiques of the imagined relationship between the teenage brain and new communication technologies. Given the ubiquity of biological explanations for undesirable youth behavior, it is unsurprising that many news items about sexting refer to these concepts. This chapter concentrates on analyzing the implications of using these ideas about teenage brains, hormones, and trend-following as explanations for sexting.

The common sense scientific, social, and technology-based understandings about youth and youth sexuality are fundamental to the counterproductive media and legal responses to sexting. One of the most powerful arguments for criminalizing sexting is the contention that it protects young people from their inability to make good, rational decisions, especially about sexuality and long-term goals. Scientific narratives offer a compelling way to confirm the common sense notion that teens are innately irrational and irresponsible and thus cannot be trusted with the rights and freedoms adults take for granted. That is, in order to recognize teen sexual agency—which is a prerequisite for accounting for both consent and harm, as will be explored in chapter 5—it is essential to first complicate the easy discourses of biological unruliness and chaos that so often substitute for a more nuanced conversation about teens' sexual choices. This chapter takes up the task of examining some of these common sense ideas and their implications for understanding and responding to sexting.

Is there a teen brain?

The predominant contemporary understanding of adolescence in many western industrialized nations continues to be informed and described by the classic "storm and stress" model (Freud, 1958; G. S. Hall, 1904). This model views adolescents as a homogenous group whose perceived moodiness, risk-taking behaviors, and lack of judgment are biologically predetermined by hormonal fluctuations during puberty. Since the late 1990s, many of these same characteristics have also been found in brain image analysis studies (e.g., Giedd, Blumenthal, & Jeffries, 1999; Johnson, Blum, & Giedd, 2009; Lenroot & Giedd, 2006). In other words, mainstream understandings of adolescence can use new information about brain structures from MRI scans to explore and often confirm the same arguments about teenage behavior that have been made for the past 100 years.

Detractors from the "storm and stress" model of adolescence note its unique incidence in western industrial societies and relatively recent emergence at the beginning of the twentieth century. In 1904, G. Stanley Hall published the first major work that popularized adolescence as a particularly problematic time that requires increasing adult supervision. Since then, many psychologists have understood adolescence as an inherently pathological developmental period that is "defined by its problems" (R. F. Hill & Fortenberry, 1992, p. 73). For example, in the recent Diagnostic and Statistical Manual of Mental Disorders (DSM-V), the criteria for the diagnosis of "conduct disorder," which specifically applies to people under 18, include the violation of "major age-appropriate societal norms or rules" (American Psychiatric Association, 2013). By this definition, truancy, breaking curfew, and running away from home can serve as evidence of a psychiatric disorder.

Critics contend that the problems teenagers experience are not biologically inevitable but should be characterized as side effects of educational and legal structures that infantilize teenagers and isolate them from adults (R. Epstein, 2007a; Lesko, 2001; Levesque, 2000; Males, 1996, 1999; Walkerdine, 1984). Mead (1928) famously argued that the turmoil adolescents experience is the result of culture, not biology, finding little evidence of "storm and stress" in her study of adolescent girls in nonindustrial Samoa. Likewise, a major review of the anthropological literature in 1991 (Schlegel & Barry) found that in most nonindustrial societies, young people spend most of their time with same-sex adults, striving to become members of the community rather than separating from their parents, and suffer far fewer social and emotional problems than teenagers in western industrial nations. Robert Epstein (2007b) argues that social structures rather than biology are primarily responsible for the problems of adolescence:

> Isolated from adults and wrongly treated like children, it is no wonder that some teens behave, by adult standards, recklessly or irresponsibly. Almost without exception, the reckless and irresponsible behavior we see is the teen's way of declaring his or her adulthood. (p. 63)

Epstein (2007a) also points to studies that demonstrate that adolescents' brains are fully developed by age 14 and that "the cognitive abilities of teens are, on average, superior to the cognitive abilities of adults" (p. 163) in reasoning ability, intelligence, and memory functions. He goes so far as to advocate eliminating adolescence altogether, which he sees as an unnecessary stage of life that unfairly labels an entire group of people as incompetent.

It is important to note that the MRI studies that are used to ground the common sense biological model of adolescence depend on a basic and unverifiable assumption that brain structures cause behavior. That is, MRI studies of the adolescent brain rely on snapshot images of the brain functioning to infer a causal relationship between brain structures and social behaviors. While there is no evidence to support this conclusion, there is considerable evidence that the brain is the product of genetics in combination with experience and that the brain changes considerably throughout a person's life (R. Epstein, 2007a, 2007b). Although brain imaging studies can show how one brain differs from another, despite media coverage suggesting otherwise, these studies are unable to offer a final verdict on the cause of such differences. For example, an MRI study could find that the brain regions related to impulse control are less active in teens than they are in adults. A journalist might then report that teenagers are not capable of impulse control because the brain structures necessary for it develop later in life. However, an equally plausible explanation might be that since most youth have less life experience, few meaningful responsibilities, and are buffered from the consequences of their actions, the results of this MRI study reflect the fact that teens are infrequently required to control their impulses.

Newspapers continue to publish articles that use studies of the brain to describe teens as psychologically distinct from adults. Teen brain research is eagerly taken up in many popular culture forms, including the *Frontline* documentary "Inside the Teen Brain," in which the narrator promises, over a sequence of brain image cross-sections, "If parents often wonder what is going on inside the teenage brain, tonight, some answers" (Spinks, 2002). Since the early 2000s, brain research has figured prominently in a number of popular books written to provide insights and advice on dealing with teens (Bradley, 2003; Clavier, 2005; Phillips, 2007; Walsh, 2005), including, *Parenting the Teenage Brain: Understanding a Work in Progress* (Feinstein, 2007) and *The Primal Teen: What the New Discoveries about the Teenage Brain Tell Us about Our Kids* (Strauch, 2004). A 2004 cover story in *Time* explains:

> Now that MRI studies have cracked open a window on the developing brain
> . . . the wild conduct once blamed on "raging hormones" is being seen as the

by-product of two factors: a surfeit of hormones, yes, but also a paucity of the cognitive controls needed for mature behavior. (Wallis & Park, 2004)

While scientific studies are usually careful to include caveats that the findings do not prove any causal relationships, correlation and causation are easily blurred in popular culture forms such as the *Time* story and how-to books for parents. Using biology to say the same things about teenagers that have been said for the past century—that they are out of control, irrational, and irresponsible, gives these common sense ideas new authority and vitality. Why does this matter? If the way teenagers act is seen as biologically predetermined, then there is no need to reform the educational or criminal justice systems. Indeed, movements to change how these institutions deal with young people enjoy much more success when they can effectively deploy biological arguments to garner sympathy for teens. This is evident in the ways organizations advocating for youth take up MRI-based brain structure research. For example, the American Bar Association draws on this literature to advocate for rehabilitation programs instead of punitive criminal sentences for underage offenders. One analyst writes that adolescents should not be treated like adults in the criminal justice system because "scientific evidence now supports the contention that the juvenile brain is often incapable of adult reasoning because of its long maturation process" (Beyer, 2000). While viewing the teen brain as temporarily defective can be used to advocate for more lenient (or simply, humane) treatment, this perspective also inadvertently infantilizes teenagers and can be used to justify their lack of rights. Sympathy for teens that relies on biological determinism can be effective in reaching short-term goals, but may be ultimately counterproductive. That is, if teens are incapable of making rational decisions and understanding the consequences of their actions, then there is no basis to grant them free speech or due process rights.

This is your brain on technology

At the same time that MRI brain studies gained prominence in the late 1990s, the internet was promising to transform culture, commerce, and politics. Young people with access quickly took up the new technology and the discourse about the unique teen brain became a convenient way to explain some of the differences between adolescents and adults in their use of digital media. The common argument, often relying heavily on general evidence of the brain's plasticity, is that teenage brains are being rewired for digital media. Some researchers view these brain changes as a positive development (Prensky, 2001, 2009), whereas others are concerned that other (superior) cognitive skills are lost in this process (Bauerlein, 2008; Carr, 2010).

In 2001, Prensky coined the term "digital natives." Stressing the generational differences between teens and adults, he contends that young people's minds have been shaped and changed by heavy technology use: "[They] think and process information fundamentally differently from their predecessors. . . . [I]t is very likely that our students' brains have physically changed—and are different from ours—as a result of how they grew up" (Prensky, 2001, p. 1). Since youth seem to be better at using digital media, commentators like Prensky praise their development of new skills and abilities, which appear to be crucial for their future success in a new digital world. He explains that digital tools offer a vital and important enhancement to the human mind, changing it for the better and opening up new possibilities for the way humans think (Prensky, 2009).

The other side of the optimism about how new media is building better brains is the concern that these new skills and habits are pushing out the old cognitive skills, potentially creating fundamental changes in how people think and act. For example, in a *Frontline* documentary, a series of psychologists and neuroscientists express their fears that gazing at computer screens for hours on end is causing changes in brain functioning. They are particularly concerned about what these changes may mean for young people, who spend more time in digital environments and whose still-developing brains are reportedly more plastic. Researcher Gary Small asks: "These digital natives, who have grown up with this technology, [w]ho are great and efficient in using it, what will they be like in 20, 30 years? Will they have fewer empathy skills? Will they have trouble putting together the big picture?" (Dretzin, 2010). Small compares using digital media to smoking cigarettes, suggesting that experts may not yet know how dangerous they are in the long term, and another researcher adds: "We worry that it may be creating people who are unable to think well and clearly" (Dretzin, 2010). Likewise, Carr's (2010) book *The Shallows* popularizes this view. He argues: "The neural circuits devoted to scanning, skimming, and multitasking are expanding and strengthening, while those used for reading and thinking deeply, with sustained concentration, are weakening or eroding" (Carr, 2010, p. 141). Carr is concerned that internet use causes human brains to take on the characteristics that the technology demands—that the human mind is being reshaped in the image of the machine, which for Carr means an increase in distractedness and superficial thinking.

Brain plasticity offers a new way to express old fears about teenagers. Critics who once saw the culture industries as a dangerous influence on the supposedly mentally weak, susceptible classes (in this case, youth in particular) can attribute all manner of problems to the interaction between the unique teenage brain and digital technologies. And the consequences of unfettered access are, for Carr (2010), potentially very dire: "[It] doesn't just threaten the depth and distinctiveness of the self. It threatens the depth and distinctiveness of the culture we all share" (p. 196). To whatever degree using the internet creates new ways of thinking, it is certainly not clear that such changes are necessarily, on balance, bad, or that new digital skills cannot coexist alongside other cognitive skills.

Many researchers argue that the generational division between "digital natives" and "digital immigrants" is overstated, since exposure to technology rather than age alone seems to have a greater impact on digital media expertise (Bennett, Maton, & Kervin, 2008; Hargittai, 2008; Herring, 2007; Livingstone, 2010; Stoerger, 2009). These studies indicate that technological expertise is associated more strongly with class and access than age and warn that educational curricula should not assume that youth do not need to be taught digital media skills (Bennett et al., 2008; Livingstone, 2010). In an uncertain economic climate, scholars and the public alike are particularly invested in viewing youth as having innate digital media skills. For example, Hamilton and Nakamura (2010) argue:

> It feels much better to assume that youth have [digital] skills "naturally" or are born with them since they are unlikely to be given access to them in any other, more systematic, way.

Many mainstream commentators and researchers are relatively optimistic about the potential of digital media, both for engaging students in the classroom and for paving the way to future economic success. Yet, referring to a range of studies, Buckingham (2007) points out, "Most young people's everyday uses of the Internet are characterized not by spectacular forms of innovation and creativity, but by relatively mundane forms of communication and information retrieval" (p. 14). Despite such critiques, the idea that the so-called teen brain is uniquely susceptible to digital media, whether the effects are seen as positive or negative, still persists.

IMPAIRED DRIVING ON THE INTERNET SUPERHIGHWAY

The biological conditions of adolescence are said to create a powder keg of irresponsibility and unfulfilled sexual energy that technology can easily set off. These conditions include adolescent's still-developing brains' supposed inability to make rational decisions, the biochemistry of their raging hormones, and the apparently overwhelming desire to conform to their peers. Especially in the mid-2000s, parents were warned that giving teens unlimited and unmonitored internet access was like letting them drive drunk—a metaphor that characterizes the internet as a dangerous technology with the lethal potential of a car and casts teenage biology as nature's judgment-impairing alcohol. As such, sexting is often positioned as a potentially devastating consequence of the combination of technology and teenage biology.

Girls in particular are seen as unable to use their technological skills in a safe and responsible manner, echoing fears in previous eras about women's unauthorized and improper use of new technologies (Cassell & Cramer, 2008; Spigel, 1992). Discussions about youth producing sexual images almost exclusively focus on girls (Draper, 2012) who are often seen as irresponsible and out of control (Goldstein, 2009; Thiel-Stern, 2009). In contrast, the sexual risks of digital media for adolescent boys are more often imagined in terms of their access to pornography, not their creation of it. The reason boys or adults sext often goes without saying: sexual desire and communication. But for girls, the reason somehow does not seem so simple. One of the most common explanations for why girls sext is the notion that it is the unfortunate result of the interaction between teenage biology and new technology. Sexual agency is conspicuously absent in this narrative.

The implicit theory of adolescent sexuality is—in dramatic terms, perhaps—that biology drives them to want an unlimited amount of sex with an unlimited amount of partners while civilization, morality, and self-control just barely hold them back from such chaos. To the extent that boys' sexual uses of technology are driven by their biology, the concern is relatively minimal, since sexual expression and desire is usually viewed as normal for boys. For girls, however, the internet and mobile phones are positioned as dangerous catalysts that threaten to destroy even the most strong-willed girl's valiant attempts to resist and delay sexuality. The key function of biology in these narratives is to shift the location of agency away from girls and teens, even away from adult abusers, and onto three elements that are each imagined to be fixed and natural: brain structures, hormones, and peer pressure.

BLAMING THE VICTIM'S BRAIN

Victims of sexual assault have long been blamed for their perceived poor choices or risk-taking. In the new version of this same narrative, essentialized notions of the developing teenage brain's lack of capacity for judgment can naturalize male sexual violence by shifting the blame for an assault onto the victim's biology rather than on the assailant.

This shifting of blame is well illustrated in one 2007 news story about a sexual assault involving a number of teenage girls who made initial contact on a social network site with a 50-year-old man. The article's focus is nearly entirely on the mistakes the victims made, which are attributed to their still-developing brains. Positioning the victims' compliance as the key problem, the article explains the reason for it:

> Teens don't fully understand the implications or risks of their behavior because their brains are still developing, said Thomas Van Hoose, a clinical psychologist with the University of Texas Southwestern Medical Center at Dallas. "The part of the brain that governs judgment is the last to develop . . . they're just not mature neurologically yet." (Jan Jarvis, 2007)

The article also quotes a psychologist who asserts that teens "believe they are bulletproof" and are "socially naïve" and offers that this "could explain why more than two dozen teenage girls might have become part of a computer pornography collection" (Jan Jarvis, 2007). In this last sentence and in a number of other cases in the article, the man's actions are described in the passive voice—a frequent trope of news writing on sexual violence that minimizes the assailant's actions. In other contexts, drinking, wearing revealing clothing, being out at night, and so on, can be positioned as excessive risks that shift blame away from assailants and onto victims of sexual violence. Here, the scientific authority of biological explanations provides a way to fault girls who might otherwise be viewed as innocent—it can be difficult to adhere blame to white, middle-class girls, but teenage biology offers a compelling way to rearrange responsibility.

Biological narratives put adolescents in a strange position; they are personally not responsible for their misbehaviors, but neither is the person who harasses or assaults them. In highlighting the fact that the girls used the internet and sent their photos to the man, this article follows journalistic conventions; unlike male sexual assault, the girls' actions seem newsworthy. These journalistic norms both respond to and reinforce the idea that male sexuality is inherently and inevitably dangerous and that potential victims are responsible for minimizing their risks. Unlike the girls, whose behaviors are extensively interpreted by three psychologists in the article, the man's actions are listed plainly in two paragraphs. Since male sexual violence is so ubiquitous and naturalized, it would transgress journalistic conventions of newsworthiness to run this story with quotations from psychologists explaining why a man would harm teenage girls or perhaps even to examine how his use of new media aided his crimes. The article concludes with a warning that parents should watch their kids, not an admonishment to adult men to refrain from assaulting teen girls. Though condemning male abusers might go without saying for journalists, following the journalistic convention to focus on the apparently new aspects of the crime, they inadvertently reinforce the idea that the assaults were the girls' fault. The end of the article suggests that parents "can protect their children by making sure there are no computers in the bedroom or other private places" (Jan Jarvis, 2007) and vigilantly monitoring their children's internet use.

Indeed, in discourses about new media and sexual risk, it is fairly common for both the responsibility for teen girls' risky decisions and for privacy violations to be deflected onto the temporarily inferior functioning of the teenage brain. For example, an op-ed on sexting stresses the need for parents to provide guidance to their teens because it is "important to bear in mind that teen brains are still undergoing development. Impulse control, the ability to weigh consequences and hormonal-emotional spikes are not the same for adults and teens" (Walsh, 2009). Likewise, testifying in front of a congressional committee on the dangers of the internet, prominent internet lawyer and online safety advocate Parry Aftab stresses that teenagers have temporarily faulty brains and need to be taught to change their risk-taking behavior:

> Pediatric neuro-psychologists tell us that preteens and young teens are hardwired, through immature brain development, to be unable to control their impulses at this age. . . . Sadly, our teens and preteens are [inviting online predators] to offline meetings, phone calls and videochats. But, as an expert in cyberrisk management, I can tell you that this is good news. Because we have a single point of risk—our children, preteens and teens. If we stop their risky and unsafe behaviors, and teach them when to reach out for help, we can manage this risk. (*Sexual Exploitation*, 2006, pp. 146–147)

Aftab criticizes teens for failing to "appreciate the consequences of their actions" and paints an appealing narrative that simple common sense rules of risk reduction can prevent online victimization. The implication is that risk-taking such as posting an image of oneself online is a main cause of sexual assault. Attempting to protect people from assault by regulating and controlling the potential victim's behavior—rather than the potential assailant—is often an ineffective strategy that implies that sexual assault is inevitable and makes potential victims the "single point of risk" who merely need to "stop their risky and unsafe behaviors" to be protected from harm. Feminist anti-rape activists and scholars have condemned such victim-blaming, but biological discourses about teenagers (and as the next chapter discusses, self-esteem promotion as well), authorizes the shift in responsibility away from perpetrators of harm and onto potential victims who supposedly failed to assure their own safety.

HOPPED-UP ON HORMONES

Hormones, like brain structures, play a similar role in narratives about technology and risk in that they offer a convenient explanation for teen's sexual behavior. In the 1940s, research on specific hormones intensified and gained new sources of funding; these biochemicals are referenced often in popular, academic, and sex education curricula explanations of gender differences and sexual behaviors (Fausto-Sterling, 2000; Whatley, 1988). Critics of the raging hormones model of adolescence note that even in the scientific literature, evidence for the direct causal influence of hormones on social and sexual behaviors is, at best, inconclusive (Buchanan, Eccles, & Becker, 1992; R. Epstein, 2007a; Fausto-Sterling, 1985, 2000; Lesko, 2001; Rosser, 2008). In discussions about sexting, mainstream media often explain adolescent girls' self-expression as the result of the so-called deadly mix of technology and teenage hormones. While this narrative at least acknowledges girls' sexual desires, it simultaneously negates sexual agency by subordinating their choices to an abstracted and dangerous druglike surge of teenage hormones. This kind of story promotes the message that girls must responsibly and safely control and manage these hormonally induced desires.

Though the influence of hormones on behavior is often presented as a neutral scientific fact, the implications are discussed in deeply gendered ways. In addition to the long-accepted narrative that adolescent hormones enable teenage boys' powerful sexual desires, raging hormones are also constructed as a dangerous liability for girls, producing sexual desires (in themselves and in boys) that girls are supposed to be responsible enough to resist. Men and boys supposedly have stronger and more frequent sexual desires that are often assumed to have a chemical origin; any of their negative effects are seen as an inevitable male condition rather than a problem to be solved. Women, in contrast, are often expected to manage and control their unstable hormones through pharmaceutical interventions and the power of their will (Fausto-Sterling, 2000; Vines, 1994; Whatley, 1988). As such, girls are dispatched to fight off the influence of young men's raging hormones until they emerge from the dangerous fog of adolescence and sexual decisions can be made rationally in marriage and/or adulthood (Fine, 1988; Fine & McClelland, 2006; Tolman, 2005; Tolman, Hirschman, & Impett, 2005). For example, a 1993 text on adolescent sexuality and childbearing explains:

> Her ability to comprehend the consequences of her behaviors, to form stable
> relationships, to communicate effectively with a partner, or to seek protec-

tive counsel may be immature whatever her hormones tell her—or tell the world about her. Thus, even when sexual onset is a matter of "choice," the young person may be as unprepared for it as if it were involuntary or coerced. (Zabin & Hayward, 1993, p. 54)

This comment positions girls' hormones as a problem for them to manage; a nefarious force that produces desires that they are so ill-prepared to act on that doing so can apparently create a traumatic experience equivalent to rape.

Many reports on sexting refer to psychological experts to legitimate the "raging hormones" theory as an explanation for why girls are sexting. One early report on sexting explains: "Psychologists said the phenomenon reflects typical teenage hormones and lack of judgment, with technology multiplying the potential for mischief" (S. Reitz, 2008), while another similarly states: "Psychologists say the phenomenon reflects young hormones and impulsivity, with technology increasing the potential for long-term humiliation" (Brody, 2008). Such narratives are so uncontroversial that they do not need a particular person as a source and can be instead vaguely attributed to psychologists in general. Since the concern about sexting focuses on girls creating images of themselves (boys are rarely described as humiliated by sexting), these comments assert that girls are not sexting in order to express sexual desire but because they lack judgment and are subject to a biochemically induced confusion. Further down in the second article, a psychologist who works with teens provides a scientific veneer to his moral judgments: "Kids today, in terms of sexuality, are much more open than previous generations. The promiscuity of it is psychologically worrisome. It's degrading to our value system" (Brody, 2008).

In the logic of adolescent sexual development, the teenage years are a dangerous battleground of unruly biological forces where hormones threaten to corrupt normative sexual morality (Patton, 1996). In an article on the dangers of online predators, Aftab justifies parents' need to monitor their kids on the internet by arguing, "When you get hormones pumping, [minors] are operating the heavy machinery of the Internet under impaired judgment" (MacDonald, 2005). A psychologist uses a similar metaphor: "[T]he parts for exercising judgment are still maturing. . . . It's like turning on the engine of a car without a skilled driver at the wheel" (Wallis & Park, 2004). Likewise, in a panicked article about online predators on MySpace, a psychologist expresses fears that "[teens'] unlimited access to pornography, mixed with a potent brew of teenage hormones, [creates] . . . a volatile mix" (Mayer-Hohdahl, 2006). A later article about sexting likewise asks, "What do you get when you mix cell phones and teenagers hopped up on hormones?" (Searcey, 2009a). These comments assert that teen sexuality is the result of "potent" hormones "pumping" to produce a "volatile brew" that teens get "hopped-up" on. For some experts, as Patton (1996) notes in her critique of safe-sex education, it follows that teens in this dangerous hormone-induced haze cannot be trusted with information about sex. The metaphor suggests that under the influence of their hormones, teens certainly cannot drive safely on the internet superhighway. Such narratives serve to maintain the contradictions of mainstream views of teenagers' sexuality: They are supposed to be demonstrating that they are heading toward heterosexuality without actually having or thinking about sex.

Just like fears about the telephone in its early days (Cassell & Cramer, 2008), there is considerable anxiety that online communication is dangerous for girls because it gives them new ways to talk (and think) about sexuality that might be less inhibited. There is no parallel widespread discourse that technology causes boys to create sexual images or to be "provocative"—being sexually inhibited is simply not expected or desired for boys. For example, in testimony before a congressional committee investigating the dangers of MySpace, online safety expert Parry Aftab (2006) argues that teenagers are "disconnected from the immediate consequences of their actions online, [so] many 'good' kids and teens find themselves doing things online they would never dream of doing in real life" (p. 16), and she notes that they post photos online in which they appear to be "drunken sluts" (p. 46). By placing the explicit blame on technology, commentators feel free to denounce teenage girls as "sluts" for expressing themselves online.

Some observers assume that digital media specifically allow and encourage adolescents to be more sexually assertive. For example, Bill Albert, a representative of an anti–teenage pregnancy organization, argues that technology is dangerous because it leads to a "casual hook-up culture" (Braver, 2009). Obviously, mobile phones offer the tools to easily create and send sexual images, but many also worry that technology itself seems to dismantle girls' supposedly natural inhibitions. An article critiquing the legal system for prosecuting teens for child pornography makes reference to "an increasingly sexualized adolescent cyberculture" (Marks, 2009). Another comment from an author of a book on MySpace for parents asserts, "[O]nline culture encourages exhibitionism" (Michels, 2008), and a psychologist says that teens "may be emboldened by technology" (Jan Jarvis, 2007). The assumption is that since the internet and mobile phones permit instant communication that is removed from traditional social contexts and consequences, when communicating with these technologies girls are more likely to make the inappropriate sexual decisions that their hormones are supposedly telling them to make.

Hormones are seen as a drug that corrupts the weak-willed and provides an explanation for sexuality in adolescent girls who are otherwise "normal" or "well-behaved" teenagers. One of the only ways that teenage girls' sexual desire is present at all in discussions about sexting is through the explanation that their sexuality is "hormonally driven" (Clark-Flory, 2008) and that they are "hormonally haywire" (Clark-Flory, 2009). While this particular argument usually advocates for the decriminalization of youth sexting, it does so by sacrificing a discussion of teen girls' sexual rights in order to make the more uncontroversial plea for sympathy on the grounds that these girls' sexual behavior is irrational because it is driven by their raging hormones. It would be much more difficult to argue instead that consensually sexting girls deserve sympathy from the justice system because they are entitled to sexual expression, desire, and pleasure.

Biological explanations can erase the possibility that some teen girls may be voluntarily choosing to sext. As long as sexting is explained as the result of out-of-control biology or a hormone-fueled mistake rather than a purposeful act of sexual self-expression, the need to protect children from their own misguided and unplanned actions is reaffirmed. In its most problematic form, however, characterizing sexting as the result of raging hormones and immature brains can mean that teenage girls are prosecuted for producing child pornography using the very laws that are supposed to protect them.

PEER PRESSURE AND "CRAZY TEEN TRENDS"

A third biology-based excuse is the long-standing trope that commentators offer to explain adolescent girls' sexual behavior: Teens are sexting because they are predisposed to follow trends. For adult observers, teenage trends seem to be separate and distinct from mainstream culture and are fed by young people's excessive or irrational devotion to an object or person. The homogenizing and essentialized assertions that teenagers blindly follow trends, coupled with the previously discussed assumptions about raging hormones and immature brains, help to reinforce the idea that criminalizing sexting protects teens, especially girls, from their own ill-considered decisions. That is, viewing sexting as a trend is yet another way that commentators can assert that teen girls are not acting voluntarily.

The dominant model of adolescence includes the assumption that teens are naturally "peer-oriented," which explains why they chase the latest trends and segregate themselves into same-age groups; even the concept of peer pressure is usually applied only to adolescents, as if adults are never influenced by the opinions of their coworkers, friends, and families. However, as Lesko (2001) and other critics of the dominant model of adolescence point out, the fact that adolescents are "peer-oriented" could merely result from the rigid age-graded structure of contemporary educational institutions that ensures that children and adolescents are frequently confined to same-age groups. These demeaning views of adolescents as weak-willed and herdlike affirms that they are "immature, dangerous, and [need] to be controlled" (Lesko, 1996, p. 153). Viewing teens as uniformly peer-oriented reinforces the idea that they lack agency and thus need to be monitored and protected from their own bad decisions.

The trend model implies that teenagers are not acting on purpose but have become infected by a sexting epidemic that is sweeping the nation. Stories framing sexting as a nationwide trend are common; an article about sexting suggests the name "Generation XXX" for contemporary adolescents (Fruhwirth, 2008). Others describe sexting as "a growing problem around the country" (Michels, 2008), an "alarming trend" (Walsh, 2009), and "a growing trend [and] concern" (Rogers, 2008). Another article quotes a law enforcement official who characterizes it as "an epidemic" (Todd, 2008). Stories in smaller papers sometimes cover the issue by announcing that the national trend of sexting has arrived locally, such as the lede in one story that explains: "A national trend of teenagers taking naked pictures of themselves on their cell phones and sending them to boyfriends and girlfriends is starting to show up in North Dakota, authorities say" ("Teens Cautioned," 2008). Another local paper headline asserts: "Sexting a world-wide epidemic: Problem hits home with 'close call' in Polk County" (Schulman, 2009). These smaller papers seem to be asserting that their hapless teens are merely falling victim to the national disease of sexting rather than engaging in it voluntarily.

The most striking thing about the discourse that sexting is a trend is that the term is mainly applied to teens and rarely to adults. Adults can and do use cell phones and the internet to share sexually explicit images of themselves, and studies demonstrate that like other sexual activities, sexting is more common among young adults than among minors (Drouin & Landgraff, 2011; Henderson, 2011). When the press covers adult sexting, it often involves specific cases of celebrity infidelity. Because adults are not seen as a homogeneous group, there are no panicked articles about a new trend among adults that threatens to break up marriages and tear apart the fabric of society. Yet for teens, sexting is often positioned in this way. Dr. Phil addresses sexting in a segment of a show called "Crazy Teen Trends" (Dowdey, 2009). In one CNN story about sexting, the background graphic reads: "SEX-CRAZED TEENS?" (figure 2). The anchor, experts, and call-in viewers to the CNN story all lament the im-

FIGURE 2. Mike Galanos asks, "Is there just no shame anymore with a lot of our young girls?" (CNN, December 4, 2008). Source: CNN

morality of both teenagers and their permissive parents who allow them to have phones with cameras (Galanos, 2008). In these contexts, the word *trend* contains a value judgment about frivolity, irrationality, and even foolish danger. After all, when a behavior is newly adopted among adults, the word *trend* often implies a passing but harmless fashion, and when it is seen as a good thing, it is not called a trend; it is often just seen as progress or as simply normal.

The developmental model of sexuality

Another dominant model in medicine, psychology, and many educational contexts, is that childhood and adolescent sexual exploration is necessary for individuals to develop naturally into sexually healthy adults. Here, teen sexuality is tolerated because it serves more important ends such as overall psychological development and maturation. When adolescent girls' sexual activity is acknowledged in this model, adult sympathizers often justify it on the grounds that they have a developmental need to explore their sexuality so that they can mature into sexually healthy heterosexual adults. While advocates who use this narrative are sympathetic to teens girls' sexual acts and desires, such excuses for girls' sexuality reinforces a slippery logic about girls' lack of authentic sexual desire. In a report sponsored by the Department of Justice, researchers invoke developmental logic to justify the need to use educational rather than legal interventions: "We should recognize that [sexting] behaviors most typically reflect natural (albeit at times misguided) manifestations of normative adolescent social and emotional needs" (A. J. Harris et al., 2013, p. 66). Rationales of development are often intended to garner sympathy for teens, but they can inadvertently subordinate desire to the supposedly more important process of overall sexual maturation.

The logic of psychological development plots out a fixed timeline of acceptable sexual behaviors, especially for girls. Adolescent boys' sexuality tends to be viewed as chaotic and uncontrollable, but inevitable and basically harmless. For girls, biology authorizes the slut-prude tightrope they are already walking by mapping out a normative path and reinforcing the idea that veering off to one side or another indicates some kind of pathology or deviance. These normative developmental discourses often produce adolescent heterosexuality as fragile and easily corrupted or sent off course and in need of protection from too much information about sex (D. Epstein & Sears, 1999; Foulkes, 2008; Heins, 2001; Irvine, 2002; Patton, 1996). Whatever sexual behavior, desire, or expression is allowed in this developmental model, the idea is that it needs to be monitored and contained to ensure that girls are heading in the right direction.

So-called sexually healthy girls have a fine line to walk and a complex sexual agency: They are supposed to follow the biology of sexual desire but keep it in check at the same time. Adolescent biology holds the potential for normative sexual development but also creates a risky, excessive desire. Thus, the role of girls' agency (which, in this model, is separate in some fundamental way from their biology) is to oppose the natural forces of sexuality—to say no, to deny pleasure, to ignore desire. The choices girls make that are recognized as such are often the choices they make to say no to sexuality; saying yes can mean that their agency has lost the battle against their biology. If girls are doing sexuality correctly, they are successfully managing and controlling the natural directives from their hormones. If they take risks and veer away from the preset path, they can be seen as succumbing to their biology's seductive and powerful forces.

In discussions of sexual victimization, the discourse of development can shift the blame from privacy violators to victims in the same way as the discourse of the still-developing brain. For example, in a series of 2006 congressional hearings on online predators, the committee chairperson asks a developmental pediatrician to explain how online predators convince their victims to perform sexual acts. The pediatrician answers:

> The adolescent's mind ... is very much in the sexually explorative phase in child development. ... So we find that many adolescents who become

exhibitionistic on the Internet are doing so partly because of sexual exploration and sexual development. . . . It is easy for me to understand how an
adolescent who is reaching out for some type of companionship online could
fall prey and become a compliant victim. (*Sexual Exploitation*, 2006, p. 20)

These comments assert that youth sexuality, which is part of a "sexually explorative phase," is a serious risk factor for assault. In an article on a sexting case,
an author of a book on MySpace safety notes that the site is "a means of getting attention, of becoming more popular. . . . It's an unhealthy extension of a
healthy adolescent exploration" (Michels, 2008). These arguments affirm that
sexual exploration is a normal phase, but that in combination with technology,
it can become unhealthy and dangerous. At the 2006 congressional hearing
mentioned earlier, Ernie Allen, president of National Center for Missing &
Exploited Children warns:

Too much technology and too much privacy, at a sexually curious age, can
lead to disastrous consequences. The teenage years are a time of personal
exploration. This is only natural. However, the new form of social interaction is over the Internet, exposing children to, literally, a world of potential
danger. (*Sexual Exploitation*, 2006, p. 138)

These kinds of comments suggest that the curiosity during young people's
"sexually explorative phase" is one of the causes of their victimization. Disturbingly, these developmental narratives seem to place at least some of that
blame with victims' developmental weaknesses for making them easy targets.

In addition to laying blame, there is something else going on in the way
that biology substitutes for adolescent female sexual agency. Attributing victimization to young persons' "sexually explorative phase" is indeed more sympathetic than merely criminalizing adolescent sex and blaming a victim for
her participation in an immoral act. Yet, by viewing adolescents' sexuality as
unformed and undeveloped, these sympathizers reproduce the logic that teen
sex is a separate, emergent form of sexuality that is fundamentally different
from what is assumed to be a fixed adult sexuality. Gray (2009) points out
that an increasing number of critical youth studies scholars contest the dominant "developmental paradigm that frames young people's identity practices
as playful experimentation rather than seeing these practices as ways of being
in the world" (p. 1169). Angelides (2004) likewise argues that scholarship
from the 1980s to the present "collapsed all forms and developmental stages
of childhood eroticism into a kind of childhood exploration that was seen to
differ from, and to precede the onset of, 'real' adult sexuality" (p. 154). Though

people's sexual desires and practices shift and change over the course of their lifetimes, adults are rarely described as exploring their sexuality unless they are engaging in non-heteronormative sex acts. The concept of exploration in this sense describes the activity as inessential, frivolous, and temporary.[4] By stressing that teens need to be able to explore their developing sexuality in order to become sexually healthy adults, this discourse implies that adolescent sexuality is not yet real and needs to be nurtured for the mental health of the future adults they will become, not for its own sake.

ALTERNATIVES TO TEENAGE BIOLOGY

The solution to these problems of assigning agency and blame is to complicate the easy narratives of biological determinism and recognize that youth sexuality is not mere experimentation, necessarily fraught with danger, or only a necessary developmental step toward adult sexuality. It is now widely accepted in cultural studies scholarship about adults that sexuality and gender are socially constructed categories; they are located not in individuals' innate identities, but in the endless reproduction and creation of discourses about them (Foucault, 1990). That is, there is no natural sexuality or gender prior to language, outside of discourse, or entirely free from power. Indeed, it is easy enough to see that the apparent binaries of gender and sexuality dissolve into vast spectra, variation, and fluidity over time and circumstance. Feminist and queer theorists, such as Sedgwick (1985), Rubin (1993), Weeks (1989), and Fausto-Sterling (2000), for example, have been advocating for the separation of gender and desire from bodies, hormones, and organs for decades now.

While queer theorists have connected discourses about sexuality to race, class, and gender,[5] age as a structural category of social exclusion and sexual regulation gets less attention. There is still considerable work to be done complicating the relationship between biology and teen sexuality. A few scholars take up this task by critiquing the personal narratives of "coming out" for their problematic production of adolescence as a volatile transitional period of sexual progress culminating in a fixed adult sexual identity (Angelides, 2004; Gordon, 1999; Halberstam, 2005; Sedgwick, 1991; Weber, 2012). The biology of sexuality—for both young people and adults—is still as popular as ever. Since biological determinism has helped secure rights for lesbian, gay, and transgender people, the gains may be worth it. After all, most people subjectively experience their sexual desires as innate and natural, not as a choice, so what's the harm? The problem is that when this genetic rhetoric biologizes sexuality, it can become ingrained in common sense and reverberate in unpredictable ways. One example is that biology-based sympathy often forecloses the recognition of nonnormative sexual choices that fall outside what Weber (2012) calls "biological homonormativity," which dictates a predictable development through adolescence to a singular stable lifelong sexual orientation.[6]

Biological determinism can also substitute for a more nuanced conversation about consent, agency, and exploitation. While states vary in their defined age of consent (16, 17, or 18 years old), each jurisdiction is certain that people below their specified age are categorically incapable of choosing to have sex. When biological assumptions authorize the use of age as a simplistic and convenient substitute for determining sexual victimization, people like Antjuanece Brown end up in jail. An ideal model of sexual victimization would better account for a range of harms. Kitrosser (1997) suggests that while age differences could indeed be one factor, the model should be based on determining imbalances of power rather than assumptions about the agency or mental capacity of the injured party. Indeed, in some cases victims are too fearful or traumatized to report incidents of exploitation, or they would retract their accusations after intimidation by their abusers, but age may be too simplistic a metric to determine which of those victims who claim consent were abused and which were not. Fischel (2010) argues, for example, that stronger standards for consent for younger people might better account for exploitation and abuses of power. Currently, age of consent laws rest on ideas about the inherent mental incapacity of the victim, which are based on assumptions about the biology of age and development. Questioning the certainties that biological narratives of sexuality and development seem to offer could open a space to begin the important task of developing social and legal frameworks that could affirm a relational consent-based model of sexuality that does not rely on homogenizing and unfair assumptions about teens. Moving away from a model based on biological incapacity raises new challenges for protecting victims, but also offers the opportunity to extend more rights and freedoms to young people and to avoid criminalizing their consensual sexual activities.

Conclusion

Many common explanations for sexting refer to biology and the supposedly innate features of adolescence. While these explanations are often intended to garner sympathy, they negate girls' agency by attributing the behavior to an external influence—hormones, brain structures, developmental needs, or peer pressure—rather than girls' own decisions. It must be noted, however, that biological excuses for sexting apply only to girls who can be seen as sexually innocent, which is connected to racial, class, and heteronormative privilege.

As long as biological narratives are being used to support the criminalization of consensual sexting, no one in particular is held accountable for sexual violence and harassment nor are these acknowledged as endemic social problems. This means that the blame for sexual violence is perversely shifted away from privacy violators and onto their victims.

The relationship between biology and adolescent sexuality is often unquestioned. Many scholars of gender and sexuality can easily see that biological sex does not determine gender and that gender does not determine sexuality, but it is less common to interrogate biological age-based assumptions about sexuality. This chapter suggests that biological assumptions about adolescence can be used to reinforce victim-blaming and an unjust criminalization of teen sexual practices. Questioning biological models of adolescence, sexuality, and adolescent sexuality is useful since these models can authorize the control and criminalization of a range of adolescent sexual practices, including sexting. The next chapter examines another way girls' sexual agency is imagined as deficient—because they have low self-esteem—and the specific interventions aimed to solve this problem and supposedly reduce their risk online.

CHAPTER 3

Self-esteem advice
and blame

Since the mid-1990s, the standard advice to parents about internet safety has been that they should restrict and monitor their teens' access to technology (Shade, 2011). But at the start of the widespread anxiety about teenage sexting in December 2008, a newspaper article offered some new advice to parents (Reimer, 2008). In this article, Bill Albert[1] suggests that parents should explain to their daughters that sending sexts to their boyfriends is "not what we meant when we talked about female empowerment." Albert also advises against rationally explaining to teens that someone might distribute a private image; according to the "Sex and Tech" (2008) survey, adolescents are already well aware of this possibility but send sexts anyhow. Given this apparent disconnect, Albert insists that parents need a more covert strategy to curtail sexting: female empowerment.

Albert's comments about empowerment do a few things: They reiterate that empowerment is an important goal for girls, they insist that empowerment is incompatible with sexting, and they suggest that the best way to reduce sexting among adolescents is for parents to address their teenage daughters—not their sons. In short, Albert's advice promotes empowerment for girls as an online safety strategy.

This chapter identifies a shift in online safety advice from a focus on predators and technology as the main culprits to an explicit strategy of encouraging girls to be autonomous, independent, and responsible online. This second model began to appear in national campaigns just a few years before Albert's comment in the mid-2000s. The new focus on self-esteem as empowerment in online safety discourses reflects self-esteem's long-standing prevalence in both abstinence-only and comprehensive sexual education programs—despite the lack of any conclusive evidence that this strategy actually works (Goodson, Buhi, & Dunsmore, 2006). By analyzing the advice for girls about online safety in public service announcements (PSAs) and mainstream media reports about sexting from 2005–2010, this chapter finds that ideas about girl power and self-esteem often have the unintended consequences of erasing the role of harassers and privacy violators and blaming their female victims for failing to adequately eliminate their risk.

Many of the major national online safety campaigns in the second half of the 2000s seek to raise girls' self-esteem in hopes of encouraging them to make safer sexual choices. This model posits that girls who are sexually active suffer from low self-esteem and use sex to seek validation, while confident adolescent girls with high self-esteem make safer, normative sexual choices (though some studies suggest high self-esteem might have the opposite effect).[2] As such, Albert argues in the article mentioned earlier that girls who sext are mistaken if they believe that their sexual choices are empowering (Reimer, 2008). Instead, he holds the common belief that true female empowerment would increase girls' will power and enable them to avoid making risky sexual decisions. Although promoting girl empowerment seems like a positive way to enhance girls' independence and autonomy, girl power discourses about online safety also operate as a form of control by defining the freedom to choose in limited ways. That is, girls' sexual choices are recognized as legitimate and freely chosen only if they conform to expectations about the appropriate time and circumstances in which adolescent girls should engage in sexual activity. Though this chapter demonstrates that self-esteem and empowerment are not inherently good, they are also not inherently bad. Cruikshank (1999) explains, "The will to empower others and oneself is neither a bad nor a good thing. It is political; the will to empower contains the twin possibilities of domination and freedom" (p. 2). The important questions are: What are the political and social effects of the kind of empowerment online safety advice promotes? What does this kind of empowerment assume and what does it leave out?

While girls do not necessarily follow online safety warnings,[3] advice directed at them that comes from mainstream sources provides an index of common sense ideas about how girls should behave. Nationally distributed PSAs and other forms of advice are good sources for common sense because the genre as a whole usually positions the advice-giver as reasonable and the advice itself as commonsensical and uncontroversial.[4] So much so that advice-giving in many forms usually does not involve the use of evidence in the way that a newspaper article would—though experts making unfounded claims appear often. The specific texts I examine in this chapter broadly represent common sense because mainstream institutions produced them for a national audience. The National Center for Missing & Exploited Children (NCMEC), which receives most of its funding from Justice Department programs,[5] is the biggest producer of nationally distributed online safety PSAs and is involved in most of the PSAs examined in this chapter. The Ad Council, a national nonprofit organization that distributes PSAs to broadcasters to fulfill public interest requirements set by the Federal Communications Commission, also distributes many of the PSAs mentioned in this chapter.

This chapter focuses in particular on the four major national PSA campaigns about online sexual exploitation that were produced in the second half of the 2000s—three of which were aimed exclusively at girls. These PSAs were produced by federal government and nonprofit national organizations. In addition to NCMEC, other organizations such as the Family Violence Prevention Fund and major media corporations such as Facebook and MTV were also involved. Each of these four campaigns were disseminated nationally across multiple forms of media, including billboards, newspapers, television, radio, magazines, and the internet. This chapter also draws on some informal advice to girls about sexting that appears in talk show segments, newspaper articles, and TV news. Taken together, the common sense in this set of texts offers evidence that the national discourse in the United States turned to self-esteem to address online safety in the mid-2000s.[6]

A range of government, educational, and corporate institutions, along with journalists, politicians, policymakers, and other authorities all seem to agree that increasing girls' self-esteem is the most effective way to protect them from harm online. They believe that girls who feel empowered and self-confident will make safer choices and avoid risk. That this strategy to address online safety is so appealing to so many diverse groups of people suggests that it reflects powerful cultural currents and assumptions about girls' sexuality. In this chapter I explore the sanctioned forms of idealized agency that online safety advice produces and I examine the problems of this self-esteem–based model. This approach to safety inadvertently blames girls for victimization, whether the perpetrator is a stranger or an ex-boyfriend, and erases sexuality from normal adolescent girlhood. I argue that online safety campaigns that promote community-based solutions to address the larger problems that underlie harassment and privacy violations would be more effective in preventing harm.

Before moving to my analysis of online safety advice for girls, I first examine the politics of girls' self-esteem.

The business of girls' low self-esteem

Since the early 1990s, many popular and academic discourses about girls have been dominated by discussions about the causes and effects of their supposed lack of self-esteem. Two widely read publications signal the beginning of this era: In 1991, the American Association of University Women released a report documenting the decline in self-esteem for girls in adolescence, and in 1994 *Reviving Ophelia* was published and became a commercial success. The market for paperbacks and educational programs about girls and low self-esteem has been described as a "veritable cottage industry . . . forced out of the fertile soil of girls' failing self-esteem" (Baumgardner & Richards, 2000, p. 179). Increasing self-esteem to reduce behaviors defined as risky is a central goal of many government and educational programs for girls. On the national level, the U.S. Department of Health and Human Services initiative Girl Power! was launched in 1996 to help educators encourage girls to harness their "power to be drug-free" and live healthy lives (figure 3). This campaign, which provides curriculum materials for educators, explains in a press release that since "girls tend to lose self-confidence and self-worth during this pivotal age . . . [they] become more vulnerable to negative outside influences and to mixed messages about risky behaviors" (Department of Health and Human Services, 1997). In PSAs for the campaign, celebrity athlete Dominique Dawes explains: "Girl Power! and drugs just don't mix. So be smart, stay away from drugs, and work hard. It pays off" (Center for Substance Abuse Prevention, 2000). Programs like Girl Power! offer individualized self-help solutions to problems—like drug use and, in the case of online safety PSAs, sexual harassment—which have significant social, structural, and systemic components. Such campaigns address drug addicts and sexual harassment victims with the cheerful message that they have the power to solve their own problems by simply raising their self-esteem and thus reducing their desire to engage in risky behaviors.

The popular and academic focus on self-esteem has been criticized for casting girls in a double bind in which they are seen both as passive victims of their low self-esteem and as active agents responsible for living up to ideals of personal strength and confidence in order to resolve lingering gender inequalities. This postfeminist rhetoric relies on the notion that since feminism has apparently achieved its structural goals for gender equality, women need to empower themselves to take advantage of all the opportunities now available

FIGURE 3. This free printable bookmark was avail-
able for download at www.girlpower.gov (1997).
Source: Substance Abuse and Mental Health
Services Administration

to them (Projansky, 2001). Focusing on self-help is still popular in government
and educational initiatives aimed at girls (Gonick, 2006; A. Harris, 2004),
perhaps because it prioritizes individual change over social change, often with
no integration between the two (Cruikshank, 1996; Kelly, Burton, & Regan,
1996; Ouellette, 2004). It is striking that self-esteem and empowerment initiatives are also common in juvenile justice systems and women's penal programs
despite little evidence of their success in either institution (Goodkind, 2009;
Mahaffy, 2004; McCorkel, 2004; Pollack, 2000).

Raising girls' self-esteem is also a popular response among feminists and
educators who are concerned about the problematic representations of gen-

der and sexuality in mass media, which I explore in more detail in chapter 4. Though the urge to empower girls to resist commercial culture is laudable, pursuing this goal can have serious unintended effects. For example, a major report for the American Psychological Association on the sexualization of girls (Zurbriggen et al., 2007) proposes solutions that focus on changing girls' attitudes and behaviors instead of trying to modify male behavior to reduce the incidence of sexual violence and harassment. The report recommends that girls should make zines, discuss sexually explicit images in mass media with their parents, and join extracurricular sports teams. These ideas all no doubt offer significant benefits to girls, but the report offers no specific recommendations for interventions or programs aimed at boys and men. The danger with this approach is that personal-empowerment solutions to social problems imply that the primary determinant of safety is girls' attitudes, not the behaviors of specific people who might harm them.

The key problem with all these self-esteem programs is that viewing girls' low self-esteem as a passively acquired pathology obscures what people and institutions do to girls that might cause trauma and difficulty in their lives, whether or not they have low self-esteem. Self-esteem–based online safety advice reproduces the same problems. Programs like these rarely consider that low self-esteem might be a symptom of social structures rather than a feminine delusion about one's potential and power that needs to be corrected. Considering female juvenile offenders in self-esteem programs, Goodkind (2009) asks: "Is it reasonable to ask girls to value themselves when they have been so utterly devalued by those around them and society more broadly?" (p. 417). Self-esteem programs often view a person's feelings of disempowerment, rather than her actual disempowerment, as the main problem and point of intervention (Pollack, 2000). Goodson and her coauthors (2006) are also concerned about the possible negative effects of programs that raise self-esteem. Their review finds a number of studies suggesting that higher self-esteem may be associated with risk-taking, aggression, defensiveness, and narcissism, meaning that self-esteem programs may be, as they explain, "reinforcing individualistic and egotistical normative patterns of behavior that contribute to the weakening of inter-personal connectedness and, thus, generate outcomes that are, mainly, unhealthy and potentially unethical" (Goodson et al., 2006, p. 317). Following Ehrenreich's (2009) work on the delusions of positive thinking, it is worth considering whether well-meaning and enthusiastic individuals who demand that girls feel good about themselves and positive about their futures are perhaps the ones who are being irrational.

Significant educational resources are dedicated to self-esteem improvement programs (Hewitt, 1998) despite little evidence that raising a person's self-esteem, in and of itself, has any long-term positive effect (Goodkind, 2009; Mahaffy, 2004). Structural inequalities remain the single largest and most significant barrier to improving one's economic standing, no matter how positive an attitude a girl can muster (Mahaffy, 2004). Though the popular and academic focus on girls' low self-esteem since the early 1990s draws needed attention to ongoing gender inequalities, it often identifies young women's inability to empower themselves as the cause. In valorizing independence and self-reliance, discourses of self-esteem encourage girls to blame themselves for their problems. Though feminists recognized decades ago that sexual violence and harassment are social and political problems, many national PSAs that address online sexual safety position girls as personally responsible for being sexual harassed.

The shift from predators to girls

When the moral panic about online predators first emerged in the mid-1990s, mainstream news coverage and PSAs often characterized teens as innocent dupes of devious internet-savvy middle-aged men. Many people believed that it was common for adult men to pose as a same-age friend or romantic interest and carefully gather small amounts of information about their target in order to locate and eventually assault them (Wartella & Jennings, 2000). This frightening scenario was reproduced and distributed in a wide variety of forms in the late 1990s and early 2000s, including news, books, PSAs, and TV shows.[7]

A typical example of these attempts to educate parents about online predators is an advertisement produced by the 2003 NCMEC Campaign against Child Sexual Exploitation, which depicts a middle-aged white man in front of a computer with the headline "Meet 10-year-old Becky's 12-year-old internet friend" and encourages parents to "know the potential dangers and report them" ("Meet," 2003). The ad stresses the contrast between the unseen "10-year-old Becky" mentioned in the text and the middle-aged man in the photo. His gaze is intently fixed on a computer screen, and high-contrast lighting illuminates dark shadows on his face, which suggests a sinister smirk, while street lights filter through blinds in the background. The text in the sidebar explains that the man intends to use the internet as "a new, effective, and more anonymous way to sexually exploit children." Exploiting children is so much easier, the ad says, that the Cyber Tipline has already received almost half a million leads—though it does not mention exactly how many of those tips led to the arrest of anonymous online predators like "Becky's 12-year-old internet friend" depicted in this campaign.

Though strangers who stalk adolescents online are extremely rare (Wolak, Finkelhor, & Mitchell, 2004; Wolak et al., 2008), mass media coverage and PSAs reproduced this fear as a primary danger of the internet from the mid-1990s to the mid-2000s (Cassell & Cramer, 2008; Shade, 2007). Many print and TV ads created as part of the 2004 "Help Delete Online Predators" campaign, produced by NCMEC and the Ad Council, include the information: "Each year, 1 in 5 children is sexually solicited over the internet." Note that the intentional passive voice in this statement implies that online predators are the ones doing the soliciting—who else would it be? Yet, the peer-reviewed study that generated this statistic defined sexual solicitation so broadly that it included comments such as "what is your bra size?" as an incident. The study makes it clear that most of those solicitation incidents were unwelcome comments from peers rather than dangerous online strangers, and most of these incidents were not seen by the young person as distressing (Wolak et al., 2008). In general, these PSAs about online predators stress the need for parents to get involved in their child's internet use and to discuss the dangers with them. Their main advice to parents is to take computers out of their children's private bedrooms and to use internet filtering and monitoring software.

In the shift to the so-called participatory web (known as "web 2.0" in the mid-2000s), girls came to be seen not as passive readers of internet content but as active producers, thus potentially taking risks in how and with whom they interacted. As MySpace, the first major social network site, gained momentum, a large user base, and media attention beginning in 2005,[8] educators and organizations began to see teen girls as content producers and to worry about what they were posting. Indeed, NCMEC's advice about online safety shifted in 2005 from educating parents about online predators and instructing them how to monitor their children to the "Don't Believe the Type" campaign, which targets girls with self-esteem and empowerment messages.[9] Likewise, a case study of the 2006 "2 SMRT 4U" campaign blames girls for supposedly attracting online predators, claiming that since girls want to portray themselves online "as fun, hip, provocative and sexy" and be connected to their peers, this creates "the perfect lure for a sexual predator" (Effie Awards, 2008, p. 1). With the shift to blaming girls for the way they portray themselves on social network sites, advice about sexual danger online looks increasingly like it does offline in that it often ignores potential perpetrators and targets women and girls instead by admonishing them to avoid supposedly excessive risks like wearing short skirts, walking alone, or drinking.

NCMEC's 2005 campaign "Don't Believe the Type" is the first national online safety campaign to focus on girls' behavior and attitudes rather than targeting parents or online predators. This campaign explicitly encourages personal strength and resilience for girls and focuses on instructing girls to distrust strangers online. A press release explains that this campaign is designed "to prevent girls from forming inappropriate online relationships with older men in an effort to reduce their risks of sexual exploitation and abduction . . . [and to] show teen girls how easily a predator can manipulate their insecurities" (2005). One PSA from this 2005 campaign intercuts a shot of a young teen girl speaking to a camera with a parallel shot of an older man, whose comments reveal that he is manipulating the girl into trusting him. The girl explains that they share interests, that he "gets" her, and that she is flattered by the attention, and says, "Other people don't understand. If you trust someone, what's wrong with meeting?" A jump cut to the man interrupts her, as he says with a sinister grin: "Meeting them is the goal. That's when things get really interesting" (National Center for Missing and Exploited Children and the Ad Council, 2005). Using the predator's voice to dispel the girl's assumptions emphasizes her naiveté, as the adult male's explanations make it clear that she is being manipulated into believing his lies, a process he describes as "easy." Concluding the ad, the narrator says, over ominous echoing musical tones, "Online predators know what they're doing. Do you?" and the screen displays the tag line: "Don't believe the type." Here the girl's online interaction with the man and her active participation in the relationship is targeted as the problematic behavior this PSA seeks to change.

This kind of ad casts men as skilled predators and positions girls as innocent dupes who need to educate and empower themselves to change their online interactions. In other words, they need to learn to distrust online relationships. The profound shift with this 2005 campaign is that for the first time since the beginning of the online predator panic in the mid-1990s, girls are now viewed as complicit in their victimization.

As fears about sexting emerge in 2009, there is a sensational and exaggerated concern that predators who find sexual images of minors will be enticed to seek out those particular people and victimize them. District attorney George Skumanick argues in his brief to the court in a sexting case (discussed in chapter 1): "Sexting provides the gateway for child predators to our children" (Donohue & Hailstone, 2009, p. 11). Likewise, a former prosecutor speaking on a CNN (2009) news program argues that criminal charges for sexting are necessary because, she says, "Adults in the real child pornography business will hunt you down and take advantage if they find these pictures, and they will." These unfounded fears about the nature of online victimization[10] tell would-be sexters and girls socializing online to take responsibility for ensuring their own online safety. At the same time, the perpetrators of sexual violence, who are actually often intimate partners, family members, and acquaintances rather than online strangers, seem to fade into the social background as an inevitable and unchangeable reality.

ONLY VICTIMS CAN PREVENT
ONLINE PREDATION

Despite the good intentions to help prevent girls from being exploited, online safety advice tends to reproduce the idea that sexual harassment is natural and inevitable and that only girls—not the men who victimize them—need to modify their behavior. These ideas reflect a long-standing problem in many mainstream rape-prevention education programs and campaigns, which position women simultaneously as victims and as responsible for preventing rape (R. Hall, 2004; Projansky, 2001).[11] Drawing on the popularity of girl-empowerment rhetoric, online safety advice reframes the familiar idea that women are to blame for sexual violence by advocating that girls curtail their online activities in order to limit their risk. In the three campaigns discussed in this section, girls' agency is limited to the power they have to self-censor, to restrict their online social interactions, and to be extremely cautious about the personal information they post online. They are allowed to explore the internet, but only if they vigilantly erase any traces of their identity.

In the mid-2000s, when fears about online predators were at a peak, many educators and parents were concerned that teens who post personal information on newly popular social network sites like MySpace and Facebook were at a high risk of being stalked by a stranger online. Many observers who hold these fears have legitimate and important concerns about violence against women, but they incorrectly assume that women are safe in domestic spaces and unsafe in public ones. Each new communication technology, from the telegraph, to the telephone, to mobile phones and the internet generated waves of panic (Cassell & Cramer, 2008). With each, the concern is similar: that these technologies are dangerous because they allow women and girls more access to public spaces—which likewise allows members of the public more access to girls. Working from this framework, parents and educators tell girls that the solution is to hide their identities online. In fact, posting personal information on the internet does not increase the likelihood that teenagers will be victimized by someone they meet online (Wolak et al., 2009; Ybarra et al., 2007). Nonetheless, two of the campaigns I examine, "2 SMRT 4U" (2006) and "Think Before You Post" (2007), advise girls to be invisible when they are on the internet.

The main practical strategy the "2 SMRT 4U" campaign offers girls is that they should avoid sharing personal information or posting pictures of themselves online.[12] Although the phrase "2 SMRT 4U" appears to be an affirming, empowering, and positive statement, the campaign limits female empowerment to the capacity to exercise caution on the internet. A press release explains, "It is essential that we empower youth to be cautious, aware and intelligent about the information they post" (Thompson, 2006). A representative for the campaign elaborates: "We're putting tools into the hands of teen girls to be safer about how they navigate online social networking sites and blogs" (Thompson, 2006). These tools for self-empowerment consist of a free silver ring embossed with the slogan "2 SMRT 4U," online safety tips, and downloadable stickers, picture frames, and worksheets. "2 SMRT 4U" advises girls to withhold all personal information and to remain silent and hidden in online public spaces. The campaign's tips advise girls: "DON'T communicate with people you don't know" and "DON'T post photos with school names, locations, license plates, or signs" ("What to Type," 2006). The campaign also suggests that girls should make sure their gender and sexuality is invisible online, advising: "Choose a gender-neutral screen name," and, of course, "DON'T post sexually provocative photos" ("What to Type," 2006). Like the other PSAs I examine in this section, "2 SMRT 4U" encourages girls to take full responsibility for their online safety, in this case by choosing anonymity when they are online.

In contrast to "2 SMRT 4U's" message of girl power and affirmation, which I return to in some detail at the end of this chapter, the next campaign I examine, "Think Before You Post" (2007),[13] offers a warning that girls should "think." This campaign, in the form of two television PSAs, as well as a print materials, radio spots, and a series of online banner ads, consists of dramatized narratives of the worst-case scenarios that can occur as a result of posting personal information or photos online. The campaign constructs girls' agency in terms of their ability to consider how they could potentially be victimized before they share personal content or photos online. The problem with this well-intentioned advice is that while it gives girls responsibility and power, the only kind of agency this constructs for girls is the ability to develop a heightened sense of personal risk and fear and to restrict their activities accordingly.

In one of the two television PSAs from the "Think before You Post" campaign, titled "Bulletin Board" (National Center for Missing & Exploited Children and the Ad Council, 2007a), a girl puts an image of herself in jeans and a tank top on a school bulletin board. In the picture, she is lying on her stomach on a bed with teddy bears and pillows out of focus in the background. Her bare toes are pointed up, she gazes coyly at the camera, and the picture is bordered

FIGURE 4. The image on the bulletin board. Source: National Center for Missing & Exploited Children, the Ad Council, and the United States Department of Justice

with pink and red hearts (figure 4). As she puts up the image, she smiles to herself, but the following shots depict an increasing number of students around the school taking the picture and passing it around—each time a person takes it off the bulletin board, there is a sound of a click, and a copy of the image reappears in its place. After everyone in school seems to have a copy, the girl returns to the bulletin board to tear it down angrily, but another appears in its place, and another, and another, as she grows more distressed and eventually gives up. The narrator explains, "Once you post your image online, you can't take it back. Anyone can see it. Family, friends. Anyone" (National Center for Missing & Exploited Children and the Ad Council, 2007a). Just as the narrator says "anyone," the camera cuts to a middle-aged male janitor who is wheeling a mop bucket past the bulletin board.[14] He stops, sees the picture, and with a devious smile takes a copy for himself (figure 5). "Remember," the narrator says, "Think before you post."

The point of the PSA is that if you would not post your image on a hallway bulletin board, you should not share it over the internet. Yet since many teens' social network pages are restricted to "friends only" (boyd, 2008; Debatin et al., 2009), the analogy that posting an image to an online profile is like posting

FIGURE 5. The school janitor takes a copy for himself.
Source: National Center for Missing & Exploited Children,
the Ad Council, and the United States Department of Justice

it on a public bulletin board may not resonate with teenage viewers. Indeed, teens are well aware—as argued in chapter 5—that just because an image is digital does not mean that it is necessarily public. The bulletin board analogy collapses the many different ways to share an image digitally, such as sending it to one person, posting it to a friends-only profile page, or posting it in a completely public place online. If the girl posted the image on a profile page that is only accessible to her online friends or sent it to a romantic interest, the wider distribution the ad depicts requires one crucial step that is conspicuously absent: Someone with access to the image needs to make the decision to distribute it without the girl's permission. Though it is easy for someone to do this, it is nevertheless a violation of privacy and consent. This understanding is completely absent in "Bulletin Board," which depicts the girl posting the image herself in a completely public place. A better metaphor might be a diary the girl shows to some of her friends but leaves in a drawer in her bedroom—certainly then it would be easy to see that anyone rifling around in her drawers to find the diary, photocopying its pages, and posting them on the school bulletin board is doing something ethically dubious. The campaign simply does not address the intermediaries who maliciously or unthinkingly distribute a

FIGURE 6. A ticket taker leers and says, "Hey Sarah, what color underwear today?" Source: National Center for Missing & Exploited Children, the Ad Council, and the United States Department of Justice

private image. As I discuss in the final section of this chapter, it is important to recognize the agency of these harassers in order to understand and curb their harmful behavior.

Another PSA from the "Think before You Post" campaign also depicts the grave consequences of posting sexual images online. The television PSA "Everyone" (National Center for Missing & Exploited Children and the Ad Council, 2007b) follows Sarah from school to the mall, the movies, and a restaurant, depicting an increasingly menacing type of attention from men who are familiar with her online pictures and posts. While she is at first flattered by the attention and celebrity status at school, she gradually becomes more distressed. The coach says, "Love the new tattoo, Sarah," and a male usher at the movie theatre smiles deviously and asks, "Hey Sarah, what color underwear today?" (figure 6). Finally, a busboy, who has scruffy facial hair and is wearing a stained white T-shirt and apron,[15] leans over and demands, "Hey Sarah, so when are you going to post something new?" (figure 7). When she is upset and gets up to leave, he calls out after her, "See you later, Sarah." The narrator explains that Sarah should not have posted pictures of herself: "Anything you post online, anyone can see. Family, friends, . . . and not so friendly people. Think before you

FIGURE 7. The busboy asks, "Hey Sarah, so when are you going to post something new?" Source: National Center for Missing & Exploited Children, the Ad Council, and the United States Department of Justice

post." By failing to think before she posted, the ad suggests, Sarah has invited this unwanted attention from strangers; the focus of the ad is to shame Sarah for her internet posts, not to criticize men's sexual harassment of young women.

The message in this PSA is that Sarah should be more careful about the content she posts on her presumably public website—it is not clear if providing personal information, such as her name or a photo of her tattoo, is thought to cause sexual harassment, or if Sarah only needs to refrain from sexually suggestive posts, such as an image of herself in her underwear. Yet nothing she does could possibly mean that she deserves to be sexually harassed by strangers. Had this nationally broadcast PSA depicted a young woman being harassed in public for wearing a short skirt and offered the advice to "Think before you get dressed," feminists would have surely responded with outrage.[16] But when the young woman in question does this online, rather than in the street, the PSA constructs her as solely responsible for her harassment. The common but mistaken idea that digital images are inherently public makes it possible to apply the idea that victims of sexual violence were "asking for it" to an online context. The message is clear that Sarah is responsible for her harassment and that to prevent such threatening encounters with strange men she needs to think more carefully before she posts anything online. Rather than criticizing people who distribute an image of someone else they know to be private, or even commenting on adult men who make threatening comments to teenage girls in movie theatres or restaurants, these kinds of messages maintain that girls' agency lies primarily in their ability to refrain from posting anything personal online.

While "2SMRT4U" (2006) and "Think Before You Post" (2007) focus on online predators, in later campaigns such as "A Thin Line" (2010), which I discuss next, and "That's Not Cool" (2009), which I examine in more detail later, the villain is a demanding, disrespectful boyfriend. The Family Violence Prevention Fund, who coined the term "digital dating violence" and brought the issue national attention with the launch of these programs, produced both of these campaigns. These later campaigns do not abandon concerns about predators but portray them as deviant, largely passive viewers of wayward sexts that are reportedly "sold on the digital black market" ("Sexting in America," 2010) rather than as people who actively seek out and stalk girls they find online. While the main villains in these newer story lines are boyfriends who demand too much attention and pressure girls to send them naked pictures, the advice is similar. Instead of addressing how abusers could change their behavior, online safety advice still asks victims to be responsible for their own safety by making the choice to never trust anyone to respect their privacy, especially intimate partners.

According to its press release, "A Thin Line" is a campaign that seeks to "empower America's youth to identify, respond to and stop the spread of . . . digital harassment" ("MTV," 2009).[17] The campaign offers yet another way of blaming victims by positioning them as the key to ending digital harassment. In a 2010 MTV News feature on sexting that is part of the campaign, the host explains, "There's a thin line between private flirtation and public humiliation" ("Sexting in America," 2010). The campaign's online banner cycles through a series of subheadlines noting that there is "a thin line" between, for example, "him/whole school" and between "private/public." These subheadlines substitute an inanimate "/" for acts of deliberate harm. The campaign is clearly set up as a warning to potential victims, advising them that, in an instant, their private images can become public. True enough, but note that like the other campaigns this chapter examines, this one—yet again—targets consensual sexters instead of privacy violators. "A Thin Line" offers no words of caution or ethical instruction to the person who might choose to willfully turn a "private flirtation" into a "public humiliation."

This same victim-blaming rhetoric is evident in a 2010 MTV News feature, that focuses on Ally, a girl who sent her ex-boyfriend a topless photo when he promised he would get back together with her and would keep the photo private. He did neither, yet the program offers no analysis or condemnation of his behavior, instead viewing it as an inevitable outcome that Ally should have foreseen. She takes responsibility for the incident, saying it was "the biggest mistake of my life," and her therapist agrees: "Because of Ally's sexting incident, she suffered a lot of consequences" ("Sexting in America," 2010). This comment subtly avoids criticizing or even referring to either the boy who betrayed Ally or her male and female classmates who harassed her at school afterward. The therapist even calls it "Ally's incident"—the shame and the blame both seem to belong to Ally alone. If MTV News wanted instead to discourage teens from maliciously forwarding private images, it could perhaps find a regretful teenage boy who can tearfully state that sending out his ex-girlfriend's private image was the biggest mistake of his life. Instead, Ally's regret is the only point to this story.

Even more disturbing, the Family Violence Prevention Fund's prominent national discourse about sexting defines the practice as inherently and typically abusive. This echoes the legal definitions that criminalize all forms of sexting. A *New York Times* article, reproducing talking points from the campaign's press release, explains: "Sending nude pictures, whether it is done under pressure or not, is part of a pattern of teenage behavior that the Family Violence Prevention Fund . . . has labeled digital dating violence" (Clifford, 2009). It is not clear how sending nude pictures without pressure or distribution could possibly be seen as "digital dating violence," but this organization insists that it is. Levine (2009) criticizes this particular article for "swing[ing] between descriptions of consensual photo-swapping and incessant, aggressive texting and Facebook or MySpace rumor- and insult-mongering as if these were similarly motivated— and equally harmful." While bringing additional national attention to intimate partner abuse is valuable, folding all forms of sexting into the new category of "digital dating violence" threatens to dilute this potentially useful concept beyond any meaningful definition of "violence." In this model, sexting is always nonconsensual, and thus anyone involved in sexting is either an abuser or victim of manipulation. The only type of power this framework offers girls is that to avoid being manipulated, they should never allow themselves to be pressured to create sexual images of themselves. Though these newer forms of advice label the manipulator as a bad boyfriend instead of an online predator, the basic message is the same. All of the PSAs I examine attempt to help girls avoid online risks but inadvertently blame victims and assert that adolescent sexual expression always leads to victimization.

Just say "no" to sexting

The next campaign I examine, "That's Not Cool," powerfully demonstrates the common assumption that girls are sexting not because they want to have sex or talk about sex, but because they have low self-esteem. Adolescent girls are routinely positioned as sexual objects but rarely as subjects. They are expected to be sexy but not sexual. So it is common for girls, and their adult observers, to offer a range of explanations and apologies for their sexual activity (Tolman, 1999). Low self-esteem is only one of a number of excuses I have found that people use to avoid considering girls' sexual agency; the other excuses, which I discuss elsewhere, include hormones and brain development, sexualization in mass media, and mobile media themselves. Each of these has been offered as an answer to the apparently difficult question of why girls would sext—pleasure, the most obvious explanation is rarely if ever suggested. Note that the excuses for sexting are typically available only to white middle-class straight girls, while less privileged girls who are sexually active are more often seen as simply deviant (Chesney-Lind & Irwin, 2008; Dohrn, 2004; Weis & Fine, 2000).

Since normative girlhood does not leave much space for sexual desire, the explanation that sexting is a result of low self-esteem asserts that girls who sext must have been influenced by male pressure, their misplaced desires for attention, or the influence of mass media. Regardless of the real or imagined cause, many commentators claim that raising girls' self-esteem is the best means of overcoming the supposedly inherent weaknesses that drive girls to sext. These discourses construct girls' ability to resist external pressures to behave in a sexual way as their only authentic and legitimate kind of sexual agency.

One version of this discourse is that girls with low self-esteem are unable to resist inappropriate or dangerous male sexual demands, such as those made by abusive boyfriends who pressure girls to send nude pictures. The second version, which I briefly turn to at the end of this section, is that girls with low self-esteem send sexts because they are foolishly seeking validation and attention in the wrong places. Both forms of advice reproduce and construct an image of normative girlhood that opposes being sexually active with having high self-esteem. The two are seen to be mutually exclusive and completely incompatible—as Albert (Reimer, 2008) contends at the start of this chapter, sexting cannot be considered a viable or authentic form of "female empowerment."

In mainstream media coverage of sexting, there is not much worry that boys might be sexting because of pressure or that they might become sexually active because they have low self-esteem. These issues are sometimes discussed in gender-neutral terms, but raising one's self-esteem and resisting sexual pressure appear to be uniquely feminine pursuits. For example, one newspaper article quotes a psychiatrist who treats children and adolescents: "Boys do it for exhibition, girls do it in response or request from a boy. That's what I've seen repeatedly" (Le Beau, 2009). This medical professional's comments reproduce the familiar narrative that girls have no sexual agency and merely succumb to male sexual pressure. TV news anchor Megyn Kelly warns about the serious consequences this can have for girls: "[I] remember peer pressure from boys to do things that most girls didn't want to do, and hopefully you've been raised right and you say 'no.' That's the problem here, a lot of these girls get peer pressured into doing it, and then they get arrested" ("'Sexting': High-Tech Flirting" 2009). Her comments reflect the belief that willpower and moral values will protect most girls' presumably innate yet fragile desire for chastity against the dangerous sexual desires of boys and peers.

Girls' willpower and moral superiority are key strategies the "That's Not Cool" campaign (2009)[18] promotes. This campaign tries to empower girls to say "no" to sexting using cheeky prepackaged quips. The campaign addresses sexting as one of six behaviors labeled "digital dating violence" and invites teenagers to download or photograph "callout cards" that they can send to other people to criticize their behavior. One of the six issues, labeled "Pic Pressure," includes three callout cards that reference sexting with sarcastic quips such as "Your boyfriend is so cute when he's badgering you for dirty photos" above an image of a puppy ("That's Not Cool," 2009). Campaigns like this one are valuable in that they keep the issue of intimate partner violence on the table, but many, including "That's Not Cool," leave the responsibility for social change to the victims. In this case, the vehicle for change is sarcasm. The campaign's characterization of adolescent girls as normally averse to sexuality and never wanting to sext consensually is also particularly insidious. All of the narratives on the callout cards are designed to help girls resist pressure from boys to send or receive nude pictures, putting girls in the familiar role of perpetually resisting male sexuality. This time, they are armed with sarcastic callout cards they can send to potential harassers and privacy violators.

To explain why the "That's Not Cool" campaign focuses on helping girls resist male sexual pressure, a press release points out that the campaign was developed in response to the 2008 *Sex and Tech* survey. In this survey, "More than half of teen girls (51 percent) say pressure from a guy is a reason girls send sexy messages or images" ("That's Not Cool", 2009). This particular statistic, reported widely in newspapers as a major finding of the survey, is a measure of teens' perceptions and assumptions about other teens, not their own behavior—only 10 percent responded that they had personally felt pressured.[19]

Such a contradiction between the respondents' views of their own behaviors and that of others is common in surveys like this one; girls may be motivated to perceive or portray themselves as resistant to male pressure or they may be accurately reporting their own experiences, but not the experiences of their peers. Either way, by choosing to use only the higher statistic about girls' perceptions of other girls and not girls' reports about their own behavior, this press release assumes that many of the girls who say they were not pressured are lying or are deluded.

The callout cards used in this campaign define being sexual as normal for boys but as repulsive or at least unwanted for girls. One card depicts a statue of David with a towel around his waist and says, "The naughty photo you sent made me gag." Another depicts a mint candy with the message: "When you pressure me for nude pics I throw up in my mouth a little." This rhetoric of physical illness is sarcastic rather than literal, but it nonetheless invokes the figure of the innocent young (heterosexual) female teenager who feels that male sexuality is repugnant. This puts girls in the position of policing male sexuality and also ignores other more salient results of the survey: Only a minority of teenagers who received sexts reported negative reactions. The responses they reported about sexting such as "grossed out," "turned off," and "creeped out" were among the lowest chosen (15–22 percent), while "excited," "amused," "surprised," and "turned on" were the most popular (40–55 percent). "To be fun/flirtatious" was the most common reason that teens reported (63 percent) for sexting on a multi-item question ("Sex and Tech," 2008). In contrast, the Pic Pressure callout cards reproduce the idea—sarcastic or not—that normative heterosexual adolescent girls find male sexual expression silly, disgusting, or unappealing. Though some have these reactions, they appear to be the minority in the *Sex and Tech* survey. Unlike other online safety campaigns that directly chastise girls for sending or receiving sexts, "That's Not Cool" does not acknowledge sexually desiring girls at all.

Many observers assume that most girls have low self-esteem and that they sext to get attention rather than to express their sexuality—as if the two were mutually exclusive. There is no equivalent concern about boys creating sexts to get attention. For example, one newspaper columnist offers the theory that girls sext because of trouble at home or a lack of self-esteem and concludes: "Our daughters need to know that this is a terrible way to get attention" (Pelham, 2010). Likewise, a high school principal explains in a newspaper article that sexting is the result of "a breakdown of self-concept and self-esteem . . . [which] leads young girls to seek venues and forums to build their self-concept and esteem because people pay attention to them. Unfortunately, it's the wrong kind of attention'" (Todd, 2008). These kind of comments depict girls as so desperate to improve their dismal self-concept that they accidentally or immorally turn to sex for attention. For boys, sexting is not usually positioned as the "wrong kind of attention," but instead as harmless boyhood sexual experimentation.

Concerns that girls who sext are seeking the "wrong kind of attention" both erase girls' sexual desires and underscore their need to raise their self-esteem through safe, appropriate nonsexual means. A final example that powerfully illustrates these concerns is the March 2009 episode of Tyra Banks's talk show on sexting in which she argues that low self-esteem is the primary driving force behind sexting. The promotional clips for this episode stress the link between sexting and low self-esteem: One girl explains to Banks, "I don't think I'm pretty. To get a guy to like me, I might have to send a naked picture" ("Teen Sexting," 2009). In this episode, Banks says to a group of apparently low-esteem sexters: "This is hurting me so bad that you guys are not feeling attractive" and she adds that being pretty is "about how we feel inside." She cautions that feeling good about yourself is important because if young men "smell low self-esteem" they will take advantage of this weakness. Banks acknowledges these girls' desires to feel attractive, but she argues that such feelings cannot come from sexting—she assumes that this particular way of feeling attractive is clear evidence of low self-esteem. Thus, her advice to girls is not just to work on being beautiful, as girls have often been told, but also to work on "feeling attractive." The importance of beauty for girls—even if it is constructed as a feeling rather than a set of physical characteristics—is, of course, unquestioned. For Banks, the importance of self-esteem is to fortify a girl's armor against malicious young men who are on the prowl for fragile girls to exploit. Here, girls are in the familiar position of being told to be sexually attractive but to never appear to be sexually active—to be a sexual object rather than a sexual subject. The form of agency Banks constructs for psychologically healthy girls is the power (and the need) to cultivate feelings of beauty and self-confidence but not the ability to express themselves sexually.

RESPECT YOURSELF TO PROTECT YOURSELF

On the surface, the "2 SMRT 4U" campaign's messages of self-affirmation and girl power might seem like a feminist model for online safety. Despite its color scheme of bubblegum pink and dark turquoise, the campaign does not explicitly promote traditionally feminine qualities such as beauty or passivity but instead celebrates girls' power and positions them as confident and assertive—the ideal girl is "too smart" to be deceived by online predators. But, in addition to the advice discussed in the previous sections that encourages girls to resist sexual pressure from boys, the "2 SMRT 4U" campaign also claims that the only path to self-respect is through exercising sexual self-restraint.

The "2 SMRT 4U" campaign distributed almost half a million silver rings embossed with its slogan to teen girls nationwide in 2006–2007, responding to nearly five times the expected demand for this safety accessory.[20] The campaign launched with a four-page advertorial in *Teen Vogue* that provided girls with online safety tips and information on how to order free 2 SMRT 4U rings from the website. A profile of the campaign for the Effie, an advertising industry award, explains that given its relatively low budget (under $500 000 for purchasing advertising) and the fact that teens are wary of mass media, they wanted to "trigger a viral, peer-driven initiative" (Effie Awards, 2008, p. 2). The campaign was promoted to *Teen Vogue*'s online reader panel of 80,000 teen girls and discussed on 300 personal blogs. As the Effie award (2008) profile explains, "Multiple rings per order would be offered, empowering girls to help spread the message amongst friends as a means of looking out for one another, while having something cool to wear" (p. 2). The 2 SMRT 4U ring resembles the pan-Christian "Silver Ring Thing," which was founded in 1995 as one of many virginity-pledging abstinence-only sex education programs. But instead of reminding wearers about their chastity pledges, the 2 SMRT 4U ring serves as another kind of self-regulatory personal reminder: to be cautious online and to refrain from posting personal information.

The "2 SMRT 4U" message on the ring is affirmative and positive, since it implicitly declares to online predators: "I am too smart for you to successfully victimize." The ring came with a literal message printed on a pink-and-white card that states: "Wear your 2 SMRT 4U ring to show you're in the know about staying safe online. Type smart. Post wisely" ("2 SMRT 4U," 2006). The Effie award profile explains that the ring is "A wake-up call for teen females about the risks of the Internet by providing them with a 'battle cry' and a new defensive attitude (as embodied in the 2 SMRT 4U ring) that they could rapidly embrace, champion and share" (Effie Awards, 2008, p. 2). While the message is well-intentioned, declaring that safe girls are smart implies that victimization is the result of being not smart enough. Though "2 SMRT 4U" is supposed to be empowering for girls, the campaign demonstrates the persistence of the idea that survivors of sexual violence are at fault for failing to heed precautions.[21] This is indeed where campaigns targeted only to potential victims often end up—the suggestion that prevention is their responsibility.

Of all the online safety campaigns I examine, "2 SMRT 4U" creates the strongest connection between self-esteem and sexual propriety. Hayden Panettiere, celebrity spokesperson for the campaign and 17-year-old star of the popular television show *Heroes* (NBC, 2006–2010) explains in a pink-rimmed bubble on the main page of the website during the initial period of the campaign: "[The ring is] like the string around the finger where it's just a little reminder everyday when you look down at it and go, I like myself, I want to be around. I want to keep myself safe" ("2 SMRT 4U", 2006). However, the assumption that a girl who likes herself is more likely to follow safety rules than one who does not have the same level of self-esteem and self-worth is not supported by previously mentioned findings that people with high self-esteem may actually take more risks (Goodson et al., 2006). The *Teen Vogue* advertorial features a full-page photo of campaign spokesperson Panettiere wearing the ring and telling readers: "There's nothing better than a girl with power, a girl with a sense of confidence, a girl with a sense of self" ("2 SMRT 4U: Safety Net," 2006). The text at the bottom of the page invites the reader to become such a girl by joining Panettiere "in wearing the 2 SMRT 4U ring to remind you and your friends to be safe online." The website also provides a number of printable items to reinforce the girl-empowerment message and connect it to online safety strategies, such as a printable photo frame that offers the affirmative declaration at the top "IT'SFUN2BME" and at the bottom, reminds girls, "BE CAUTIOUS OF anyone you don't know who asks you for personal information, photos, or videos" ("2 SMRT 4U," 2006). In keeping with its upbeat message, "2 SMRT 4U" only vaguely refers to online predators and offers no specific depictions of them.

The campaign encourages girls to yoke self-worth to self-protection by explicitly stressing the link between practicing strategies of personal safety online and feeling confident and positive about oneself. What's new is that campaigns like "2 SMRT 4U" do this by telling girls that sexting and other presumably reckless online behaviors are not forms of rule-breaking but are dangerous warning signs of low self-esteem and negative self-concept. Conversely, teenage girls who have high self-esteem are characterized as those who regulate their sexuality and take responsibility for preventing sexual violence and harassment. In this paradigm, sexting is not a rebellious or disobedient act that needs to be punished but is instead a problem that needs to be corrected through the targeted interventions of educators to improve girls' self-esteem. While appearing to promote empowerment and free choice, the kind of sexual agency this offers to girls is quite narrow: It gives girls the power to say "no" to sexuality but also the obligation to do so. Refusing sexual advances requires and asserts a kind of power, but without genuine choice about whether or not to refuse, the campaign barely offers girls any agency at all.

Alternative forms of advice

Self-esteem–based advice constructs cautiously abstinent girls as extremely autonomous, responsible, and self-aware—indeed some may be. Likewise I do not assert that girls who sext are necessarily liberated, self-confident, and completely in charge of themselves. Given that girls often lack power and resources compared to adults and boys, they are not in an ideal position to negotiate with partners and satisfy their needs and desires—or as Tolman (1994) would assert, to even know and articulate these desires. In chapter 4, I examine constructions of girls' agency; for now, note that girls' agency (like adults') is neither totally constrained nor fully free—all forms of agency are necessarily relational, contextual, and limited to some degree (Ortner, 1996). Since sexual practices are always situated within a larger field of power relations, the point is that scholars and educators should avoid making normative assumptions about what girls' sexual agency will look like.

In the campaigns and other forms of informal advice mentioned in this chapter, the kinds of agency the self-esteem model of online safety endorses are limited to girls' capacity to be afraid and to curtail their risk accordingly, to never trust intimate partners, and to avoid sexual expression. The challenge is to craft models of empowerment and agency that both further social justice and reduce the incidence of victimization. With this in mind, I turn now to some alternatives to the types of agency that self-esteem discourse constructs and evaluate their political implications. Each of these alternatives separate personal safety from self-esteem and thus avoids the problems of demonizing girls who fail at practicing personal safety. However, most of these still offer individualistic approaches, whereas community- and school-based programs, as I argue later, are likely to be more effective in reducing and addressing harm.

There may still be a role for advice targeted to potential victims, as long as it does not constitute the majority of the discourse about sexual dangers online and is based on empirical evidence of risk and victimization. But there is too much at stake to waste resources on messages like "don't post personal information online," which has common sense appeal but is ultimately ineffective, shaming, and alienating to most youth, who routinely do this without incident. As with sexual education and messages about drug use, youth need to hear accurate unbiased information about the risks, since an overwhelming number of studies show that fear-mongering is ineffective (Jones, 2010). Further research is needed to investigate and promote strategies to make sexting safer, such as creating images that do not depict faces[22] and deciding whether or not to sext by considering the trustworthiness of potential recipients. Indeed, some lighthearted articles about sexting for adults encourage the practice but offer advice such as: "Delete them every so often" (Leshnoff, 2009). An online safety campaign that could counsel strategies for exercising caution without attaching them to self-esteem or demanding abstinence would still make girls primarily responsible for preventing their own victimization, but could do so without resorting to sexual shaming.

Online safety campaigns could construct a different form of personal empowerment if they began with the assumption that adolescents have the right to sexual expression and privacy. For example, just like the callout cards in "That's Not Cool," a new campaign could give girls tools to demand respect for their online privacy. On the "That's Not Cool" website (2009), a section called "Privacy Problems" addresses people who monitor their intimate partners' cell phones and demand access to their email accounts. These messages actually affirm the right to privacy, but only for nonsexual personal information. The callout cards here include statements like, "Congrats on totally violating my trust" and "Now that you've violated my email account I won't feel bad dumping you." The former would work just as well in the context of sexting, and the latter could be revised to read, for example, "Now that you've sent out my sext I won't feel bad dumping you." If educators insist on targeting girls for educational interventions, at least the girl who sends these callout cards to a malicious ex-boyfriend would be asserting her right to sexuality and respect for her privacy. Though it is still an individual response to a social problem, encouraging such a caustic retort might be a better form of girl power.

Concentrating on all adolescents' capacity to reduce privacy violations could create alternative models of agency and responsibility as well. Instead of focusing exclusively on girls' behaviors, safety campaigns could target potential distributors of private images. By speaking to sext receivers rather than just producers, antiforwarding messages could promote a conversation about digital privacy that facilitates holding the distributors of private images responsible for their actions. In chapter 5, I develop a model of explicit consent for personal information distribution and offer a number of technological, educational, and legal ways to implement this model, including user-controlled restrictions on photos taken by mobile phones, campaigns to discourage forwarding, and greater privacy protections for users.

Another way to target potential forwarders could be to manipulate norms of masculinity for positive ends in online safety discourses.[23] For example, a message about sexting that targets heterosexual young men as potential privacy violators could focus on their ability to choose not to breach trust by appealing to their masculine egos. Such a campaign slogan could read something like:

"You got a sext? Congrats! Want another? Respect her privacy." While this would reproduce a number of the problems with self-esteem–based messages, including the gendered construction of adolescent sexuality and the individualization of social problems, at least it would target potential privacy violators rather than victims and would not pursue the ineffective goal of promoting abstinence from sexting.

While some of these strategies might reduce personal risk, it is vital to recognize that sexual privacy violations occur within the larger context of gender- and sexuality-based victimization (Ringrose et al., 2012). These widespread forms of harassment reflect norms of discrimination and marginalization that some teachers and school administrators promote or tolerate (E. Meyer, 2009), such as by suggesting, for example, that gender-nonconforming boys dress differently to avoid being targeted for violence rather than addressing the perpetrators. As such it is clear that none of the individualistic forms of agency I have discussed so far—including the dominant self-esteem model and the various individualistic alternatives I just examined—can offer satisfying solutions for reducing victimization.

Youth who work together with the support of teachers and administrators to respond to gender and sexual harassment and to change the attitudes and policies that underlie these problems might feel (correctly) that they have the power to change their environments. As such, campaigns to promote online safety and to combat digital dating violence might be more effective if they followed existing models of community-based responses to social problems. For example, research demonstrates that gay-straight alliance groups in schools can improve the school climate while offering resources and social acceptance to the youth who participate (C. Lee, 2002; Russell et al., 2009; Szalacha, 2003). While the self-esteem model equates power with positive feelings about oneself, addressing sexuality- and gender-based victimization through community-based action would instead position agency as the ability to work with others to create broader change. If agency could be reimagined in this way, educators could help youth to understand the impact of sexism and slut-shaming and develop and reinforce the importance of respecting privacy online.

Conclusion

The earliest online safety advice in the mid-1990s targeted parents, raising their awareness of online predators and suggesting that they closely monitor their children's internet use. Later on, at the same time that social network sites gained popularity and media attention (the mid-2000s), the online safety advice began to shift. Instead of maintaining the focus on parents, mainstream national online safety advice started to target girls with a combination of the victim-blaming advice commonly found in rape-prevention tips for women (e.g., don't walk alone at night) and the rhetoric of girl power and self-esteem that has been dominant in discussions of girlhood since the early 1990s. Despite its good intentions, the new self-esteem–based safety advice tends to (1) blame girls for online victimization rather than those who violate privacy and harass others; (2) construct girlhood as nonsexual; and (3) attach girls' self-respect to their ability to exercise extreme caution and self-censorship online.

All of these online safety advice campaigns impose narrow expectations on teen girls' sexuality through forms of soft power. That is, although none of these campaigns directly coerce girls or punish them for misbehaving, they all advocate self-regulation. As such, self-esteem programs are perhaps appealing to institutions such as the Justice Department and the Ad Council because they seem to put power in the hands of girls themselves and offer them positive messages of responsibility and self-confidence. This kind of governing "at a distance" is a key strategy of neoliberal modes of controlling and managing populations (Bratich, Parker, & McCarthy, 2003; Cruikshank, 1996). Self-esteem programs may be popular precisely because they do not pose any significant threat to the entrenched gender norms that legitimate sexual harassment. In fact they inadvertently reaffirm these norms by idealizing the psychological health of extremely cautious teenage girls who abstain from all sexual activity.

The focus on girls' low self-esteem in the national debates about sexting is a major roadblock to developing nuanced understandings of youth, gender, and sexuality online and to creating privacy protections that work in the context of digital media. The online safety advice I examine in this chapter relies on the misguided assumptions that girls who sext do so because they have low self-esteem, and that low self-esteem is an attitude problem that can and should be corrected. By telling victims that their main problem is not sexism or rape culture but their own negative attitudes about themselves, the larger social issues that give rise to these problems remain unaddressed. Self-esteem messages tend to idealize a limited version of girls' sexual agency and thus exacerbate the legal, educational, and public policy failures to respond to sexting effectively. Promoting a community-based sense of agency among students, parents, and administrators to address the larger underlying social problems may be a more effective way to reduce harassment and privacy violations.

Many assume that sexting girls must be misbehaving because of some outside corrupting influence. This offers a comfortable substitute for their agency—in the previous chapter the substitute I discussed was biology, in this one it is low self-esteem, and in the next chapter it is depictions of sexuality in mass media. I shift now to the book's second half, continuing my critique of common sense discourses about sexting but spending more time developing new models of agency, consent, and privacy as well. In the next chapter, I analyze the assumption that sexting is a result of sexualization in mass media, picking up where this one left off in its theorization of agency.

PART II

Alternative ways to think about sexting

CHAPTER 4

Sexualization
and participation

If the question is: "Why are girls sexting?" one answer that might seem appealing is "sexualization." The theory is that girls create suggestive images of themselves on their mobile phones because they are imitating what they see in mass media. Instead of considering how sexting might be, in some cases, a choice to express oneself sexually (Goldstein, 2009; Karaian, 2012), many people assume that sexting girls are misguidedly reproducing the sexualization of women in mass culture.

Since at least the mid-2000s, sexualization has been identified as a crisis in news media, documentaries (Newsom, 2011; Palmer, 2012), reports (Papadopoulos, 2010; Zurbriggen et al., 2007), and best-selling paperbacks (Durham, 2008; Levin & Kilbourne, 2008; Oppliger, 2008). International attention to this issue is particularly concentrated in the United States, Canada, Australia, and the United Kingdom. Concerns about sexualization usually rely on a deterministic media-effects argument that objectifying depictions of female sexuality in mass culture cause girls to be too sexually active too early and in an unhealthy or unnatural way.[1] A number of feminists have criticized discourses about sexualization for conflating sexuality with sexualization, erasing girls' agency, pathologizing working-class femininities, flattening differences among girls and women, and promoting a simplistic version of media effects (Attwood, 2006; Egan, 2013; Egan & Hawkes, 2008; Lerum & Dworkin, 2009).

Sexualization positions girls as both its victims and its agents. That is, sexualization is thought to victimize girls by undermining their capacity to make authentic, healthy, self-determined choices about their gender and sexual embodiment. At the same time, sexualization also posits that girls are agents because their choices and actions affect others and society in general. Specifically, girls who sext are sometimes blamed for promoting child sexual abuse because their private images end up on the internet and in the hands of child abusers who use this material to fuel their desires and groom potential victims. Girls are also blamed for sexualization in general and are expected to help solve this problem by raising their self-esteem and abstaining from objectifying themselves in sexts.

Sexting is often seen as a symptom of acquiescence to sexualization and is thus excluded from the discussion (and celebration) about participatory culture. I argue that viewing sexting as a form of media production highlights the pleasures and benefits of consensual sexting and positions it as a choice. Nevertheless, participation and agency may be overvalued modes of interacting with mass culture, and conformity may not be the problem that many observers imagine. Consider as well that accusations of ideological passivity can serve to validate particular choices: Good choices are seen as authentic and self-determined while other nonnormative choices can be dismissed as evidence of victimization by culture. I argue that sexting can be (potentially, but not inherently) a valid and authentic choice, but at the same time I suggest that the concepts of agency, participation, and choice are often excessively idealized.

In a different era (before the invention of adolescence) or for different (less privileged) girls, it might be possible to view sexually expressive girls as immoral, accountable, and responsible. But many observers explain sexting as a consequence of girls' acquiescence to mass media, thus not only preserving the fundamental innocence of normative, privileged, teenage girlhood but also maintaining teen girls' inferiority as incomplete agents. This is a familiar strategy: Chaotic biology and deficient self-esteem, which I examined in the previous two chapters, also offer alternative explanations for sexting that similarly do not acknowledge sexual agency.

Blaming sexualization for sexting

The cultural context of sexualization is often constructed as one of the possible reasons that girls might be sexting.[2] For example, a *New York Times* article about sexting provides this background information: "[The teenager's] world is steeped in highly sexualized messages. Extreme pornography is easily available on the Internet. Hit songs and music videos promote stripping and sexting"

(Hoffman, 2011). Since this comment is not attributed to any particular person, the article suggests that it is obvious and uncontroversial to say that teenagers are "steeped" in a toxic brew of sexual depictions in entertainment, advertising, and pornography. Likewise, writers at the *Christian Science Monitor* and the *Washington Times* describe sexting as "a sign of the disconnect between the legal system and an increasingly sexualized adolescent cyberculture" (Marks, 2009) and "an increasingly sexualized culture" (Fields, 2011). On a segment about sexting on NBC's *Today Show*, one guest expert argues that sexualization causes sexting: "We live in a hyper sexualized culture right now. And kids can't escape from it" (NBC, 2013). Another *Today Show* guest expert agrees:

> Unfortunately, there are so many messages out there that say that [sexting] is normal. Whether it's what's on TV, what's on the internet, the marketing campaigns that are out there for teens that objectify and sexualize women, we know that this is the message that teens are getting. (NBC, 2013)

Comments such as these assert that teens are sexting because they are imitating the sexual depictions they see in mass culture. In a newspaper article, media critic Jean Kilbourne is quoted as saying that girls are not to blame for sexting because "they grow up surrounded by these images. . . . Girls are just encouraged to present themselves as porn stars" (Frank, 2010). As noted above, sexualization is commonly positioned as an all-pervasive and all-powerful force that determines how girls think about sexuality and gender. Journalists and the experts they quote claim that adolescents are "steeped in" (Hoffman, 2011), "bombarded by" (Knowles, 2010), and "surrounded by" (Frank, 2010) sexualized imagery. The passive voice in these sentences positions media as a force that acts upon teenagers in a way that is overwhelming, unstoppable, and even violent.

In thoroughly mainstream sources like the *New York Times* and the *Today Show*, sexualization is not positioned as a controversial explanation for sexting, or even as an untested new theory, but as an obvious common sense reason for why teens sext. These discourses tend to rely on a deterministic media-effects paradigm that sexual representations in mass media have direct and inevitable negative effects on young people. One final example: A Canadian documentary distributed by the Media Education Foundation examining how "the accelerating pressure to be sexy—and sexual—is changing kids' behavior and undermining their health" is titled: *Sext Up Kids: How Children Are Becoming Hypersexualized* (Palmer, 2012). The fact that sexting is a pun in the title of one of the latest documentaries about sexualization is a strong indication that the link between sexting and sexualization is seen as so obvious and self-evident that it needs no explanation or evidence.

BLAMING SEXTING FOR CHILD ABUSE

The idea that society is harmed when a sexual depiction of a minor is created is sometimes used as a rationale for criminalizing sexting. Conversations about sexualization often assume that most (if not all) mediated representations of female sexuality have negative effects on viewers—just as sexualization in media is thought to have an impact on girls, it is also seen as a cause of sexual violence in general. Girls' self-produced sexual images are thought to increase the incidence of child sexual abuse. As such, some people support using child pornography laws against sexting teens. This is made possible because these laws specify no age limits or exceptions for teen sexting; thus a 17-year-old can be charged for creating and possessing a photo of herself if it is explicit enough. Child pornography laws were passed in the 1980s in a moment of renewed public concern about child abuse when new video recording technologies emerged that facilitated its documentation (Adler, 2001). While child pornography laws were not designed to apply to the consensual sharing of private personal sexual media among teenagers, as discussed in chapter 1, legal reforms are nearly impossible because legislators do not want to be perceived as decriminalizing child pornography in any form.

Indeed, a former prosecutor speaking on *The O'Reilly Factor* argues in favor of the criminal prosecution of a 15-year-old girl who posted images of herself online because she believes that such images harm "all children." She explains: "This isn't a crime just against this one child [herself]. This is against all children. Because those pictures, while they may not have injured her, led perpetrators to seek more images, more pictures of kids, which puts more kids at risk as victims" (O'Reilly, 2004). Likewise, legal analyst Mary Leary (2007) insists: "If we are to combat the sexual objectification of children, we need to prosecute, regardless of the age of the creator" (pp. 41–42). The logic is that any sexual depiction of a teenager, regardless of consent or the conditions of its production, contributes to the sexual objectification of children and thus promotes sexual violence against them.

It may seem like common sense that private sexts would routinely end up in the hands of child pornography collectors. For example, one judge justifies convicting a consensual teen sexter whose images were never distributed by arguing that the girl should expect that her boyfriend would eventually widely distribute the private photos (*A. H. v. State*, 2007). In fact, there is little evidence that private sexting images are regularly distributed online, and the prevalence of any type of child pornography online is still unclear. To date, there are no peer-reviewed studies of the type and quantity of child pornography available on the internet.[3] One reason for the lack of data is that researchers cannot legally view child pornography for scholarly purposes. Since it is impossible to determine whether or not private sexts regularly become part of the underground child pornography market, panic about this can circulate unimpeded by empirical evidence that might contradict these fears. At the very least, the existing data suggest that the vast majority of teenage sexts are shared consensually among peers, and in cases in which they are distributed without permission, they are usually shared among teens and are rarely uploaded to public websites.[4] Nonetheless, many online safety campaigns and advertisements dramatize the relatively unlikely scenario of a middle-aged online predator viewing a girl's private sexual image (Shade, 2011).

While some studies have found that a majority of people convicted for possessing or distributing child pornography have also abused children (e.g., Alexy, Burgess, & Baker, 2005; Kim, 2004), these findings are based on an atypical sample since most people who view child pornography are never arrested or convicted. Moreover, such studies cannot determine whether individuals would have abused children if they had never viewed child pornography—or whether others might view child pornography as an alternative to abusing actual minors. If child pornography indeed causes the abuse of children, the rates of victimization might have increased since the mid-1990s as more people gained internet access, yet the available data shows a steady and significant decline in reported cases in the United States since 1990.[5] This is not to say that viewing child pornography has no impact on potential abusers—the point is that because sexual violence has existed since long before the invention of photographs and videos, the relationship, like any effect a media representation might have on an individual, is unclear and complex.

In more concrete terms, the vague possibility that a sext may contribute to a potential abuser's fantasies or grooming techniques is not a good enough reason to prohibit consensual sexting for teens,[6] especially given all the other problems this prohibition creates. Even if evidence emerged that errant sexting images floating around the internet play a significant role in child abuse, consensual sexting should still not be criminalized. This is because abusers who are using sexting images to groom victims or who might be incited to abuse by viewing such images are still the only people who can bear any significant, meaningful, or measurable responsibility for the specific incidents of sexual violence they have committed.

Given the quantity of sexually suggestive images of teenage girls produced commercially and circulated legally by adults, including in fashion magazines, advertisements, and other forms of mainstream popular culture, the fears about self-sexualization cannot be entirely about these representations or embodiments causing harm to society. Why is an adolescent girl creating a sexually explicit image of herself viewed as more disturbing than an adult male photographer producing a similarly sexually charged image of a teenage girl for the pages of a magazine or for an art gallery wall? Prohibitions on sexting may originate from a desire to protect girls from sexuality and to control what its production indicates: adolescent female sexual agency. In contrast to sexting, commercially produced suggestive images of teenage girls are widely accepted and are often defended, or at the very least debated (Bray, 2009), as a form of free expression.[7] The difference with sexting, and perhaps the central feature of sexting that makes observers uncomfortable, is that it provides tangible evidence that teenage girls are choosing to express themselves sexually. Mainstream commercial representations of adolescent female sexuality are perhaps seen as less threatening than sexting because the models and actresses are evidently appearing in such images for profit rather than for their personal sexual pleasure.

In order to avoid treating sexting like child pornography and citing it as a cause of sexual abuse, it is necessary to think through the unintended consequences of trying to remedy the injurious potential of representations. The feminist debates about pornography in the 1970s and 1980s that aimed to curb harmful representations never found a way to resolve the problems of censorship.[8] Censorship is such a thorny theoretical and practical issue because it raises concerns both about the state's authority to censor and about the power of speech, in and of itself, to cause a particular action or form of harm (Butler, 1997). Since the meanings and effects of representations are always context-dependent, developing an absolute definition of injurious representations is essentially impossible. Representations can, in general, exacerbate social problems, but the costs of censorship are usually too high to justify regulating this type of harm. In the case of sexting, it becomes all too easy to blame victims of privacy violations who created images of themselves and to heap punishment for such sexual transgressions on people who the prison system already disproportionately targets for other sexual crimes: people of color, queer people, and trans people (Filler, 2004; Spade, 2012; Sullivan, 1996). Consider also that whatever vague and immeasurable harm to "all children" a single image out of many millions might possibly produce, an act of sexual violence observably and significantly harms a specific person. Yet the prison sentences for possessing child pornography images can equal or even exceed those for committing an act of sexual assault. My position is that it is unjust to hold a consensual sexter responsible, even in part, for the sexual abuse another person has committed.

BLAMING GIRLS FOR SEXUALIZATION

The widespread concern about the sexualization of girls is rooted in serious problems, including sexual violence, harassment, and continuing gender inequalities. But the discourse about sexualization identifies girls' supposedly passive media consumption as the primary point of risk and intervention, holding girls responsible for ending sexualization. When sexualization is positioned as the primary problem, recommendations usually center on formal and informal self-esteem and media literacy training for girls (Karaian, 2014). Though there are indeed some indications that programs for girls using media literacy and self-esteem to foster a positive body image can have positive effects on individuals (LeCroy, 2004), an exclusive focus on these strategies can implicitly blame sexters, hold them to impossibly high standards, and divert attention from privacy violators and harassers.

The antisexualization rhetoric reinforces the idea that girls can prevent sexual violence—at both an individual and social level—if they embody a particular type of gender presentation that adheres to norms of respectability by appearing to be middle-to-upper class (Egan, 2013). In the American Psychological Association report on the sexualization of girls, one of the examples of the phenomenon is "a 5-year-old girl walking through a mall wearing a short T-shirt that says 'Flirt'" (Zurbriggen et al., 2007, p. 2). There are no details about whether the girl picked out the T-shirt or if an adult chose it for her, but viewing the girl wearing the shirt as a problem in and of itself contains the dangerous implication that if she were harassed or assaulted, her clothing would be partly to blame. The report dispels this problematic conclusion later on, noting: "Girls do not 'cause' harassment or abusive behavior by wearing sexy clothes; no matter what girls wear, they have the right to be free of sexual harassment, and boys and men can and should control their behavior" (p. 34). But disturbingly, the report also positions women and girls as the link between media images and sexual exploitation, since the majority of the solutions proposed in the report focus on changing girls' attitudes and behaviors to solve the problem of sexualization. One favored method is through media literacy programs, which can "teach girls to critique and understand the salience of sexualizing images in the media . . . [and] be better protected from these images" (p. 42). Throughout the report, and in most discussions of sexualization, girls' passive acceptance of objectifying media representations is identified as a key problem.

By focusing on increasing girls' agency, this approach fits with contemporary discourses about girlhood that valorize self-determining, individualistic girls and concentrate anxiety on girls who do not achieve these ideals (Gonick, 2006; A. Harris, 2004). These discourses put girls in an untenable position: On one hand they are portrayed as passive victims of sexualization, and on the other they are expected to solve this social problem. However, in producing the ideal girl as strong, powerful, flexible, and constantly self-improving, girls' sexual choices bear far too great a burden for accomplishing the broad structural changes feminism seeks. The problem is that maintaining sexual propriety can become yet another project of self-regulation for girls (Duits & Zoonen, 2011) and part of "endlessly working on a perfectible self" (McRobbie, 2007, p. 718). Eisenhauer (2004) argues that some feminist advocates assume that girls need to work on resisting sexism and gender conformity in order to join the supposedly enlightened and self-actualized ranks of adult womanhood.

Resisting sexualization is often portrayed as an empowering act that will increase self-esteem and assure mental health, but in many ways it also means rejecting the personal pleasure, privilege, and safety that can result from going along with it. If sexualization is anywhere near as dominant and powerful a force as people assume, resisting must be a difficult task. As Peterson (2010) explains, "We cannot expect adolescent girls to achieve unambivalent sexual empowerment when most (or all) adult women (and men) have yet to accomplish that goal" (p. 312). As such, some antisexualization advocates have unfairly high and unrealistic expectations of girls to manifest more personal strength and resolve than most adults.

What social responsibility do individual women and girls have to fight against sexualization? If sexualization is more of a symptom than a cause of gender inequalities, blaming particular women and girls who embody sexualized gender presentations seems unfair.[9] It is not clear how reducing self-sexualization would actually help accomplish any of the broader goals of feminism to redistribute resources, reorganize society, end discrimination, and end violence. In most discussions of sexualization, the links between representation and systemic discrimination and violence are imagined as tantalizingly clear and direct—it can seem like eliminating the representations (or the miniskirts, or the sexting) results in an end to the violence. Unfortunately, the relationship between actual and symbolic violence is far more complicated.

A particularly problematic implication of blaming girls for sexualization is that it diverts attention and blame from the typical perpetrators of gender- and sexuality- based violence: men and boys. Objectifying portrayals of women no doubt reinforce the idea that it is acceptable for men to view women as sexual objects, which is linked to misogyny, sexual assault, and physical violence. Indeed, in some parts of the APA report (Zurbriggen et al., 2007), sexual images in media are said to cause harassment and abuse by teaching men that women and girls are sexually available to them. Yet, in contrast to the many mass-market books and hundreds of studies of girls and objectification, the effects of sexualization on how men view sexuality, their identities, and their relationships are rarely studied or discussed (Garner, 2012). Men and boys are rarely asked to do any work to resist the ill effects of sexualization; instead this task falls almost entirely to girls and women. For example, in the opening monologue of the documentary *Miss Representation* (Newsom, 2011), the narrator draws a link between beauty ideals in mass media and her own experiences of sexual violence. The men she describes as "prey[ing] on her vulnerabilities" are positioned as an inevitable and natural part of the cultural landscape and her narrative implies that women and girls need to work on resisting and fixing the problem of sexualization in media in order to become less vulnerable to sexual assault. Sexualization is positioned as a problem here not because it encourages men to view rape as acceptable, but because it weakens women and girls.

Viewing sexualization as a cause of sexting implies that the focus should be on girls' supposedly bad choices. Like the other explanations I previously examined, such as unruly biology, low self-esteem, or pressure from boys, the idea that sexualization in mass media is to blame for sexting also diverts attention away from privacy violators. Indeed, all of these explanations serve to mask the widespread lack of attention to the issue of consent in sexting (Albury & Crawford, 2012) and reinforce the belief that all sexting, consensual or not, is simply wrong for everyone involved (Slane, 2009). Moving the conversation back toward the structural and community-based solutions that feminists have been advocating for decades to end the rape culture (e.g., Friedman & Valenti, 2008) may require rejecting the easy explanation that sexualization and girls' failure to resist it is the cause of sexting. Sexualization saps attention from the continuing challenge to promote sexual ethics based on consent and pleasure (e.g., Carmody, 2005) and to apply these ethics to mediated sex acts like sexting.

Sexting is not necessarily an inherently radical act that helps dismantle structures of oppression. But neither is abstaining from sexting. The point is that both are choices about sexual embodiment, with various risks and benefits, which may be reasonably and authentically chosen in some contexts. The objectification of women is certainly worth resisting, but I suggest that it may be ineffective and even unreasonable to attempt to fix this problem by asking girls to correct their supposed deficiencies of agency. After all, the correction most interventions have in mind is that girls simply conform to a norm of sexual propriety instead of succumbing to norms of sexual self-objectification.

The relentless focus on the need for girls to increase their agency and media literacy is even more puzzling given sexualization's supposed effects on men as compared to women. At worst, girls who passively accept sexualization wear skimpy clothing and overvalue their sexual attractiveness, which some researchers believe is a cause (rather than a correlate) of depression, low self-esteem, and eating disorders (Zurbriggen et al., 2007). Yet for men and boys, the effects of sexualization may be much worse: Accepting the premise that women and girls are little more than sexual objects could lead them to discriminate against women and even to commit acts of sexual violence. In short, the discourses and research about sexualization suggest that it may cause women to be unhappy and men to commit rape. And yet the tendency is still to concentrate on girls as the primary point of intervention and to allow the ubiquity of discrimination and rape culture to fade into the background. A more effective approach to ending sexual violence may be to focus on changing male behavior (for example, Garrity, 2011). One way to do this, as the APA report (Zurbriggen et al., 2007) recommends for girls, might be to create intervention programs that offer men and boys the tools to help them become more critical mass culture consumers and producers.

Sexualization, agency, and choice

Viewing sexting as a result of sexualization makes it difficult to recognize or understand the complexity of girls' choices and obscures complicated interrelationships between mass culture and the individual. By positioning girls as dangerously and excessively obeying dominant media culture, discourses about sexualization inadvertently pathologize conformity and exalt resistance to mass culture as the only healthy or genuine form of agency. These assumptions lead to a simplistic view of sexting that entirely erases girls' capacity for choice—as explored in previous chapters, erasing girls' agency can have the problematic effect of conflating consensual and harmful uses of sexual images.

Concerns about sexualization rely on normative definitions of healthy sexuality. While social conservatives often define healthy sexuality for young women as practicing abstinence until marriage, liberals are more likely to define it in terms of using birth control and STI-prevention measures effectively and having sex within monogamous, loving, long-term relationships. Many people justify focusing antisexualization interventions on girls by arguing that girls need to be taught to resist it for the sake of their own mental health.[10] As such, the concept of "healthy sexuality," Smith and Attwood (2011) explain, "is intensely normative, ruling out many pleasurable, non-coercive practices including, at the very least, casual sexual encounters" (p. 333). The construction that normative sexual choices are healthy and freely chosen is common. For example, in most U.S. states, teenagers can marry earlier than they can legally have sex (Cocca, 2004). In this way, consent is preapproved for sexually normative choices like marriage. In the context of girls and sexting, abstaining from it is often viewed as a genuine choice while engaging in sexting is often positioned, for privileged girls at least, as a loss or lack of agency and as a sign of victimization by peers, mass culture, or their own low self-esteem. Not all girls who sext are making the choice with the same (or, necessarily, any) degree of agency, but the point is that assessments of another person's choices inevitably rely on the observer's normative assumptions.

Such assumptions about sexualization are particularly problematic because they often facilitate and depend on implicit classism. The politics of respectability authorizes a central myth of rape culture: that certain forms of femininity, marked as lower class or associated with sex workers (and the two are often conflated), invite sexual attention and assault while other forms of femininity communicate innocence and deserve protection. Indeed, most of the examples observers provide of sexualized dress, such as midriff-exposing shirts, fishnets, thongs, high heels, and miniskirts, are seen as lower class. The supposedly classier version of femininity is still thoroughly sexualized but seen as appropriately sexual rather than excessively sexual. This is a fine line, but one that girls are routinely asked to walk when they are advised to dress and behave appropriately. The message is that girls should stop self-objectifying and resist sexualization. But it is not a simple task to accomplish this while maintaining a sufficiently feminine gender presentation.[11]

Since neoliberalism defines success as class mobility, observers may worry that girls who embody apparently lower-class feminine identities are destined for economic failure as well. Egan and Hawkes (2008) explain that debates about youth and sexualization produce "a particular type of sexually precocious girl," sometimes referred to as a Lolita, kinderwhore, or prostitot, who has been corrupted by media to become "seductive and transgressive" and "socially disruptive" (p. 305). This is about class contamination, they argue: "The discourse on sexualization paints a picture of overly sexual displays of 'low culture' rupturing the innocence of middle and upper middle class girls" (p. 306). Antisexualization advocates believe they are concerned with girls' mental and sexual health, but the definition of sexualization clearly rests on normative assumptions about sexual behavior and embodiments that are based largely on class distinctions. The idea that self-sexualization is harmful to one's health and to society in general legitimates a program of instruction in appropriateness and feminine respectability—and confirms that women and girls who embody sexualities marked as lower class do not deserve respect. This advice is targeted almost exclusively to white middle-class girls, for whom the privileged option of embodying innocence is more readily available.

The discourse of sexualization often flattens the distinctions between depictions of sexuality and depictions of sexual violence. Bratz dolls, for example, who wear heavy makeup and miniskirts, are particularly reviled by antisexualization advocates, and the dolls are often held up as evidence of sexualization alongside examples of violent pornography (Levin & Kilbourne, 2008; Zurbriggen et al., 2007). The logic is that depictions of so-called inappropriate forms of sexuality—identified as slutty or trashy by less careful authors—are on a continuum that runs unbroken from false eyelashes to rape. That is, the panic about the representation of sex in mass media tends to vilify sexuality in general rather than sexism or objectification in particular (Egan & Hawkes, 2008; Gill, 2009; Heins, 2001; Lamb, 2009). Failing to differentiate among representations of sexuality implies that all representations of it are bad and damaging and that sexuality without sexualization is impossible.

Girls are often expected to develop sexual desires and modes of sexual expression that bear little evidence of their interaction with mass media representations of sexuality. For example, some researchers who examine girls' sexuality online are disappointed and frustrated when girls seem to reproduce the conventions of commercial pornography (Grisso & Weiss, 2005; Thiel-Stern, 2007). Yet, poststructural and queer theory demonstrates that gender and sexuality are constituted by discourse and culture. So if mass culture is wholly sexualized, then how can women and girls inhabit gender and sexual identities that are not tainted by sexualization and self-objectification? Critics challenge the view that teen girls' choices to express their sexuality are necessarily inauthentic and criticize the presumption that the natural state of adolescent girlhood is completely asexual (Caron, 2006, 2008; Egan & Hawkes, 2008; Gill, 2009; Lamb, 2009). As Egan and Hawkes (2008) explain, "Girlhood sexuality is conflated with sexualization; as a result sexuality, outside of the context of exploitative corporate messages, is rendered impossible" (p. 303). The idea that there is a normal, healthy, girlhood sexuality prior to and separate from sexualization in media works to legitimate normative assumptions about what natural, healthy sexuality looks like. Sexting, especially between casual partners, is linked to pornography and exhibitionism and thus is typically viewed as an unhealthy form of sexuality and as evidence of the negative effects of sexualization on girls.

Discussions about sexualization often do not grapple with the complication that many women who engage in behaviors that researchers describe as self-objectifying experience them as pleasurable and freely chosen (Lamb, 2010). Lerum and Dworkin (2009) point out that the APA report (Zurbriggen et al., 2007) offers only negative examples of the impact of sexualization on girls, and does not consider "the possibility that some forms of self-generated sexualization (some of which may come from viewing sexualized images) may actually nurture the development of sexual health" (p. 259). Vanwesenbeeck (2009) points out, "We still do not know if, how, and under what conditions self-sexualization or self-objectification can function to serve the self; foster autonomy, assertiveness, and self-esteem; and, last but not least, serve one's own sexual lust, arousal, and satisfaction" (p. 270). Dobson (2011) likewise argues: "There is a need to complicate straightforward readings of hetero-sexy material as 'harmful,' 'oppressive' and so on when viewed in the context of female self-production." Without such interventions, arguments about sexualization can remain unquestioned and tautological; the choice to self-objectify is offered as proof that the person's choice is a symptom of victimization by sexualization in media.

Moreover, consider the privilege that comes with being a person who is typically seen as making choices freely, actively, and rationally—often these assumptions adhere best to white, able-bodied, economically advantaged adult men. As I discussed in chapter 2, youth are often considered peer-oriented, pathologically delinquent, and biologically unruly. Analogously, women are seen as more social and subject to their hormonal cycles and biological clocks; working-class people are considered more likely to lack personal responsibility and be dupes of mass culture (Walkerdine, 1997); and people of color are sometimes thought to blindly follow cultural norms (Volpp, 2000).[12] Crucially, the implicit assumption undergirding structural inequalities is that these explanations (biological, cultural, or otherwise) do not serve as excuses; people are usually told that they must work to overcome these personal weaknesses to achieve equality.[13] Moreover, assuming people's choices reflect only cultural and biological constraints on their free will means that those choices need not be taken seriously or considered authentic. The discourses about sexting girls' false consciousness bear a striking rhetorical similarity to those about so-called "third-world women." For example, Abu-Lughod (2002) critiques mainstream feminist discourses that position Muslim women who wear veils as dominated by men and incapable of agency. Like choosing to wear a veil, sexting is such an incomprehensible choice for some observers that they insist that the choice is inauthentic and thus the practice should be banned or criminalized in order to protect women from themselves.

Assumptions about agency also have other normative gendered dimensions. Devaluing the desire to be looked at, desired, or admired might be a symptom of the tendency to privilege forms of agency that are seen as masculine. Lamb (2010) explains: "Using active vs. passive, subject vs. object as ways of describing good vs. bad sex, suggests to girls that there is only one correct position from which to have sex, the position that has traditionally been associated with men" (p. 299). Likewise, it may be difficult to separate any potentially negative effects of being an object of desire or objectifying oneself from the fact that this role in the heteronormative sexual script may also be devalued simply because it is marked as feminine. Studies on sexualization and objectification typically examine only the negative outcomes for women and rarely examine any potentially positive effects (Lerum & Dworkin, 2009; Vanwesenbeeck, 2009). The point is not that self-objectification is inherently good but that the discourses about sexualization assume, without much evidence, that it is always bad.

MEDIA EFFECTS

While the perceived impact of mass media on adults has waxed and waned over the past century, there is a consistent belief that youth are particularly vulnerable to media and technology (Mastronardi, 2003). Panics about youth and new media have recurred with the introduction of film, radio, comics, television, video games, the internet, and cell phones (Mazzarella, 2003; Wartella & Jennings, 2000). This is especially true since the advent of the modern internet in the mid-1990s. Since then, concern has shifted among a number of issues, including online predators, cyberbullying, and, of course, sexting. For example, an educational campaign promoting safe texting asks young people to make this pledge: "I will enjoy all of the technologies available to me, but I will not allow them to control me" (Canadian Centre for Child Protection, 2010). This potently captures the attitude many adults have about the impact of new media on youth. What kind of people need to be asked to promise they will not allow technologies to gain control of their behavior? What, exactly, does it mean to be controlled by technology? Or to resist such control?

A central assumption about sexualization is that mass culture has a strong, one-way effect on girls, who are supposedly uniquely susceptible. The idea that sexualized images are pervasive and controlling is dominant in a couple of documentaries about sexualization. For example, the voiceover in the opening sequence of *Sext Up Kids* argues: "From very early on, it's a non-stop barrage of sex, sex, sex" (Palmer, 2012). The visual imagery in these types of films often show a range of unannotated, undifferentiated sexual images of women and girls to illustrate their ubiquity. These images often appear too quickly to examine what is depicted in each, whether they are shown one after the other or are displayed all at once in a collage. *Sext Up Kids* (Palmer, 2012) employs

FIGURE 8. The documentary *Sext Up Kids* (Palmer, 2012) calls sexualized clothing and toys an "avalanche" and employs collages, rapid
successions of images, and this "hall of screens" animation with a
bewildered girl in the center to communicate that sexualized images
of women are ubiquitous and powerful. Source: Maureen Palmer

both these techniques (figure 8), and *Miss Representation* (Newsom, 2011)
likewise begins with a montage of black-and-white photographs of famous
feminist figures, such as Eleanor Roosevelt, Rosa Parks, and Shirley Chisholm,
juxtaposed against grainy color video clips of female celebrities, models, and
reality TV stars, posing and performing in sexual ways or fighting with one
another. At the end of the *Miss Representation* montage, the music swells and
the images of sexualized women appear in extremely rapid succession, finally
turning into a collage for a split second and then exploding. The visual rhetoric
of these films suggests that sexual imagery is everywhere, that it is inescapable,
and that girls are wholly incapable of navigating or negotiating it.

Debates about structure and individual agency have been ongoing for many
decades, particularly in media and communications research. Despite feminist
media studies research reclaiming agency for girls by viewing them as actively
interpreting media and representations of sexuality (Durham, 2004; Kehliy,
2004; McRobbie, 1999a; Weekes, 2004), there is still considerable scholarly
anxiety about mass media victimizing girls. As decades of audience research
has demonstrated for adults (Bobo, 1995; Radway, 1984), researchers such
as McRobbie (1999b) and Walkerdine (1997) have found that girls are also
neither entirely free in interpreting and remaking media texts nor are they pas-

sive dupes of media representations. In Driver's (2007) study of queer girls' responses to mass media, she finds that they "combine textual enjoyment and critique with detailed subtlety" and that they "work around and with commodified representations" (p. 11). In short, young people are indeed aware that mass media offer unrealistic depictions of gender and sexuality (Vanwesenbeeck, 2009). As Lerum and Dworkin (2009) point out: "Girls' and women's consumer activities are undoubtedly more complicated than simply 'buying into a sexualized image' out of false consciousness" (p. 254). The discourse of sexualization suggests that there is only one version of sexuality available in mass media and that girls are incapable of negotiating or resisting that dominant representation.

To say that in some cases girls may consent to sexting does not mean that it occurs in a context free of coercions. The choices teenage girls make about how to embody and express their gender and sexual identities occur in environments in which sexual harassment from peers can be ubiquitous and where adult authorities might unfairly discipline them for their sexual choices. The stakes are even higher for girls of color, queer girls, and working-class girls, who are often punished more harshly when they commit the same crimes as more privileged girls (Dohrn, 2004; Tolman, 2005). At the same time, consider Fine's (1988) observation: "[D]iverse female sexual subjectivities emerge through, despite, and because of gender-based power asymmetries" (p. 41). Like adults, girls make choices within complex social and media contexts they do not control. The representations of gender and sexuality in media are part of this context, but it is useful to recognize that girls' responses to them are varied and complex.

Sexting as media production

For some girls, one way they negotiate and respond to representations of gender and sexuality in mass media might be through sexting. That is, I suggest that sexting is a form of media production. Media production (like media viewing) is neither inherently liberatory nor inherently oppressive—but thinking about sexting in this way highlights that it can be a choice, however complicated and situated in a political and social context that choice may be. If sexting is media production, then it is not sufficient to assume that people create and share images of themselves because they are simply imitating sexualization in mass culture.

Though most new media scholars do not position participatory media as universally positive and empowering, many hope that media production will help youth express themselves and challenge mass culture. For example, the

MacArthur Foundation devoted a volume of its Digital Media and Learning series to the topic of civic engagement (W. L. Bennett, 2008). In many discussions of youth media production and participatory culture, the logic is that if given the tools to make their own media, they will use them to express their own authentic points of view. Since girls are seen as especially susceptible to the effects of mass media, media production is particularly celebrated in girls studies. Many researchers argue that media production can offer girls an important way to respond to the objectifying media portrayals of women (Driver, 2007; Durham, 2008; A. Harris, 2004; Kearney, 2006). The APA states that by becoming cultural producers rather than just consumers of media, girls can resist sexualization because it "enables them to be more effective cultural critics" (Zurbriggen et al., 2007, p. 40). Likewise, a range of government- and nonprofit-sponsored programs provide funding to groups that facilitate youth access to video- and media-making equipment. Giving girls video cameras is thought to help empower them. Yet observers often portray girls negatively when they turn the camera on themselves to produce sexual images (Goldstein, 2009; Thiel-Stern, 2009).

People who create photos of themselves with their cell phones may enjoy the same benefits of creativity, critical engagement with mass culture, and self-reflection that are often noted for nonsexual media production. Yet, a discussion of the potential benefits of sexting is typically absent from the popular and scholarly attention to participatory media. Henry Jenkins (2006) briefly refers to sexting in his introduction to *Convergence Culture*, offering a vivid example of drunk high school girls creating "their own soft-core porn movie involving topless cheerleaders making out in the locker room" that then circulates around the school (p. 17). He contrasts this kind of media use with a parent saying goodnight to a child via instant message, explaining: "When people take media into their own hands, the results can be wonderfully creative; they can also be bad news for all involved" (H. Jenkins, 2006, p. 17). The remainder of his book focuses on positive ways people actively engage with mass media, portraying users who are empowered and entertained by the ways they participate and become media authors. The main problems he notes are the challenges that convergence poses to producers and the fact that not all people can access this new cultural realm. Girls reappear in only one chapter, as Harry Potter fan fiction writers. There is no room in this celebratory overview of media production practices to say that while a practice like sexting might be "bad news" in some cases, it does not mean it cannot also be "wonderfully creative" at other times.

The risks are clear enough, but the value of sexting remains largely unexamined. To learn more about what pleasures and benefits consensual sexters gain from the practice, researchers should pursue questions about the unique opportunities that technology affords: When girls use mobile media to produce their own pornography, how are they challenging the sexism of the commercial media industries and how are they reproducing it? Could mobile phones help girls be more assertive and confident in expressing their sexual needs and desires? How do girls produce their sexualities by producing social media? More scholarship is needed, but at the very least, the limited research about sexting and the popular discourses about adult sexting (as a fun way to spice up your love life) indicate three potential reasons girls might sext that challenge the assumption that they are merely passive victims of sexualization: interpersonal communication, self-expression, and pleasure.

INTERPERSONAL COMMUNICATION

For many couples, communicating via mobile phones is a key part of their relationship and their daily interactions, including sharing affection and intimacy and arguing (Ito, 2005; Lasén & Casado, 2012; Prøitz, 2005). As Ito (2005) outlined, camera phones can be used to create an "intimate visual co-presence," and couples in particular "were more likely to post very mundane photos that conveyed ambient visual information rather than explicit communication" (p. 13)—that photos were nonetheless important to their feelings of connectedness. Crawford (2009) likewise highlights the importance of mobile communication itself, without even much substantive content, to create a sense of intimacy between people. Mobile phones, she explains, "offer intimacy that travels with you" (p. 256). As such, texting, talking, and sending photos that appear to serve little practical purpose is a common practice in some relationships. It follows that a sexual image or text could serve a similar function in a romantic and/or sexual relationship to maintain an intimate sexual copresence that reaffirms attraction and affection while the two partners are physically apart.

Lifestyle articles about sexting aimed at adults also highlight the positive role sexting can play in communication between partners in sexual relationships. Such a function might be especially valuable for teen girls, as research indicates that they sometimes struggle to communicate their sexual needs to partners, including talking about safer sex practices and about their sexual desires (Fine & McClelland, 2006; Tolman, 2005). The press release about the Sex and Tech (2008) survey highlights the finding that "nearly one-quarter of teens (22 percent) admit that technology makes them personally more forward and aggressive." While negatively connoted words like "admit" and "aggressive" indicate that this is supposed to be bad thing, there may be particular benefits—especially for girls—to being more "forward" or assertive about their needs and desires. Indeed, articles aimed at adults often promote sexting on the grounds that it can increase sexual communication between partners and help them discuss their sexual desires in new ways. One article aimed at retirees quotes a 50-year-old woman who says: "It makes you a little more brave. It takes the fear away, your inhibitions. I might be a little more bold in a text message than I would be over the phone or in person" (Leshnoff, 2009). Here, lack of inhibition is not positioned as a cause for concern but as an important feature of sexual health and clear communication of needs and desires.

Some researchers maintain that digital communication offers important advantages for women and girls in navigating sexual relationships.[14] One study of teenage mobile phone use in dating relationships suggests that girls might be more assertive when communicating through texting than speaking face-to-face (Cupples & Thompson, 2010). Likewise, a study of 10–12-year-olds found that though many children felt ill-equipped to deal with sexual attention in person, "children who talked about receiving sexually harassing texts and emails also talked about how they could be deleted or blocked, and almost all of the children described in detail exactly how to achieve this" (Renold, 2013, p. 14). Döring (2000), also suggests that physical separation from an online sexual partner could also help women resist the gender norms that dictate that they should politely tolerate sexual harassment. Another study of online chatting is even more optimistic: "Girls may be able to initiate online relationships with the opposite sex without much of the weight of traditional gender roles and without the possible stigmatization for being too forward" (Subrahmanyam, Greenfield, & Tynes, 2004, p. 662). Other researchers suggest that text messaging and image-sharing might help disrupt traditional gender roles. For example, Prøitz (2005) discusses the complex ways that teenage couples communicate via text messages and suggests that the medium might encourage young men to be more emotionally expressive.

These claims represent a radically different way of looking at how mobile phones and the internet might affect the way girls talk about sex. Although this research might be accused of excessive optimism, it highlights that digital communication technologies might enhance sexual communication and assertiveness, which could be an especially positive feature for girls and women. Could sexting help girls find new ways to express their sexual needs and desires? Is there some way sexting might even destabilize the gender norms that ask girls to be passive and acquiescent in heterosexual relationships? Clearly, sexting can expose girls to familiar forms of harassment and slut-shaming, but future research that takes such questions seriously might demonstrate that there are unique benefits as well.

SELF-EXPRESSION

Most of the depictions of sexuality young people consume (legally or otherwise) consist of images created of, by, and for adults. Media scholars have written for decades on the social and emotional consequences of being misrepresented or underrepresented in commercial mass media (e.g., hooks, 1996), including the effects of symbolic annihilation (Gerbner & Gross, 1976). The solutions scholars usually suggest are that girls, women, and people of color should have more power to influence how they are represented and that a greater diversity of depictions is necessary. Kearney (2006) argues that media production and publication can be radical and worthwhile for girls or anyone else who is routinely excluded from the process of creating mass media representations. Indeed, many sex-positive feminists[15] argue that the best response to sexist representations of women in mass culture is to create better representations of sexuality. However, teen girls are explicitly prohibited from creating and sharing sexual representations of themselves.

Even though a sexual image might be created for an audience of only one other person—or just for oneself—such mediated practices of self-representation may facilitate media critique, creativity, and self-reflection. For example, Tiidenberg (2013) finds that some participants in a Tumblr group gain confidence and the ability to reflect upon and resist normative standards of beauty by creating and sharing sexual images of themselves. As Döring (2000) suggests, the features of digitally mediated communication make it easier both "to explore one's own sexual desires and to critically reflect on the experiences associated with them" (p. 880). Hjorth (2007) also wonders if camera phones offer "new emerging modes of self-presentation and identification that both, paradoxically, reinforce, and yet subvert, gendered imagery in mainstream media" (p. 231). Dong-Hoo Lee (2005) likewise reports that the camera phone users she interviewed take pleasure in objectifying themselves with their own cameras and learning how to manipulate and construct images. While these images sometimes conform to dominant beauty expectations, she maintains that it is significant that young women are producing these images themselves rather than being photographed by others, deeming the camera phone "a tool of self-exploration."

This research suggests that girls' sexual media production practices, like more celebrated forms of media production, might provide new ways for young people to negotiate, respond, and speak back to sexual representations of youth and femininity in mass media. While most experts are convinced that girls use sexting to get the wrong kind of attention because they lack self-confidence, in an atypical newspaper article, a psychologist offers an alternate explanation: Girls who sext "are very impressed with their growing bodies and the way they look... [and] they think it's a mark of being cool and gives them bragging rights. ... It's daring, exciting and, they think, kind of safe" (Jan Jarvis, 2007). Speaking in early 2007, prior to the start of the epidemic of coverage of sexting, this expert provides the unusual interpretation that teens post sexual pictures online because they are proud of their bodies. She casts these girls as self-confident, "daring" girls who take pleasure in the attractiveness of their bodies and want to "show themselves off" to others. Though she chastises these girls for behaving recklessly, these girls are not the low-self-esteem, eating-disordered girls that commonly appear in mass media discourse. While the psychologist offers a rarely seen picture of girls who feel great about their developing bodies—not embarrassed and awkward—and take pleasure in their appearance, most experts offer a harsher condemnation of this as an inappropriate and dangerous sign of low self-esteem.

Viewing sexting as a form of media production makes it possible to consider the creativity of teens who consensually produce their own sexual images. While the technical skills gained in using a point-and-click mobile phone camera might be relatively limited, having a degree of control over one's representation is nevertheless significant. If sexting is media production, it is important to investigate how the practice could facilitate critical reflection on gender and sexual representations in mass media.

PLEASURE

Viewing consensual sexting as media production highlights a basic motivation for sexting that is often unmentioned in discussions about girls: desire for sexual expression and pleasure. This much is clear in lifestyle news items about sexting for adults. Without the weight of the moral panic about teens, these articles offer an interesting alternative discourse about sexting that is often positive about the practice, usually focusing on how sexting can enliven readers' sex lives (Colon, 2010; Leshnoff, 2009). An American Association of Retired Persons newsletter article begins by noting that teens who sext are getting into trouble and exercising "bad judgment," but the rest of the article explicitly promotes the practice for its adult readers (Leshnoff, 2009). In this article, a number of experts tell readers to have fun with sexting, and the article offers a step-by-step guide that includes: "When you're comfortable, try texting something slightly suggestive." For adults, sexting is not seen as a sign of "bad judgment," and the only warnings the article provides are to "keep expectations . . . in check" and to "periodically houseclean" one's mobile phone:

> If you're sending or receiving racy notes or photos, delete them every so often. . . . If you lose your cell phone or it's stolen, pictures can be uploaded in a heartbeat—and that's not to mention the possibility of your teenage kids innocently flipping through your texts or photos.

Similarly, an *AOL Personals* article advises, "Flirting over a text message or instant message on the computer can be a great way to spice up your relationship. It's especially useful for long-distance couples" (Colon, 2010). In contrast to the focus on risk in media coverage of teen sexting, such articles about adults frame the practice primarily in terms of sexual pleasure and note concern only as an afterthought that private texts or images could be distributed without permission.

Popular discourses of adult sexting as "fun and flirty" indicate the need for further research on the pleasures of sexting and its role in sexual relationships. There are indications that teens, like the imagined adults in these lifestyle articles, often sext consensually for pleasure. Recall, for example, that in the Sex and Tech survey (2008), the most popular reason teens selected for why they engage in sexting is "to be fun/flirtatious." Albury and Crawford (2012) find that some young adults sext to maintain connections in long-distance relationships, and as one young woman explained, for "just a different form of erotica," while others might take or send nude photos as "more of a joke than the serious sexual type of thing" (p. 468). Focus group research finds that many teenagers explain that sexting can be a part of their intimate sexual relationships and that a few view sexting as a safer alternative to sex (A. J. Harris et al., 2013; Lenhart, 2009). For example, Lenhart (2009) reports that a younger high school boy said, "Most people are too shy to have sex. Sexting is not as bad" (p. 8). Although many researchers recognize that nonsexual media production can be a pleasurable leisure activity, it may be useful to understand the ways that sexting could offer unique sexual pleasures. As one essayist points out, "Seduction is language, bodily or verbal, not action" (Prickett, 2012). She describes sexting as taking the distinct sexual pleasure of written communication one step further:

> In some ways the speed and ease and volume of texts have devalued the content, but in others texting and IMing and g-chatting are improvisational evolutions of letter-writing, making it automatic and collaborative, not single-handed and static. Making it, in one word, hotter. . . . Good sex I can usually leave wherever I found it, but good sexters I keep forever in my pocket. (Prickett, 2012)

As Karaian (2012) suggests, there is a need for more research and theory addressing how sexual pleasure exists alongside danger and risk, particularly for teenage girls.

Complicating participation

Thinking about sexting as media production also suggests a need for skepticism about participation. While the radicalizing effect of media production and participatory culture may hold some promise, recall Carey's (1989) observation about the frequent recurrence in U.S. history of inflated hopes that new communications technologies will usher in progress and solve the most pressing social problems. With that in mind, perhaps some of the benefits of new media and participation are overstated. After all, distributing a sext without permission is still a form of participatory media use. Any popular video on YouTube will garner thousands of comments, some of them irrelevant or hateful—yet all are participation. Arguments about the benefits of media production and participation rarely consider banal, complicated, and even harmful forms of media production and distribution. The harm caused by privacy violations makes it clear that interaction and engagement with media is not necessarily consensual, pleasurable, democratic, or radical. Indeed, there is nothing inherently good about participation, and the form of agency it presumes to offer is often overvalued.

As critics such as van Dijck (2009) and Andrejevic (2004) point out, many people believe that new media facilitate interaction and return power and control to the user while old media supposedly create passive recipients of information and ideology.[16] Andrejevic (2004) explains:

> The hope offered by the advent of the network society is that . . . the return of public participation via interactivity might revitalize not only politics and production but also culture—that the interactive aesthetic is a more democratic one than either of those provided by mass society: high culture and the culture industry. (p. 46)

For girls, who are said to be especially influenced by sexualization in mass media, the expectation is that new media would facilitate their resistance to sexism in media. The high hopes for new media are based on the assumption that being a victim of culture is a condition of passivity while being a participant means actively engaging with culture. Consider that the opposition between active and passive is often too starkly drawn. A fundamental insight of cultural studies is that users and audiences accept, negotiate, and oppose the terms of mass culture in complex ways (S. Hall, 1980), and that perhaps viewers—and sexters—are usually in some kind of gray area between resistance and acceptance. The general celebration of audience interaction and engagement in new media might even obscure how user participation benefits media companies and does not necessarily reflect or enhance political engagement (Andrejevic, 2004, 2007; Barney, 2010; Dean, 2009). Sterne (2012b) points out that commercial media platforms that rely on monetizing user participation are not so different from "the so-called passive media of previous decades, . . . [since] the most compliant gesture we can make is to consent to interact on the terms presented to us by our software and machines." Voting for one's favorite singer on *American Idol*, for example, may be valorized for bringing democracy to mass culture, but it also provides the show with an unprecedented volume and detail of information it can use to market more effectively to viewers (Andrejevic, 2004). Audience involvement generates the data that fuels the information economy and facilitates state surveillance but it does not, as claimed, necessarily constitute empowered democratic citizenship. Barney (2010) suggests: "Participation is ambivalent, as open to stabilizing prevailing arrangements of power and injustice as it is to disrupting them" (p. 143). Participation, then, is not necessarily in opposition to power but can just as easily reinforce power relationships.

As those concerned about sexualization might fear, participating in media production by sexting is not necessarily a form of resistance to sexualization. When girls create sexual images, they might reproduce and reinforce the misogynistic parts of commercial culture. Women are frequently called upon to perform a normative version of commercialized sexually attractive and sexually empowered femininity, which is portrayed as an indicator of a woman's self-confidence. Some feminists, such as Pitcher (2006), argue that the mainstream commercial culture version of this "sexual empowerment" offers "a depoliticized, empty model of choice" (p. 215) that demands that women participate by performing a particular type of sexual agency. Gill (2008) argues that sexual depictions of adult women in popular culture are still objectifying, but that now (some) women are called upon to "understand their own objectification as pleasurable and self-chosen" (p. 45). She explains: "A 'technology of sexiness' has replaced 'innocence' and 'virtue' as the commodity that young women are required to offer in the heterosexual marketplace" (Gill, 2007, p. 72). She notes that these commodified representations are no more accurate or authentic than previous discourses that erased and silenced girls' sexuality.

The point here is that what may seem like an opportunity to participate can be in fact a coercive demand. When such a demand comes from a specific person, the victimization is clear. For example, threatening someone in order to compel them to produce a sexual image constitutes sexual abuse. However, when the imperative to participate is located in a culture more generally, be it the conditions that the digital economy creates inducing users to interact or the pervasive objectification of women, the relative agency and victimization of a participant are more difficult to discern. A key problem with the explanation that sexualization causes sexting is that it reduces the extremely complex relationship between media representations of sexuality and sexual desire to a simple one-way effect. Like all people, girls are no doubt influenced by sexualization in media, but their sexualities and modes of sexual expression are not determined by it. In any case, girls' agency or lack thereof is still the wrong target for intervention.

Sexting, as a form of media production and participation, might still offer unique forms of resistance and agency. However, these forms of action are perhaps overvalued and idealized. Sterne (2012b) explains: "Neither activity nor passivity are goods in themselves; both have roles to play in culture, politics and personal life." Indeed, conformity to cultural norms is not unique to girls, working class people, and "third-world" women, nor is it a pathology—most people, most of the time, accept or negotiate rather than resist most norms. The discourses about sexualization rely on a problematic fundamental assumption about agency: that culture, especially mass culture, is opposed to and separate from individual freedom and agency. For example, Mahmood (2005) critiques liberal humanism for often viewing agency as "the capacity to realize one's own interests against the weight of custom, tradition, transcendental will, or other obstacles" (p. 8). It is easy to pathologize and target conformity to mass culture because agency is often viewed in a limited way as the struggle of the individual against the will of others—other individuals, other forces, and other structures.

Conclusion

Communication practices and technologies constantly fail to live up to high hopes that they will solve social problems, reinvigorate the public sphere, or facilitate a perfect distortion-free dialogue (Barney, 2000; Carey, 1989; Peters, 1999). Sexting may be particularly disturbing for some observers because it seems to disrupt the hope that media production will liberate viewers from the negative influences of mass culture. Sexting perhaps bears the burden of broken dreams that new media, this time, will finally create agency, resistance, and meaningful cultural and political participation. Of course, such feelings depend on a particular celebration of resistance and a definition of liberation for girls as freedom from certain forms of sexuality.

If it is obvious to say that media users and audiences are both active and passive, that they both negotiate and accept the terms of mass culture, then why is it so hard to remember this when it comes to sexting and the debates about sexualization? It seems that normative ideas about gender, sexuality, and age have the power to erase all this hard-won nuance that the fields of cultural and media studies has provided and replace it with claims that girls who self-sexualize or who sext are passive carriers of a cultural disease. Indeed, many conversations about sexualization assume that girls hold the solution to problematic media representations, gender inequality, and the prevalence of sexual violence. The discourse of sexualization is especially troubling because it has the uncanny ability to both evacuate girls' agency and blame them for their own victimization at the same time.

The intervention offered here of viewing sexting as a form of media production helps shift the discourse away from these problems and instead to assume that the typical sexting girl is not necessarily a victimized automaton rendered passive by a pressuring boyfriend or the supposed avalanche of sex in media but may be producing sexual media for her own reasons. At the same time, it is valid to ask: How can girls and women express and embody sexuality in a cultural context that offers overwhelmingly sexist, objectifying representations of femininity? Blaming girls who sext for contributing to child abuse and for the privacy violations they experience is clearly an unfair victim-blaming response to complex social problems. Thinking about sexting as media production suggests that participation is not necessarily resistant or even positive, but it is still useful to acknowledge and grapple with girls' agency and choices—like all our choices, they are made within contexts we did not create. Dismissing a girl's choice to sext as inherently inauthentic or coerced by sexualization might be appealing, but erasing a girl's subjectivity leads to unfair and misguided responses to sexting.

Why are discussions about sexualization so appealing and popular? For people who are passionate about ending violence against women, girls who seem to sexually objectify themselves offer a highly visible reference to the structural problems and incidents of harassment and assault that are less easy to see in everyday life. People who see a preteen wearing a crop-top in the mall might cringe or sigh with sad resignation—such powerful affective responses come from the connection these observers make between this girl's self-sexualization and the problems with a culture that objectifies women and tacitly authorizes sexual violence. But consider that these problems would persist even if that girl (or all girls) abstained from self-objectification. At the same time, if we actually did solve those larger problems, the crop-top would likely no longer be worrisome because it would no longer seem to reference inequality and violence. Who benefits the most when we ask girls to resist sexualization and to avoid objectifying themselves? It is not clear that either girls or society in general stand to gain much from fewer exposed midriffs—but concerned observers would have to cringe less, to sigh less, and to be reminded less often of the gendered and sexualized violence that continues despite our best efforts to end it.

The fact that mass market paperbacks, newspaper articles, and academic studies alike are united in viewing the solution to sexualization as a self-help project for women and girls should raise some serious suspicions (Duits & Zoonen, 2011). Condemnation of sexualization in media even unites people across the political spectrum—liberals might view it as sexism or the commodification of intimacy and conservatives might call it indecency or vulgarity, but they are all worried about similar things (Gill, 2009). The discourse about sexualization is so appealing in these diverse markets and contexts because it reproduces common sense ideas they all share. These widely held beliefs include: that girls are passive media consumers; that mass culture is an outside force that has a negative impact on individuals, primarily on those imagined to be vulnerable; that sexuality is fundamentally dangerous and best restricted to so-called healthy or otherwise normative expressions; that only women who embody a particular version of class-marked femininity deserve respect or recognition as agents; and that men and boys bear little responsibility or capacity for change. The dominant discourse about sexualization is so popular and marketable because, while it is often feminist in origin and in intent, it is a fundamentally conventional discourse, which offers little that is new or challenging to how people already tend to understand media, sexuality, and gender. The solutions that discussions about sexualization often advocate—self-esteem and media literacy for girls—are popular precisely because they ask for nothing from potential perpetrators of violence and harassment and do not disrupt the ideas about gender and sexuality that still badly need changing.

CHAPTER 5

Information and consent

There is an interesting contradiction in how we think about the capacity and right to control information. On one hand, there is broad legal and public support for the control of commercially produced information and media. From intellectual property and patent laws to copyright infringement lawsuits, the law and the public seem to generally support companies' rights to own and control the information and media content they create. Yet, on the other hand, users are told that the inherent qualities of digital media make privacy impossible and that giving up control over their information and personal content is necessary for the success of the information economy. They are told that "information wants to be free" and "privacy is dead." Most forms of data mining are legal, governments engage in sophisticated surveillance programs, and public records that were once difficult to access are now freely available online. Why does it seem feasible and important to control commercially produced information while limiting the flow of personal information seems impossible? For example, a Kindle will allow users share an ebook with only one other device, but most mobile phones can forward any photo to any number of users.

With regard to personal information, there is a problematic consensus that seems to be developing that everything that is digital is public by default. Ideas about consent and privacy seem to be shifting in the new information economy, often in the interests of media companies and the state rather than individuals. While copyright and crime prevention are often seen as legitimate reasons to restrict the flow of information, other interests, such as privacy and cultural preservation, are weakly and inconsistently protected (Nissenbaum, 1998; Seeger, 2005; Solove, 2007; Weintraub & Yung, 2009). In this chapter, I challenge the idea that personal information is impossible to control and explore how this assumption operates in discussions about sexting.

The key variable missing in the way we think about information flows is consent, and in the discussion that follows, I suggest that explicit consent should be required for the circulation of private media and information. Such a change would lead to some alternative ways of protecting privacy, including developing social norms and technological mechanisms for obtaining meaningful and informed consent before circulating private information. The explicit consent standard developed in this chapter might mean, for example, that by default users should not be able to forward all images they receive on their mobile phones—instead, the person who creates the image should be able to decide whether the recipient can forward it to someone else. Adopting an explicit consent model could lead to a range of policies, norms, educational interventions, and technological architectures that are tailored to address the most common form of harm, which occurs between people who know one another rather than strangers. As such, the key intervention should be to reinforce consent as a norm in the flow of private information and to find ways to address violations without resorting to incarceration.

It is tempting to simply abandon privacy on the grounds that freeing information is often positive and that new technologies make the wide distribution of all information inevitable. However, in this chapter I suggest that constraints on the free flow of information are both important and possible to establish. Recall the story of the Star Wars Kid, a teenage boy who was widely mocked on the internet and at school beginning in 2003 after classmates uploaded a video of him acting like a character from the movie. Vaidhyanathan (2011) argues that the blame for incidents like these lies in "our willingness to ridicule others publicly and our ease at appealing to free-speech principles to justify the spreading of everything everywhere, exposing and hurting the innocent along the way" (p. 96). Just because something can be distributed—technically or legally—does not mean it should be distributed.

Thinking about the importance of consent in the distribution of information sidesteps the victim-blaming rhetoric that maintains that one should simply know better than to create any private images. Though taking and sharing a private photo might be risky, accounting for privacy norms that operate in digital media contexts makes it clear that it is not necessarily an unreasonable risk. Consider that people routinely trust lovers, doctors, cashiers, and loan officers with personal information that they expect will not be distributed. While protecting individual privacy in the information age is no easy task, it is possible to adapt existing offline privacy norms for new media by prioritizing consent and accounting for a variety of information-based harms.

Rethinking "free information"

The attitude that the distribution of digital personal information is inevitable may be rooted in the libertarian utopian ideology associated with the early internet. The dream was that because this new network was supposedly impossible to regulate and censor, there would be unprecedented levels of free market competition and unrestrained political discourse. Barbrook and Cameron (1996) dub this the "Californian ideology," which they describe as "an anti-statist gospel of hi-tech libertarianism: a bizarre mishmash of hippie anarchism and economic liberalism beefed up with lots of technological determinism" (p. 56). For example, in his 1996 Declaration of the Independence of Cyberspace, Barlow describes the internet's resistance to control and governance as natural properties: "[The internet] is an act of nature and it grows itself through our collective actions. . . . Your legal concepts of property, expression, identity, movement, and context do not apply to us." A similar idea is that the internet wants to free information from constraints. Gilmore argues: "The Net interprets censorship as damage and routes around it" (Elmer-DeWitt, 1993, p. 64). In the heady rhetoric of the early 1990s, the internet is naturally democratic, anticensorship, and virtually impossible to regulate. As Willis (2002) points out, metaphors positioning the early internet as a "wild west" frontier space justified the idea that it was an unsafe place that women should avoid. The key idea is that the internet could not (and should not) be governed.

While these dreams of an unrestricted internet have been scaled back since the 1990s, there is still a common belief that personal information, data, and content are nearly impossible to control online—that privacy is dead and users must adjust their behavior accordingly. Users are routinely told, through policy decisions, the terms of service they agree to by using social media, and in mainstream advice about online safety, that their personal information and content can be freely distributed and sold. While legal precedents are still evolving, a number of decisions reflect the widespread belief that personal privacy is impossible online. For example, in one case the judge asserted that on social network sites, "Privacy is no longer grounded in reasonable expectations, but rather in some theoretical protocol better known as wishful thinking" (*Romano v. Steelcase Inc.*, 2010, p. 434). In another case, the judge commented: "The concept of Internet privacy is a fallacy upon which no one should rely" (*People v. Klapper*, 2010, p. 226). While the norms and challenges of privacy are indeed different in social media and digital environments, in the final section of this chapter I examine many policy, technological, and social changes that could increase users' ability to exert some control over their personal content.

The idea of freeing information from regulation and control may be appealing because it seems to support individual freedom and progress. Indeed, when software and commercial media are freely distributed, such as in open-source formats, this seems to generally benefit users. Brand (1987) famously stated, "Information wants to be free," because it is so easy to copy. At the same time, he explained that "information [also] wants to be expensive" because it is an increasingly vital commodity (p. 202). Technological advances that facilitate information distribution exacerbate this constant tension. The complex and divisive debates Brand refers to about copyright and intellectual property persist decades later; unauthorized file sharing continues unabated while laws like the Digital Millennium Copyright Act (1998) and digital rights management systems seek to restrict this flow. Yet, since the digital economy has developed around "free" information, many of these debates are not between users and companies but among various sectors of commercial interest. Indeed, users do not always want information to be free and media companies do not always want to restrict it. As Sterne (2012a) explains in his work on the MP3, "Piracy may not itself always be an economic activity, but it enables all kinds of other market activities" (p. 203), including generating profit for the broadband and consumer electronics industries. Even the free circulation of commercially produced media is monetized by other means—for example, through advertising on BitTorrent websites like the Pirate Bay.

Whether information is commercially produced or user-generated, its free movement is not necessarily a form of resistance to the digital economy. Instead, the beliefs that information is impossible to control and that privacy is dead are in fact cornerstones of this economy, sometimes at the expense of individuals' rights. How does an economy that relies on free raw material (information) generate profit and what are the hidden costs? Users pay for some commercially produced content, for internet and mobile phone service, for electronic devices, and for the use of social network platforms as they view pages with advertisements and create the content that will appear on these pages. Scholars such as Andrejevic (2009) and Terranova (2004) illustrate that in the economy of the internet, much of the profit relies on the free labor of users who generate online content and the free flow of their personal information. Balsamo's question in 1996, "What rights do individuals have *vis-a-vis* the information they produce in the course of their daily lives?" (p. 347) is still unresolved, both in terms of evolving social norms and the uneven legal precedents established since then. In social media environments, there is an inherent conflict between users' desires to maintain some control over their privacy and website owners' desires to find ways to distribute user-generated content with advertisements attached and to aggregate and resell as much personal information as possible.

The point is that refrains about the death of privacy serve particular commercial interests. As boyd (2010) argues, "By continuously arguing that Privacy is Dead, technologists justify their efforts to make publicly available data more public." There is little incentive for social media companies to help users truly understand and maintain the privacy of their personal information. Instead, the more such information is produced, gathered, and distributed, the more these companies stand to gain, as long as users are unaware of these processes and their potential impact. Many ways data is collected and used, for targeted advertising, for example, are completely invisible to users. Websites can also make changes to their privacy policies without fully informing users. For example, facial recognition was enabled by default on Facebook (Fiveash, 2011), and users must keep track and opt out of new features like this one to maintain their privacy. Solove (2004) argues that state and commercial collection of personal information pose new threats that the legal system is not well equipped to recognize and address. It is increasingly evident that there is much at stake in protecting privacy. Left to the free market, protections for and norms of privacy will only continue to erode.

While the basic idea that information wants to be free (or should be free) is attractive, there are a number of problems with this view of information. The idea that restrictions on information are always bad serves a variety of commercial interests while disproportionately affecting people who depend on privacy for their safety or who lack the skills and resources to maintain it. The assertion that privacy is impossible online is inaccurate, but it can still have powerful effects on users' rights and expectations. Such claims about digital information ignore the issues of consent and harm and surrender agency to information itself and to the technologies that are used to distribute it. The common sense belief that personal information cannot be protected erases both larger systems of power and specific incidents of abuse, which I turn to now in the context of sexting.

DO SEXTS WANT TO BE FREE?

Many people think that sexting is foolish and unsafe because they assume that it is impossible to keep any image private. Sometimes people assume that all digital images, regardless of content, are inherently public; that users should expect all images created on mobile phones to be forwarded. There is a common assumption that consent is always either irrelevant or unclear in the context of digital media. Sexters whose intimate partners have violated their privacy are often chastised for trusting the wrong person and for engaging in foolish and risky behavior. The attitude that digital information cannot and should not be controlled is especially prevalent in public discourses about sexting. News coverage of sexting often contains comments such as, "Children must learn that any images they send out never disappear" (Steele, 2008). The typical advice to youth about sexting is: If you do not want your private images all over the internet, do not create them in the first place. This advice might seem simple and obvious. Yet, it has damaging effects, particularly for girls, who are more likely to be both humiliated and punished if their sexual images circulate widely. The idea that private information will always be distributed contributes to the widespread problem of blaming sexters and ignoring privacy violators that this book discusses in detail.

In many cases of privacy violation, Barrigar (2013) explains, there is a troubling tendency to "blame the stupid user," an attitude that constructs individuals as solely responsible for ensuring their privacy and obscures the responsibilities of institutions, companies, developers, and the state to contribute to protecting privacy. She argues that while taking steps to protect one's personal information remains important, not taking these steps by choice or because of a lack of understanding does not justify the appropriation or exploitation of personal information.

Consider the response to users whose credit card numbers were hacked from an insufficiently secured Sony Playstation network (Arthur, 2011). In the typical media coverage of this incident, users were not blamed for giving Sony their credit card numbers, held responsible for this company's failure to protect their privacy, or criticized for being taken in by Sony's false promises of security. Instead, Sony was blamed in this incident. Here, it is clear that all digital information is not inherently public—there are standards, laws, and expectations for every context and every kind of information.

Likewise, the potential to own and control information is also seen as viable and important in discussions about commercially produced media and other intellectual property. For example, an attorney for the National Press Photographers Association is quoted in a newspaper article explaining, "Like anything of value, people need to ask permission, give credit and pay fair compensation for those images, and when they don't, photographers need to be able to stand up for their rights" (Estrin, 2013). In the mainstream commentary about commercial media, the fight against unauthorized uses and forms of distribution is viewed as challenging but important. In other words, few media or legal authorities would tell a studio executive that the way to avoid piracy is to stop producing blockbuster movies. Instead, there is an extensive set of laws, policies, and technologies to protect the profits derived from the ownership of media content. These protections for intellectual property are not entirely successful—and internet users are indeed collectively inclined to find ways to "route around" restrictions on commercial media distribution—but in mainstream political discourse, these so-called pirates are still seen as destructive lawbreakers who, if caught, may be subject to huge fines or even incarceration. While mainstream media and legal discourses find it important and possible to protect information that has the potential to generate profit, private sexual content is seen as especially impossible to control.

PRIVACY IS DEAD; LONG LIVE PRIVACY

Sun Microsystems' CEO Scott McNealy famously stated: "You have zero privacy.... Get over it" (Sprenger, 1999). While the much-heralded and greatly feared end of privacy as we know it is not yet upon us, discussions of the death of privacy online are commonplace. Since at least the beginning of the modern internet, individuals have been viewed as complicit in this so-called end of privacy for sharing too much information and exposing their private lives online. These judgments are sometimes gendered and typically centered on youth, who are both the early adopters of social media and the frequent focus of discourses about the decline of society and moral values. Ranging from critiques of shallow, self-centered, exhibitionist bloggers to fears that predators will stalk girls who post any personal information online, observers often view the internet as corrupting standards of personal propriety and privacy. For example, a late-1990s newspaper article on webcams states: "Voyeurism is the latest Internet rage, and technology is blurring the lines between public and private lives" (Kennedy, 1998). A later piece on teenage bloggers suggests that their sense of privacy may be "degraded" (Nussbaum, 2004). The idea that privacy is dead works in two ways in discussions about sexting. One assumption is that creating a nude or suggestive image of oneself indicates a lack of personal privacy. A second assumption is that given how easy it is to distribute media online, no sexters should expect their privacy to be respected.

Viewing teens as having no concept of privacy is a gross oversimplification. For example, though not all users of social network sites understand or use the privacy settings (Debatin et al., 2009), Marwick, Murgia-Diaz, and Palfrey (2010) assert that youth are indeed concerned with online privacy. They find that young people often view privacy in terms of maintaining control over who (friends, parents, or teachers, for example) has access to their information. Though many social media users share personal information and media content online, controlling what information is available to which audiences still matters to them. Though norms of privacy have evolved as a result of technologies like social media, privacy is by no means dead.

While inefficiency and impracticality once prevented the wide distribution of most personal information, the technological changes of the past century or so have significantly altered the challenges to privacy (Nissenbaum, 1998). Indeed, one of the earliest known U.S. publications on privacy is concerned with the impact of photography and the printing press on maintaining privacy in public space (Warren & Brandeis, 1890). Nissenbaum stresses that even in public spaces, people generally follow widely accepted information and privacy norms (2004). As boyd (2010) explains, "Just because something is publicly accessible does not mean that people want it to be publicized." Nissenbaum (2004) points out that each social context has specific norms about information collection and circulation, whether they are formal or informal. The topics that are discussed, the distribution of information, and the directions in which information moves vary widely depending on the social context. For example, information a patient shares with a doctor is formally protected, while the privacy of health information shared between friends or family members relies on informal norms and expectations. Some online spaces are public, or in boyd's (2008) terms, they are networked publics, but as publics they still have particular informational norms and expectations of privacy.

Likewise, there are common social norms about distributing an image with private intimate content. Research on this is just emerging, but a study from Albury and Crawford (2012) as well as research I conducted with Tamara Shepherd (2014) indicates that the unauthorized distribution of a personal sexual image is widely considered a serious violation of privacy. It is a myth that all or even most private sexts will be distributed to third parties. Though further research is required to determine how often and under what circumstances this occurs, a minority of teen sexters report on surveys that they have had this experience. The largest and most representative peer-reviewed study reports: "Photographs were distributed in 10 percent of incidents when youth appeared in or created images and in 3 percent when youth received images" (Mitchell et al., 2012, p. 5).[1] In another report, 14 percent of young people who voluntarily sent sexts said that their images were forwarded to one or more unintended recipients (Englander, 2012).[2] For such an image to become available publicly, at least one recipient would have to upload it to a public website, and for a family member or future employer to find the image, some identifying details would also need to accompany the image. While distribution is clearly a significant risk and is devastating to many victims (Powell, 2010b; Ringrose et al., 2012), in a range of studies reflecting different methodologies, study populations, and survey questions, a large majority of teens report that the intended recipient of their private sexts did not distribute the images.

Though privacy norms may shift and evolve over time, the notion that they have disappeared is not reflected in users' attitudes or practices. While a digital image can be easily distributed, the technological form it takes does not erase all the norms and expectations about appropriate use and circulation. Though a sexual image sent from one person to another passes through service providers' networks and infrastructures, users typically do not consider their private images to be public simply because of their format. To argue otherwise, like the judges and commentators quoted earlier, is to assert that everything digital is public and everything public can be publicized. It is vital to challenge these creeping and unwarranted assumptions about privacy in digital media.

INFORMATION AND POWER

Privacy may not be dead, but the right to privacy is unevenly distributed. For example, Andrejevic (2007) points out that many companies enjoy such strong privacy rights that users cannot even find out all the personal information a company has gathered about them. Yet, some individuals who rely on privacy for their safety can be vulnerable. As boyd (2010) explains, consider the privacy needs and what is at stake for an undocumented immigrant, a person trying to avoid contact with an abusive ex-partner, or a person who is gay and chooses not to reveal this in a homophobic work environment. The default settings on social media applications often assume that people want to share all their personal information, which affects the least skilled users (boyd & Hargittai, 2010), who are also more likely to have lower incomes (Livingstone & Helsper, 2010) and lack access to legal resources. boyd (2010) points out: "The 'public by default' environment . . . isn't always the great democratizer; for many, it's exactly the opposite." While the idea that "information should be free" seems to support individual freedom, the unrestricted circulation of data is not a benefit to everyone.

Like issues of privacy and personal safety, cultural reasons for restricting information that do not conform to commodity-based regulations are also not well addressed by the copyright model. As digital reproduction technologies allow for the archiving and circulation of sacred cultural objects, there are new concerns about the intended audiences of these artifacts. Christen (2011) explains that online archives pose challenges for some indigenous communities who wish to "maintain some traditional cultural protocols for the viewing, circulation, and reproduction of some materials" (p. 185). For such groups, creating completely open-access online databases can be at odds with cultural norms and goals—in this context, unrestricted access to cultural products is not always desirable. Christen (2012) describes a digital archive project for one group that addresses these issues by requiring users to create profiles tagged with affiliations that determine what content they can access, thus coding pre-existing social norms into the architecture of the system.

The lack of control over information is another problem some indigenous groups experience, as Seeger (2005) explains: "Most intellectual property legislation excludes folklore and anonymous works from consideration . . . [and usually] fails to recognize collective ownership of knowledge" (p. 79). Since such cultural products and knowledge belong to the public domain, they can circulate freely without restrictions and royalties and can be repacked and commodified by third parties for profit. Seeger (2005) argues: "The same people dispossessed of their lands in previous centuries are today dispossessed of control over (and income from) their artistic life" (p. 81). This can also be a problem for individual artists who work in commercial media production and, like in other industries, lack control over the profits of their labor. For example, for much if not all of the history of recorded music in the United States, people of color working as musicians and composers have been disproportionately deprived of the profit from royalties for their creations (Vaidhyanathan, 2001).

There is a striking similarity in how two very different types of information—indigenous knowledge and sexual images—are constructed as somehow inherently public. The assumption is that both types cannot be owned or controlled by their producers and thus are free for others to use and circulate. Both types of information are viewed as outside their producers' control: Indigenous knowledge can seem to differ too much from commercial modes of information production and ownership, while private sexual images can be seen as a nonnormative sexual behavior and thus not deserving of privacy.

While there is a broad acceptance of sexual images commercially produced for public consumption, there is little support of the right to create such images for the sole purpose of private pleasure or interpersonal communication. In this sense, sexting seems to be outside what Berlant (1997) identifies as the private intimate sphere of normative heterosexual behavior, which is relatively protected by a legal and social zone of privacy. Though women and girls are typically criticized more then men when their private images are distributed, even male politicians who appear in sexual photos are often told: You should have known better. For example, congressional representative Anthony Weiner was forced to resign after suggestive photos and text messages he sent to adult women were widely distributed (McAuliff & Bendery, 2011). While politicians are often held to high standards of marital fidelity, Weiner was particularly reviled for creating and sharing sexual photos of himself. That this type of behavior is seen as deviant means, in Berlant's (1997) terms, that it enjoys none of the privileges of privacy that protect more normative sexual behaviors.

AGENCY AND THE MEDIA VIRUS

Information is sometimes positioned as an agent with the desire to distribute itself. For example, Barlow (1994) explains: "'Information wants to be free' . . . recognizes both the natural desire of secrets to be told and the fact that they might be capable of possessing something like a 'desire' in the first place." These ideas are related to the concept of the meme, a term coined by Dawkins (1976) and popularized in the 1990s (e.g., Rushkoff, 1994). In contrast to the one-to-many model of broadcast media, the concept of the "meme" describes information that seems to self-replicate. In this framework, humans' role is to be efficient but passive copiers who are compelled by the power of the meme itself to replicate the information. The idea that information has an innate desire to be circulated has waned since the height of interest in memetics in the late 1990s. Yet, it implicitly reappears in the common myth that sexts are always distributed. This concept underlies the common passive-voice assertion in many discussions about sexting incidents that "the image was distributed," which avoids naming a subject who is responsible for distributing that private image. Instead, the grammar suggests that the blame might lie either in the ambulant image itself or with the person who created the image.

Critics of memetics and the concept of "viral media" argue that the erasure of human agency is a serious problem. Henry Jenkins and his coauthors (2009), for example, point out: "The idea of the 'media virus' breaks down because people are making conscious choices about what media they are passing along." In contrast, biological viruses typically move from one host to another without any deliberate human action, agency, or choice to replicate that particular piece of information. For example, for a virus to spread, it requires only that we go about our daily lives, sneezing and touching doorknobs—even better if we are oblivious to how this works. When humans spread information and culture, they often choose to share these things with others, sometimes modifying them before transmission. The critics argue that evolutionary principles cannot be applied to culture: "Culture is not in any meaningful sense self-replicating—it relies on people to propel, develop and sustain it.... Cultures are not something that happen to us, cultures are something we collectively create" (H. Jenkins, Li, et al., 2009). Likewise, neither sexual privacy violations nor the gender and sexual dynamics from which they emerge are imposed upon us from sources outside human culture and agency—we collectively both create and work to resist these conditions. As such, the distribution of a private image is not caused by the image's inevitable desire to circulate, but by individuals who deliberately decide to distribute it.

Toward an explicit consent model

Given the quantity of personal information created and stored in digital formats and the ease of its circulation, I suggest that scholars, policymakers, technology developers, and users alike should adopt an explicit consent standard for the production, distribution, or possession of private media and information. As Nissenbaum (2011) points out, it is important to find ways to adapt existing offline norms for privacy for online contexts. My proposed explicit consent standard can help address the complexities of privacy in digital media and challenge the current attitudes that information should always be free from constraints. The new norm I propose is simple: It asks everyone—individuals, companies, and the state—to actively seek consent if they want to distribute another person's private media or information. Before explaining this model in more detail, I first turn to why it is needed: because age can be a poor proxy for consent.

AGE-BASED RESTRICTIONS AND THE MISSING DISCOURSE OF CONSENT

Child pornography laws offer some of the only restrictions on the free flow of information that are not designed to protect intellectual property. These laws rely on a strict age-based framework to determine an offense. This means that instead of asking whether the person consented to appearing in or sharing a sexual image, child pornography laws categorically criminalize all images of people under 18 that are sufficiently sexually explicit. The irrelevance of consent in these laws makes it easier to prosecute but creates a range of unintended consequences.

Statutory rape laws also rely on age rather than consent to determine whether a crime has been committed. Ideas about age and the capacity to consent to sex have long been fraught with contradictions. For example, statutory rape laws did not originate with concerns about sexual consent but, as Cocca (2004) points out, were originally conceived as property crimes in order to protect the commodity value of white girls' premarital chastity.[3] Though statutory rape laws now attempt to address the sexual exploitation of all minors, chaste or unchaste and regardless of gender, expectations about female sexual propriety still influence court decisions (Anderson, 2002; Little, 2005) and figure prominently in mass media discussions of rape cases (Benedict, 1992; Cuklanz, 1996; Worthington, 2005). Statutory rape and child pornography laws do offer some young people legal recourse against rape, coercion, or a privacy violation. However, these laws are inflexible, overly harsh, and can be misapplied. Moreover, though child pornography laws classify filming a sexual assault as an extremely serious offense against a minor, this type of harm is barely recognized legally when committed against an adult.

Many legal scholars writing about sexting have also reproduced the problem of ignoring consent. Though some have developed taxonomies of sexting to address the problem of conflating benign and malicious incidents, these models often refer to consent only obliquely. For example, one model distinguishes "primary" from "secondary" sexting (Ryan, 2010) and another refers to "self-sexting" and "downstream sexting" (Calvert et al., 2010). Some models focus on harm by, for example, describing "sextbullying" as type of cyberbullying (Eraker, 2010) or distinguishing between "aggravated" and "experimental" sexting (Wolak & Finkelhor, 2011).[4]

Erasing consent is particularly problematic when legal and school officials completely ignore malicious behavior and choose instead to punish everyone involved equally. Recall that a girl who creates a sexual image of herself can be punished in the same way as her peers who distribute the private image without permission. For example, in the Miller case discussed in chapter 1, the girls who created images of themselves as well as their classmates who circulated these images without their permission were all handed the same punishment: Everyone was asked to enroll in a "re-education" course and serve a term of probation. Likewise, in the Seattle case noted in this book's introduction, two cheerleaders were punished for creating images while the boys who distributed them were ignored (Blanchard, 2008). Responding to this case, CNN commentator Mike Galanos exclaims, "It's the girls that are to blame, not the school!" and calls it "ridiculous" that the parents tried to sue the school for their unequal treatment (Galanos, 2008). Bill O'Reilly is likewise unsympathetic, commenting that even if the girls did not distribute the photos, they are still at fault because they "were allowing themselves to be put in this position" (O'Reilly, 2008).

The attitude that consensual sexters share equally in the blame is especially problematic when digital privacy violations are severe and devastating (Powell, 2010a; Ringrose et al., 2012). Powell (2010b) explains that nonconsensual distribution can be "a direct violation of the individual's sexual autonomy, with the effect of humiliating, intimidating, and otherwise harming the victim" (p. 112). In some egregious cases, when a sexual assault incident is recorded and distributed, the harm and trauma is even greater. While schools and justice officials usually do not punish victims when it is clear that they did not "participate" in the creation of the video or photos, peers can still turn against them. In one tragic case, Rehtaeh Parsons' peers photographed themselves sexually assaulting her and then shamed and humiliated her, while adults in her school and local justice department repeatedly failed to address the perpetrators. These injustices reportedly drove Parsons to suicide (Mendoza, 2013; Visser, 2013).

At the same time, the absence of consent in child pornography and statutory rape laws means that some teens in consensual relationships are unable to prevent their parents or the state from prosecuting their older partners. Sutherland (2003) explains that parents who are upset about the race, class, or sexual orientation of their teen's older partner are responsible for a substantial proportion of statutory rape prosecutions. It is likely that sexting prosecutions for young adults will repeat the same biases. Recall Antjuanece Brown, who was convicted despite the fact that her girlfriend Jolene Jenkins explicitly stated that their relationship and their image-sharing was consensual. In another case reported in a local newspaper, a 17-year-old girl's father found her sexual photo on a mobile phone and reported it to the authorities ("Illegal," 2007), ending her relationship with her 21-year-old boyfriend and leading to his incarceration and lifetime placement on the sex offender registry. Though these young people could legally have sex in their respective states, in the United States, no 17-year-old can legally consent to the creation of an image of those sex acts. A state official explains: "It doesn't matter . . . whether she consented to appear in the picture. . . . Whether the victim realizes it or not, she was exploited by this man" ("Illegal," 2007). Here, the photographic documentation redefines the girl's otherwise-legal, consensual sexual relationship with her 21-year-old boyfriend as "exploitative." Finally, in another case of a young adult in a relationship with a minor, the victim told investigators that sexting was "a normal part of [her] relationship" with her girlfriend and that "she doesn't believe she is a victim" (DeLea, 2009). Because age alone is often used to assess consent, neither the press nor the legal system can account for the claims of so-called victims who explain that their relationships with their young adult partners were consensual. Thus, relying on age instead of consent in child pornography laws can create problems both for teens who sext consensually and for teens who have been harmed.

THE EXPLICIT CONSENT MODEL

One solution to these problems might be to rethink private media distribution from a perspective that prioritizes consent. The explicit consent model I develop here is based on the concept of affirmative consent that feminists advocated in the late 1980s and early 1990s. These anti-rape legal reformers were then and still are frustrated that the criminal justice response to rape operates on an oversimplified model of sexual consent that is best at recognizing sexual coercion when it involves a stranger, physical force, and a victim who embodies social fantasies about innocence (Anderson, 2002; Estrich, 1987; Gotell, 2008; Oberman, 2000; Pineau, 1989). Estimates based on Department of Justice data suggest that if unreported rapes are accounted for, only 5 percent of all rapists are ever convicted ("Reporting Rates," 2012). In short, there have been many failures to adequately address sexual violence.

In response to these problems, particularly the low rates of reporting for non-stranger rape, feminist reformers seek to change the way people think about sexual consent. Scholars including Estrich (1987), Pineau (1989), and Remick (1993) argue that assumptions and nonverbal cues are insufficient to determine consent in sexual activity. They point out that prosecutors working with conventional understandings of rape must prove that the person resisted; in some states this resistance must still be physical, while others require verbal resistance (Little, 2005). In contrast, according to the affirmative consent model, rape is defined by the absence of a clear and voluntary "yes." That is, these reformers argue that the sexual initiator has a responsibility to always obtain clearly articulated consent. While there are some critiques of the affirmative consent standard for sexual contact,[5] I suggest that such a standard could be easily adopted for the production, distribution, or possession of private images and information. As Kasubhai (1997) points out, there are already strict standards of informed, voluntary consent in nonsexual situations of potential personal intrusion, such as participating in research, undergoing medical procedures, and agreeing to warrantless searches. Though some laws imply that silence or even agreeing under duress constitutes valid consent to sex, the standards for meaningful and active consent are much stronger in these other nonsexual situations and could easily be applied to the distribution of private information as well.

The power of an explicit consent standard is that it clearly establishes that the default is that it is not acceptable to distribute private information. Requiring explicit consent means that the burden shifts to the person who wants to produce, distribute, or possess private content. In such cases, that person would need to obtain some formal or informal agreement (or strong precedent) to establish consent for the circulation of any private explicit sexual image.[6] Explicit consent is especially important for private images and information because the act of distribution can occur without the presence of the person depicted. Since data mining and online surveillance are typically invisible processes, the victim of a privacy violation is often unaware of it and thus not able to resist or refuse at the time it occurs. Crucially, an explicit consent standard clarifies that consenting to sex in no way implies consent to sexual photography; likewise consenting to sexual photography does not imply consent to the distribution of the photos.

An explicit consent standard has a range of implications, from suggesting that one should always ask for permission before distributing a private photo of someone else, to requiring that websites that aggregate and resell personal information should obtain informed and meaningful consent from users. There are legal changes that could come out of the explicit consent model, but the idea of adding consent to media is most powerful as a new social norm that can help transfer existing ideas about offline privacy to an online context.

There are already many privacy norms for offline social interactions that can provide a meaningful guide for how to interpret what content should be considered private. Nissenbaum (2011) argues that privacy is possible online by pointing out that many of our activities on the internet involve a variety of preexisting social and commercial relations, from banking and shopping to conducting research and chatting with friends. For example, a commercially produced sexual image is not intended to be private; thus a person buying pornography would not need to obtain consent. However, since people usually view their sexual acts as private, they can likely also recognize that others' personal sexual images will be typically private as well. While further study of the expectations of privacy and understandings of consent in social media is necessary, emerging research indicates that young people understand that personal sexual images are private (Albury & Crawford, 2012; Hasinoff & Shepherd, 2014). Consider that before the internet and mobile phones, people created and selectively shared personal sexually explicit photos, using a Polaroid camera, for example, and would be able to reasonably expect that person to refrain from showing it to parents, friends, and future employers. Mobile phones make it far easier to violate privacy by digitally forwarding such an image, but Nissenbaum's (2011) argument stipulates that the old information norms can and should remain when social behaviors become mediated and digitized.

Explicit consent is already a norm in commercial media production and circulation. That is, people who appear in still and moving images for commercial mass media usually negotiate their compensation and record their consent to distribution in written contracts. These market norms and regulations are so well established that while youth-produced sexual images are often seen as dangerous, commercial versions of the same types of images are viewed as legitimate business. Teenage fashion models, for example, can sign contracts to appear in widely distributed sexually suggestive images—some of which could even possibly be classified as misdemeanors if the model had taken the photo of herself on a mobile phone, especially considering the range of images criminalized by the broadest of the new antisexting laws discussed in chapter 1.

Commerce is such a strong justification for the production of sexual images that even companies that distribute sexual images of minors without their meaningful consent can face less punishment than consensual sexters. For example, a judge ordered the *Girls Gone Wild* company to pay $1.6 million in fines (12 percent of their 2005 profits) and to perform community service for their use of intoxicated underage girls in their videos ("Girls Gone Wild," 2006). This company distributed sexual images of minors without their consent to a global audience for great financial gain, and yet faced relatively minor penalties. In contrast, young adults like Antjuanece Brown have suffered far greater criminal penalties for their private consensual sexual behavior. Indeed, the motive of financial gain seems to insulate adults like the *Girls Gone Wild* executives from the stigma of "predator" or "sex offender." What these discrepancies also suggest is that the law is primarily concerned with regulating sexual deviance and is in fact relatively unconcerned with the impact on society of the wide circulation of sexual images of minors or the harm to young people who cannot legally consent to appearing in such images. While legal discourses stress the importance of consent, the standard is, of course, unevenly applied. Though child pornography has been carved out as an exception to free speech and the free market, there is much less concern about adults who create sexually suggestive images of adolescents for profit than about a teenager creating the same type of image for her personal sexual gratification.

COMPLEXITIES OF CONSENT

As noted above, age is such a common proxy for consent because the concept of consent can be tremendously complex. Fischel (2010) argues that the concept of the "consenting adult" is used as a substitute for more nuanced sexual ethics, making victims and predators out of consenting minors and failing to adequately recognize victimization between adults. Indeed, typical constructions of sexual consent often imply that adults are rational agents uninfluenced by any structural constraints or forms of power. In advocating for an explicit consent model, I rely on relativistic models of agency and the capacity to consent. In the last chapter, I explored context-based models of agency; here, I argue for assessing consent by considering contexts and relationships as well—this is necessarily imprecise and determined on a case-by-case basis. The explicit consent standard is an attempt to codify norms and thus potentially clarify the absence or presence of consent in the distribution of private media and information.

The problem with consent is that not every "yes" is necessarily a meaningful voluntary agreement. As Kate Harris (2012) points out, a simplistic transmission model of sexual communication in which a verbal "yes" is sufficient to establish consent can fail to account for context. Legally and ethically, what mitigating factors should render a "yes" invalid? This is an important question because while not every "yes" is valid, the implications of imposing victimhood on a person against her will are profound. This is evident in the range of nonnormative sexual behaviors that have been legally defined as inherently nonconsensual (Berlant, 1997; Rubin, 1993). Though they had rarely been enforced, prohibitions against sodomy (anal or oral sex) and fornication (sex between any unmarried partners) only became unconstitutional in the United States in 2003. Such laws formerly defined anyone involved in such sex acts as either a victim or a perpetrator, making legal consent to these acts impossible.[7] That is, consent is a particularly fraught concept because it can be used as a proxy to maintain socially constructed divisions between deviant and normal sexual behavior.

The other side of the heteronormative definition of consent is that normative sex acts can be constructed as inherently consensual even when they are not. For example, until the late 1970s, the marital exemption made it impossible to charge a man for raping his wife in many states. Despite feminist legal reforms, in some states, being married to the victim still reduces the penalties (Anderson, 2003). As these examples demonstrate, sex acts that are seen as nonnormative—personal sexual media production among them—are more likely to be viewed as innately nonconsensual. So how is it possible to identify the circumstances in which a stated "yes" should not be viewed as meaningful and freely given without imposing moralizing judgments of sexuality?

It is beyond the scope of this book to definitively answer this extremely complex question, but for now I look to the definition of consent added in 1992 to the Canadian Criminal Code[8] as a guiding framework. The Code defines consent as "voluntary agreement" and enumerates factors that invalidate consent: when the person is incapable of consenting (including intoxication); when consent is expressed by someone else; when lack of agreement is expressed or consent is withdrawn; and in situations in which the accused has incited the sexual activity by abusing a position of trust, power, or authority. The Code also sets the age of consent at 16 but has a number of age-span provisions.[9] It is vital to consider the factors that could negate consent without relying on simplistic age-based models or on judgments about the supposed deviance of particular sex acts.[10] Such a model could be useful for thinking about consent in cases in which private media has been distributed. If someone claims their private information has been distributed, the explicit consent standard requires that the person distributing private information would need to prove that explicit consent was given. At the same time, a person's stated "yes" to the distribution or production of sexual images might not be meaningful if, for example, she was intoxicated, she was blackmailed by a classmate, or the request came from a coach. But without such mitigating conditions, third parties like parents or prosecutors would need to accept the statements of people like Jolene Jenkins when they explain that they are sexting consensually with their partners.

For any type of private information, it is important to account for imbalances and abuses of power in the process of obtaining consent (Bartow, 2000). For example, people often are not asked for permission when public records are placed online (Nissenbaum, 2004), and the consent forms users click through online are so complex and difficult to understand that the consent may not really be informed or meaningful (Nissenbaum, 2011). One study estimates that it would take 76 work days per year to read all the privacy policies of all the websites a user visits in that time (McDonald & Cranor, 2008). The social pressure to be on sites like Facebook or to have a mobile phone also means that some users might find it difficult to resist using these platforms. If using a particular social network site is a social necessity, like having a phone number or a bank account, it becomes untenable to argue that consent to the terms of service is truly voluntary. Eubanks (2011) also illustrates the limits of meaningful consent for social services clients who are required to provide personal information to receive benefits:

> If clients do not sign away their right to control their own information, they will not receive any kind of benefits: food stamps, transportation vouchers, Medicaid, housing assistance, child care, emergency cash assistance, and other basic necessities of life. Under these conditions, notions of "free choice" and "informed consent" are stretched to their breaking points. (p. 93)

Determining what constitutes informed and meaningful explicit consent in relation to private information requires developing nuanced models that draw on existing sexual, medical, research, and legal frameworks of consent.

Despite the messy complexities, it is nonetheless a vital intervention to bring consent to media. Focusing on consent in social media circulation offers a new perspective that is less burdened with the contradictory legal assumptions that explicit teen sexting is inherently nonconsensual and that victimized youth are as culpable as privacy violators since they both participated in sexting. In order to accurately recognize harmful or malicious behaviors, it is necessary to understand that sexting can be consensual. As Slane (2010) argues, if sexting is seen as simply deviant and criminal for all parties involved, then the malicious distribution of private images becomes normalized. Unless this changes, any teenager who is victimized by a privacy violation and reports the incident can be harshly judged and even prosecuted for participating in the production of child pornography.

How to use consent to protect privacy

The explicit consent model suggests a range of new options for protecting privacy in the circulation of digital media. This standard provides a simple guiding principle that lawmakers and educators can draw on when creating policies and responding to specific incidents. The remainder of this chapter offers a few technological and legal ways to support privacy and address harm in ways that avoid blaming victims, criminalizing consensual behaviors, or expanding the prison system. Just as increasing criminal penalties for other forms of gendered and sexual violence have failed to reduce their incidence (e.g., Corrigan, 2006), criminalizing harmful and exploitative uses of media is unlikely to have much lasting positive social impact. Addressing the issue requires thinking beyond the prison system to find ways to change gendered expectations about sexuality and broader ideas about privacy online. Both the legal and technology-based solutions offered here are best conceived as a reflection of broader social changes in ideas about privacy and digital media rather than the substitute for them.

TECHNOLOGICAL ARCHITECTURES

Despite the early hopes that the internet would be impossible to regulate, it is monitored, controlled, and structured by the code that creates it (Lessig, 2000). The important question is: Whose interests are these digital architectures designed to serve? (Lessig, 2000). As Balsamo (2011) points out, coders and product designers make decisions based on their perceptions of social norms and the needs of the company, creating a complex feedback loop between design and use. That is, social media and mobile devices are designed with the assumption that people expect the content they create to be distributed; by making this the default, the design encourages the wide distribution of content. The design often also assumes that users are uninterested in the monetary value of the content they create and thus need no mechanisms to protect copyright. Such design decisions are also likely motivated by profit: Any capacity to control distribution of one's personal media potentially limits the financial gain for the service provider. Though perhaps unintentionally, the mobile phone industry profits from privacy violations—it may collect fees whenever an image is sent from one phone to another regardless of consent. Thus, it is convenient for service providers and mobile phone manufacturers to take the position that users should simply avoid creating images they do not want forwarded.

Incorporating existing norms of privacy at the level of design (Cavoukian, 2009) might better serve users' interests. Indeed, some commentators argue that both individual participants and the people who design digital environments or platforms are responsible for anticipating and preventing harm to others (Huff, Johnson, & Miller, 2004). In this framework, developers and mobile phone companies may have an ethical obligation to minimize the potential for privacy violations. For example, information could have a user-defined expiry date, which would artificially replicate the once-natural process of forgetting over time (Mayer-Schönberger, 2009). Design features could be built to support an explicit consent model for private media. While most mobile phones can forward any image stored on the device, an explicit consent model might suggest that phones should be able to forward only the images the device created—or images that have been expressly marked as public or unlocked by the original sender. A range of existing mobile phone applications demonstrate how mechanisms for personal content management could work. Snapchat, which has an estimated 26 million users, allows people to send messages and pictures to others that disappear after up to 10 seconds (M. Duggan, 2013). Another app (Encrypt A Pic, 2012) allows users to add passwords to photos they store on their device or send to others. Yet another (Peek: Sexting Awesome, 2012) offers user-defined limits on view time, claims to protect against screenshots by allowing recipients to view only a small portion of the image at a time, and allows users to add stars and pixelation effects to censor parts of their images.

While there are ways to crack these apps and any digital rights management system, doing so often takes effort, which may be sufficient to discourage some forwarders. Some might lack the skills to break the protection but others may find that overcoming such obstacles encourages them to reflect and think twice about violating someone's privacy. Moreover, breaking an electronic lock on a photo also might help legally establish a privacy violation as malicious and deliberate. However, as Kerr (2010) points out in the context of copyright-based digital restrictions, using a lock as a substitute for an ethical decision may have broader social implications. Furthermore, if the option to put restrictions on photographs becomes widely adopted, people who do not use these digital tools to protect their private images could then be blamed if someone maliciously distributes their image. In order to protect the privacy of the least-skilled users, it might be best to implement these kinds of privacy protections on mobile phones and social network sites as default settings rather than as opt-in choices or applications. With this kind of system of default privacy protections, users who want to share their content widely would need to learn how to remove the preset privacy restrictions.

LEGAL REFORMS

Currently, the two most common ways that the law addresses unauthorized image circulation are through child pornography laws and copyright laws. Neither is appropriate or effective for dealing with privacy violations involving personal sexual images. The problem with child pornography laws is that they are designed to address sex crimes committed by an offender who is often imagined to be a predatory, middle-aged white man. However, the harms of sexual privacy violations typically do not fit this scenario. Whether the victim of a privacy violation is a teenager or an adult, the perpetrator is often not a predatory stranger, but a peer or former romantic partner. Most victims in such cases would likely be unwilling to press charges when the consequences are extreme and severe, as is the case in sexual assaults that fit this profile (Corrigan, 2006). As for copyright, victims of malicious distribution are not suffering from loss of profits; thus copyright is an inadequate tool.[11]

One alternative is civil law, which potentially offers victims some ways to address privacy violations, especially if existing privacy laws were adjusted to reflect the explicit consent model. Unlike criminalizing sexting, the civil law system might provide restitution for harm to individuals without stigmatizing offenders. The serious limitation to civil law remedies is that they are accessible only to those with financial and legal resources, and can, like criminalization, have a disproportionate impact on defendants who lack such resources.

PERSONAL LAWSUITS Prioritizing consent in private media circulation would mean fine-tuning the way harms are recognized by law as grounds for lawsuits. Though a range of torts could apply to a privacy violation case, so far courts have responded unevenly to such claims. Calvert (2009) argues that instead of using child pornography law, victims could file lawsuits for "intentional infliction of emotional distress" in cases of malicious private image distribution. Others point out that a range of existing privacy-related torts are also relevant for some victims of privacy violations (Eraker, 2010; Nunziato, 2012). Some legal scholars argue that images and information shared online could be protected by reviving the concept of "implied confidentiality," because users have shared expectations of trust (Hartzog, 2014), particularly in the context of an intimate relationship (McClurg, 2005). This type of reform could help people address a privacy violation by establishing that their expectations of confidentiality were breached.

One major barrier to better legal protections for digital privacy is that judges' sympathies are often limited by their assumptions of what constitutes a reasonable expectation of privacy. For example, one judge in a sexting case explains that a girl should be held legally responsible for producing child pornography because she had no reasonable expectation of trusting her boyfriend to preserve her privacy. The judge writes in his opinion: "A reasonably prudent person would believe that if you put this type of material in a teenager's hands that, at some point either for profit or bragging rights, the material will be disseminated" (*A. H. v. State*, 2007, p. 237). In this case, the teenage boy did not actually distribute the images—it was the parents who disseminated them when they found these private images on their child's computer and turned them over to the police. This judge argues that a "reasonably prudent" person should know better than to ever create a sexual image. But expectations of prudence and responsibility are subjective and are also of course gendered; the judge in this case seems to believe that the girl should be held criminally liable for failing to be "reasonably prudent," but that the average teenage boy cannot be expected to restrain himself from distributing a nude picture of his girlfriend without her permission.

A few adults who have been victimized by the malicious distribution of private sexual images have fared better than teens in the legal system by using privacy torts (Nunziato, 2012). For example, in one case a woman's ex-boyfriend distributed sexually explicit photos via email to her family members, boss, and coworker. A jury awarded the woman punitive damages on the grounds that the man caused her emotional distress and publicized private facts about her ("Outrageous," 2009). While the photo was sent to only five people, the court decided that since the images were sent digitally and thus could easily be widely disseminated, this constituted publication (E. Brown, 2009). Though the definition of *publication* in this tort typically requires wider distribution, this type of interpretive change could help victims of such privacy violations successfully sue for damages. As Solove (2007, 2008) argues, civil law could be strengthened to better protect minors' and adults' privacy. He suggests modifying both this "public disclosure of private facts" tort and the "breach of confidentiality" tort for the forms of publication, authorship, and distribution that are unique to digital media.

In other cases involving the malicious distribution of private photos, courts have found that such behavior can qualify as infliction of emotional distress (J. Kelly, 2011). Yet, this determination relies on subjective interpretations, since liability for causing emotional distress depends on the court's view that the defendant's actions are "extreme and outrageous." The requirement is that an average citizen, upon hearing about the case, would be moved to spontaneously exclaim, "Outrageous!" Fully incorporating explicit consent into popular and scholarly views of private media circulation would help to establish that unauthorized image distribution among teens or adults may indeed be outrageous. As argued in this chapter, it is reasonable to have some expectations of privacy, even in digital media environments.

LIMITING WEBSITE IMMUNITY A broader way to protect privacy would be to develop a notice-and-takedown system for private content posted publicly online. Currently, Section 230 of the 1996 Communications Decency Act provides website operators with immunity from liability for the content their users publish, which helps maintain free speech on the internet. However, this immunity does not extend to intellectual property violations once the website owner has been notified (Digital Millennium Copyright Act, 1998). Some legal scholars argue that websites that refuse to remove private content after being notified should also lose their immunity and be liable for prosecution for invasion of privacy (Nunziato, 2012) and for defamation (Solove, 2007). The rationale is that while the financial impact of a copyright violation can be significant, a privacy violation can irreparably harm a person's reputation (J. Kelly, 2011). While most people would not pursue lawsuits against websites, such changes in the law might encourage websites to remove problematic content quickly from their sites when they do receive a complaint (Marwick et al., 2010). Similarly, mobile phone service providers could potentially be required to block the distribution of an image once they receive notice that it violates someone's privacy.[12]

Hunter Moore's now-defunct website isanyoneup.com illustrates the need for limits on website immunity. His site collected nude and sexually explicit images from angry ex-lovers and former friends and posted these photos along with detailed personal information of the people depicted, including screenshots of their Facebook and Linkedin profile pages (D. Lee, 2012). The site was basically legal as long as it did not post images of minors, since Moore was largely immune from prosecution under Section 230. He publicly reveled in this freedom and constructed his image as a rogue internet bad boy; for example, he often responded to lawsuit threats by posting them on his website and mocking the victims further (Dodero, 2012). The mainstream media coverage of the site was overwhelmingly negative, and some observers seemed particularly offended that Moore profited off others' misfortune. One headline reads: "Hunter Moore makes a living screwing you" (Dodero, 2012). Clearly there is no sympathy for the privacy violator here.

While the risks to free speech are considerable, a carefully designed notice-and-takedown system for privacy violations—improving on the current process for copyright—would help prevent more sites like Moore's, which profit from violating privacy. Because the Digital Millennium Copyright Act can be abused to suppress speech rather than to address legitimate copyright claims (J. Kelly, 2011), specific limits on such a system of takedown notices for privacy violations would be necessary. For example, being able to issue such a notice might be limited only to the person depicted. Google Street View offers another approach: The service has worked around privacy laws and public backlash by automatically blurring out faces and license plates (see for example, the debate in Germany: Albanesius, 2011). Developing a notice-and-takedown system that relies on blurring out the person who issues the request might help balance free speech with privacy. While there would be many details to consider, if legislators do not develop better privacy protections, sites like Moore's could proliferate. Regardless of how it is implemented, my explicit consent standard suggests that users should be able to remove their private images or information from websites, commercial databases, and even some government records.

CHANGING SOCIAL NORMS

None of these technological or legal solutions can shift attitudes about privacy or resolve complex social problems. Research indicates that like other forms of gender- and sexuality-based victimization, sexual privacy violations reflect and reproduce the same larger issues (Ringrose et al., 2012). Many education researchers stress that bullying and harassment reflect broad social norms and school cultures and can be addressed effectively only through collective action by administrators, teachers, and students (E. Meyer, 2009). This work would be more complicated, time-consuming, and difficult than showing a public service announcement at an assembly or punishing individual sexters, but it has the capacity to address forms of gender and sexual marginalization in lasting and meaningful ways. The legal and technological suggestions outlined here might prevent some unfair prosecutions and offer more effective remedies for some victims of privacy violations, but they can be truly effective only as part of larger efforts and cultural shifts.

Adopting the norm of explicit consent for private information distribution is not as complicated as it may seem, nor does it even necessarily require any new laws or new technologies. For example, Solove's (2007) simple code of ethics for bloggers could apply to anyone using cell phones or social networking sites. Two of his suggestions are: "People should delete offensive comments quickly if asked . . . [and] should avoid posting pictures of other people without getting their consent" (Solove, 2007, p. 195). Another example is MTV's 2010 online safety campaign, which includes a message advising against forwarding images. The website explains: "When you get a sext, you might not know if the person would be cool with you sending it around, so better to hit delete rather than forward." This seemingly mundane piece of advice is actually a radical departure from typical online sexual safety campaigns, which often exclusively target girls as the potential producers of digital sexual images and simply advise them to abstain from creating them. By addressing sext receivers rather than just producers, this type of message can facilitate a more effective conversation about digital privacy. The explicit consent model could help solve some of the problems in the legal, educational, and media responses to sexting as well as open up new avenues of research. Most importantly, it urges social media users and youth educators to initiate conversations about digital privacy and to find creative ways to bring offline norms online.

Conclusion

By using the internet and mobile devices, people deliberately and inadvertently generate personal artifacts and data that can be persistent, easily replicable, and even searchable (boyd, 2008). While most people have significant interests in protecting their private personal information against commercial exploitation, the existing tools to do so—both rhetorical and legal—are limited. Many people are convinced that information is impossible to control. The only people consistently acknowledged as victims of the free-information economy are commercial media producers—some individual artists are viewed sympathetically while larger entities like the RIAA (Recording Industry Association of America) who pursue lawsuits against file-sharers are perhaps less so. Freeing information is often viewed as benefiting individual users, or even as favoring individuals over commercial interests. Yet, the digital economy relies on the free flow and monetization of personal information and user-produced media. The public benefit of unrestricted information flows has been ceaselessly promoted without careful consideration of the possible harms.

If there are such strong protections for generating profit from information, why not have the same kind of protections for individuals' privacy? Bartow (2000) suggests, "If society can tolerate ownership of information by companies, there is no compelling reason not to accord analogous property rights to individuals" (p. 694). While the explicit consent model is based on norms, it also implies that personal information is property in a general sense and that individuals should have the right to make decisions about where their personal information goes and how it is used. A strictly property-based model of privacy has some problems (Andrejevic, 2012; P. Schwartz, 2004), but drawing private content and personal information into the powerful system of laws and social norms set up to protect private property is appealing and could be effective (Lessig, 2006). Either way, it is vital that any new protections we build for privacy are able to address harm and individual interests in ways that reach beyond economic interests. We need policies and norms that account for the range of reasons people may have to limit the free flow of their personal information and content, including privacy, cultural preservation, and personal safety. Surrendering all the decisions about the circulation of private information to market forces is unlikely to result in sufficient protections for our privacy.

Conclusion

Since the beginning of the media attention to sexting, a number of high-profile suicides have appeared in the news. In some cases, peers maliciously distributed girls' self-produced images and then inflicted further sexual shaming and name-calling upon the victims (Celizic, 2009; Inbar, 2009). In other cases, victims of rape killed themselves after peers harassed them and circulated videos of the assaults (Mendoza, 2013; Visser, 2013). These tragic cases attracted particular interest because of the heightened shaming these girls experienced through social media. The evidence that is left behind when people socialize online makes once-private locker-room talk and whispers in the hallway newly public and visible to adults. What these girls experienced was not an exception but merely a highly visible (and, I hope, extreme) version of what all too often happens to survivors of rape and youth who are subjected to homophobic and sexist harassment.

Though social media brings slut-shaming and rape culture into the light of day, it is important to recognize that these attitudes are not unique to teens or to a few bad people; they are endemic in mainstream culture. Consider, for example, the disproportionately high rate of suicide among gay and transgender youth (Ryan et al., 2009). None of these deaths—queer teens and rape victims alike—should be understood as outliers, but rather as the result of the enforcement of problematic but widespread gender and sexual norms. We reinforce these norms when we respond to harassment and privacy violations by punishing and blaming the victims for sexting consensually and by disavowing girls' sexual agency. Our common sense beliefs about gender and sexuality can mean the difference between social acceptance and shaming, incarceration and freedom, and even life and death.

Part I of this book focused on three dominant problems in how people tend to think about sexting. Chapter 1 considered the fact that sexting is viewed as a crime and made a case for the decriminalization of consensual sexting, chapter 2 questioned the assumption that adolescents sext because they are biologically irrational and irresponsible, and chapter 3 contested the common explanation that sexting is a psychological problem of girls' low self-esteem. Part II offered not only a critique of the dominant discourses but also new frameworks for thinking about sexting as a media practice and an intimate sexual practice. As with any other sexual act, consent is paramount, and as with any sensitive information, protecting privacy is important. Chapter 4 advocated viewing sexting as a form of media production and interrogated both the theory that sexualization causes sexting and the idea that new media participation is inherently good. Finally, chapter 5 criticized the ideas that "information wants to be free" and "privacy is dead" and instead advocated a model of explicit consent for all private media circulation.

One of the most heartbreaking things I found in the course of this project is that the majority of adults who respond to sexting so poorly seem to believe that they are protecting girls from harm. These adults include feminists who think self-esteem is the solution to sexualization in mass media, educators who advise sexting abstinence, and legislators who think that new anti-sexting laws send the right message. When faced with a problem that looks new, well-intentioned people often fall back on familiar assumptions about girls' sexuality and new technologies to develop a solution. The fact that such good intentions so often fail so badly to shield girls from danger speaks to the enduring power of common sense assumptions. It is only by examining such beliefs more closely that we can expose the misconceptions that underlie the problematic responses to sexting.

Fear and anxiety about sexting are valid responses. There are serious problems with harmful and exploitative uses of technology. But when we blame consensual sexters, we are misdirecting our attention and interventions. The two real problems—privacy and sexual violence—are big, complex problems that are difficult to solve. The ideas presented in this book for dealing with privacy violations are not wholly satisfactory: Creating user-controlled digital rights management options, strengthening privacy laws, and creating better educational campaigns each addresses only a small part of the problem. After all, if there were already adequate solutions to sexual violence or privacy violations, they could simply be applied to new media. Anyone peddling an easy answer, such as new misdemeanor laws, mobile phone bans in schools, or sexting abstinence campaigns, is missing the larger picture. Nevertheless, we do know where to begin: We can rethink agency and consent in how we understand new media.

The erasure of teen girls' sexual agency can be difficult to critique because it is often framed as a gesture of sympathy. Indeed, viewing a girl as sexually knowing or assertive would, in many contexts, indicate her deviance or moral failure. Yet, assuming that sexting girls lack sexual agency leads to a failure to address the real causes of their victimization and a denial of their right to express themselves.

When I began this project, I expected to find that the newest way of talking and worrying about girls' sexuality—in terms of their use of digital media—would be as sexist, racist, classist, and heteronormative as previous panics about girls' sexuality. I did not anticipate that these conversations would be so thoroughly dependent on interpretations and assessments of girls' agency. The implicit focus on agency in the discourses about sexting seems to arise from the dominance of self-help, personal responsibility, neoliberal "girl power" narratives. This fits into an ongoing shift away from an explicitly moralizing framework of sexuality to one that obscures its moral judgments with pseudo-scientific assertions about health (Arney & Bergen, 1984). That is, instead of condemning sexters for their innate immorality, it is more common to locate the cause of their deviance in external factors. Crucially, the implication for these observers is that girls can and should fight against such influences in order to achieve health and happiness.

According to the dominant models, the only sexual agency teenage girls have is the agency to resist male sexuality and sexuality in media. It is far easier, more comfortable, and less disruptive to these common sense assumptions to interpret girls' consensual sexting as evidence of their subconscious victimization by outside forces. These forces include (1) digital media, which is said to disinhibit girls (but not boys); (2) brain structures and hormones, which are viewed as separate from the idealized figure of the innocent girl; (3) other desires, such as the desire for self-esteem; or (4) media representations, which again are viewed as separate from so-called authentic sexuality and desire. Why is it so difficult to see the interrelationships between these elements and to understand how individual agency is always working both with and against media, other people, and even biology? Part of the answer is that in order to convince ourselves of our own agency, we tend to construct classes of people (younger people, women, people in other places and times, people with less money, etc.) as having less agency than we do. This confirms for us that, despite the dubious evidence, we are fully agentic and self-determining subjects. Perhaps we do not want see girls as having the capacity to make choices as freely as we do because that would mean that we have less agency than we imagined.

As with girls' sexuality, a similar problem reappears in how we think about individual agency in relation to new technologies. The focus on danger and victimization in discussions about youth online—whether in newspaper articles or academic studies on girls' sexuality and digital media—can be as one-sided as the popular and scholarly discourses that make overbroad claims about the inherent democratic effect of social media. Both the panicked discourses about sexting and the rosy assessments of youth media production need to account for power, gender, and sexuality more thoroughly. The overwrought pessimism of the former and the improbable optimism of the latter persist because each exaggerates legitimate hopes and fears about new technologies. For instance, we celebrate the ways that new communication technologies can connect us across time and space, and at the same time we worry that they could have irreparable negative effects on our social relationships.

Although we may consider young people, who are perceived to lack agency already, as being particularly susceptible to the perils of technology, everyone is seen to be vulnerable. Part of the problem is that we construe technology as wholly separate from us. Yet as we create it and make choices about how to use it, culture and technology are intertwined in profound and unpredictable ways. It is important to remember that our agency is always relational and contextual, and that perhaps the more agency we imagine we have, the more upset we become when something appears to threaten it. Often it is something new, since the familiar preexisting norms that structure our agency (gender roles, for example) usually fade into the background. The problems with how we think about technology and girls' sexuality are similar: Both create anxiety because they can disrupt our fantasy that we have the capacity to know and act upon our authentic will. Our response to girls is to think of them as weak and passive, which perhaps reinforces our own sense of agency. New media's threat to our agency is less easily contained; thus there is a proliferation of both celebratory narratives and anxious speculations about emerging technologies. The endless discussion about the effect of new media on society may indicate deep-seated apprehension that new technologies cause us to lose our agency and autonomy—which is even easier to imagine if we do not realize that our values, desires, and identities are always structured (though not determined) by the technologies, institutions, norms, discourses, and contexts with which we interact.

We need to resist the strong temptation to try to prohibit sexting. As one report cautions: "Threat-based messages that rely on instilling fear are unlikely to work, and may do more harm than good. Teens [in our focus groups] were consistent in their view that efforts to banish sexting outright would fail" (A. J. Harris et al., 2013, p. 84). Instead, this book offers three key recommendations (see appendix 3 for a summary of practical recommendations and tips). First, we must recognize that granting youth the right to sext will offer them a significant defense against possible harms that the state and peers can commit. Adding age-spans to child pornography laws is a simple way to do this, but it may nevertheless be politically difficult. Second, we need to incorporate consent into how we think about private media circulation. In technology design, policy, and social norms, we can adapt the privacy expectations we take for granted in offline contexts for digital media. Finally, we need to accept girls' sexual agency. This is less abstract and challenging than it may seem, as it simply involves taking people at their word. That is, when girls say they are sexting intentionally, instead of resorting to explanations about raging hormones, sexualization in media, or low self-esteem, we can believe them.[1] We can allow their words and actions to change how we think about how girls negotiate sexuality in and through mass media and communication technologies. Granting sexting girls some agency may also be productive in other ways, since it can destabilize agency itself and challenge assumptions about privacy, information, and consent.

These three recommendations may be difficult to implement, but they are possible. In 2013, the Law Reform Committee of the Parliament of Victoria in Australia conducted an inquiry on sexting. Drawing on interviews and submissions from a range of experts, including feminist academics working on sexting, the report reaches a number of ground-breaking conclusions. It criticizes current antisexting educational campaigns and curricula and recommends that they shift their focus to "people who distribute intimate images or media without consent, rather than on the person who initially creates the intimate images or media" (Newton-Brown et al., 2013, p. 71). The report also suggests a number of reforms to child pornography laws: to make it impossible to charge teens who create photographs of themselves with producing child pornography, to decriminalize sexting between minors who are close in age, and to give discretion to judges to leave teens off the sex offender registry. These legal reforms are a radical departure from the response in many U.S. states to criminalize youth sexting further and would be a significant step forward if they were adopted. As chapter 1 explained, Vermont's attempt to decriminalize sexting for teens was met with national outrage. In contrast, the

Victorian government's initial response has been to accept most of the report's recommendations, and they have even begun to implement some of them ("Victorian," 2013; Maddocks, 2014).

I hope that by critiquing the dominant discourses about sexting and advocating for legal, educational, and social reforms, this book has opened some space for imagining a future in which teenage girls' sexuality is not demonized or erased and all people are protected from sexual harm and are free to pursue consensual sexual pleasure. Asking for both the technologies we use and discourses we create about digital media to address consent is a simple request, but it will be neither an easy sell nor uncomplicated to implement. These difficulties demonstrate that we still have a lot more work to do.

APPENDIX 1

A brief history of the sexting panic

While sustained media attention to sexting began in December 2008 after the release of the National Campaign to Prevent Teen and Unplanned Pregnancy's study ("Sex and Tech," 2008), both the practice of sexting and the discussion about it have a longer history. The term "sexting" may have originated as "sex-texting," a phrase that appeared in U.K. and Australian media as early as 2001. Since European countries adopted cell phones and text messaging earlier than the United States or Canada (Ahonen, 2008), this might partly explain why the terms "sex-texting" and "sexting" appear in the newspapers of European countries and Australia long before these words were seen in North American papers.

Especially in the U.K. and Australia, sexual uses of mobile phones were occasionally discussed in the context of celebrities and infidelity through the 2000s. "Sex-texting" is mentioned in a few dozen U.K. newspaper articles in reference to a 2004 scandal involving an adult police officer and an underage teenage girl as well as in reference to celebrity athlete David Beckham's unfaithfulness to his wife. In 2005, Australian papers also covered a cricket star's "sex-texting" infidelity in a small number of articles. Media coverage in the United States was also concerned with celebrities, including athletes Tiger Woods in 2009, Brett Favre in 2010, and politician Anthony Weiner in June 2011. In discussions of adult sexting, then and now, there is typically little analysis of it as a phenomena, though some celebrity cases have sparked debate as to whether sexting without any physical sexual contact should count as infidelity.

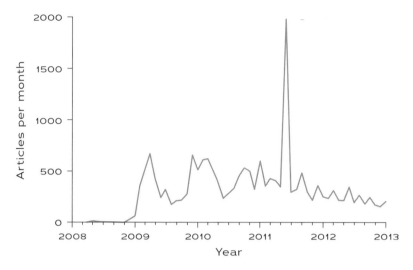

FIGURE 9. This graph depicts the number of U.S. newspaper or newswire articles and transcripts containing the word "sexting" archived in the NewsBank database, calculated monthly January 2008–May 2013. The peak in June 2011 is likely due to politician Anthony Weiner's sexting scandal and subsequent resignation.

In media coverage before 2008, sexting is neither a significant social issue nor is it specifically related to adolescents. Though Australian newspapers also covered a survey by *Girlfriend* magazine in late 2007 reporting that 40 percent of teen girls had been asked by someone to send them a naked or semi-naked photo (Walliker & Critchley, 2007), this study did not set off a wave of international media attention like the one in the U.S.

Prior to the beginning of the moral panic about sexting in December 2008, U.S. media also covered a few incidents of adolescents producing sexually explicit digital images of themselves but framed these as isolated incidents rather than a new trend or a cause for serious widespread concern. These early incidents were discussed as legal curiosities because teenagers were charged with producing child pornography of themselves. In one of the earliest reported cases to enter the U.S. legal system, a 15-year-old Ohio girl was arrested in 2004 on child pornography charges for sending photographs of herself to people she met in chat rooms (O'Reilly, 2004; "Teen Girl," 2004). In another 2004 case, two teens were charged with creating and distributing child pornography when a parent discovered photos a girl had emailed to her boyfriend. This case was

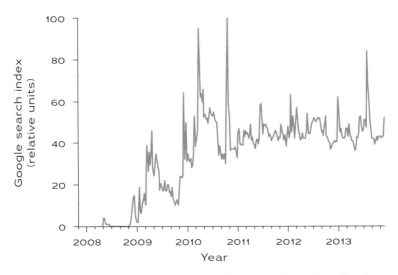

FIGURE 10. This graph depicts the relative search volume (peak = 100) over time according to data from Google Trends, calculated weekly November 4, 2007–November 24, 2013. This data indicates that Google users in the United States searched for "sexting" most frequently in March 2010 (possibly due to the Third Circuit Court decision in the Miller case [Podlas, 2011])—and in December 2011 (which could be due to the release of a study that defined sexting narrowly and found a very low rate [Mitchell, 2012]). A number of newspaper articles covered these two landmarks. A third peak occurs in late July 2013, likely due to Anthony Weiner's second sexting scandal. As a search term, *sexting* has remained relatively high since the beginning of 2010. Not all this interest is in sexting as a legal issue or moral panic about teens—a Google search for *sexting* also returns many pages of sexting tips and commercially produced pornography.

briefly discussed online in 2007 after a judge's decision denying the girl's appeal was published (Brown, 2007; *A.H. v. State*, 2007; McCullagh, 2007). Neither of these incidents involved cell phones, nor were they labeled as "sexting," but the cases address the same legal and social issues since they use child pornography laws against adolescents who create and/or distribute digital sexually explicit images of themselves or other minors.

Though the practice of sexting no doubt began with the earliest mobile phones that had text messaging and picture messaging capacities, the sustained attention to sexting in U.S. mass media began much later at the end of 2008 and has continued at a relatively high level ever since (figures 9 and 10).

APPENDIX 2

Discourse analysis:
How to find common sense

This book examines discourse from the beginning of heightened panic about girls sharing information on social network sites in 2005 to 2013, which includes the panic about sexting that began in 2008. I focus my analysis on various forms of nonfiction mass media that both draw on and produce common sense. Taking a discursive approach (Rose, 2001) to studying what constitutes "mainstream" or "boilerplate" discourse (Treichler, 1999) in policy and media, I examine themes and assumptions across a variety of texts.

In Foucault's terms, the common sense about sexting is one part of the "discursive formation" about sexting, since all these statements share the same object and the same basic approach to the topic. Common sense could also be understood as the specific set of frames that are agreed upon by a range of institutions. As Gitlin (1980) describes, media frames are "persistent patterns of cognition, interpretation, and presentation, of selection, emphasis, and exclusion" that people use to "organize discourse" (p. 7). Likewise, in Entman's (2004) words, frames "promote a particular interpretation, evaluation, and/ or solution" for an event or issue (p. 5). The set of dominant, common sense discourse that I focus on is not the only type of commentary about sexting, nor is it so all-powerful that it subsumes all other discourses. However, as this project demonstrates, it is the discourse that underlies many legal and educational policies that impact youth.

During the course of my research, I collected more than one thousand items about sexting, internet safety, teen sexuality and technology, social network sites, sex offenders, and child pornography. These came from newspaper articles, television news clips, talk show episodes, magazine articles, web pages, educational materials, legislative debates, legal texts, and policy documents. I gathered these items from a range of online sources, including NewsBank, LexisNexis, the Vanderbilt television archive, and search engines such as Google and YouTube. I obtained some news articles and videos from the websites of news organizations and TV shows, and I found U.S. government and state documents and transcripts in online databases such as GPO Access and THOMAS.

To analyze these materials, I identify mainstream, dominant discourse by assessing what experts, institutions, and media campaigns most commonly discuss and agree upon in mass media and in legal and legislative debates. To decipher the assertions, I evaluate formal elements as themes and tropes, metaphors and similes, syntax and sentence structure, headlines and section headings, images and photographs, sources and quoted statistics. Together, such features help determine which assertions each text positions as common sense and which are positioned as controversial.

This approach requires a thorough qualitative analysis of specific examples from mass media, legal, and policy texts to understand the dominant ways a current social problem is imagined. I analyze the common sense they contain through a combination of close textual analysis, described earlier, and by intense familiarity—which Stuart Hall (1975) describes as a "long soak" (p. 15) in the materials—with the dozens or hundreds of similar texts, such as newspaper articles about the same incident, comparable sexting bills in different states, and television morning show reports on sexting. Any particular example I analyze is representative of common sense not because it appears in a majority of newspaper articles or sexting bills (though often it does), but because of what text it appears in, how it is framed and positioned in that text, who it is attributed to, and the rhetoric that authorizes it as commonsensical. My approach to analyzing the discourse about sexting requires looking more at how a statement or idea is expressed as factual, true, objective, and obvious rather than the quantity of times it is expressed. Certainly, most items are expressed over and over in different contexts, but it is not the repetition itself that makes them common sense, it is the *way* they are repeated.

All of the mainstream nonfiction texts I examine draw on specific rhetorics and practices to produce themselves as truthful and legitimate. I highlight the similarities between various media and do not substantially discuss the differences among the wide variety of nonfiction texts I examine. While a newspaper article is produced according to significantly different conventions than a prime-time news report or a talk show episode, I focus on the continuities between them and the shared common sense assumptions in these different nonfiction media formats and genres. For example, talk show hosts such as Dr. Phil, Tyra Banks, and Bill O'Reilly perform the role of providing information, opinion, and analysis that reflects their point of view but which they work to position as obvious, reasonable, and correct. Many commentators, like Dr. Phil in particular, draw on the legitimacy of science and the discipline of psychology to authorize their statements.

News uses and produces common sense in slightly different ways. While it also relies on experts, journalistic rituals and strategies of objectivity operate according to a set of professional norms (Fishman, 1980) that validate official sources such as government communications, press releases, and certified experts as the most authoritative, interesting, and important (W. L. Bennett, 2007; Cook, 2005). In marking out what is new and interesting about sexting, journalists rely on, and thus reproduce, common sense assumptions about girls and sexuality. As Stuart Hall and his coauthors (1978) argue, in journalism, events are "assigned to a social context . . . [through their placement] within a frame of meanings familiar to the audience. . . . An event only 'makes sense' if it can be located within a range of known social and cultural identifications" (p. 54).

It is a structural bias of journalism to respond to new phenomena like sexting with familiar story lines. Often, common sense statements will appear without a specific person or institution named as the source for this knowledge. In a newspaper article, for example, the phrases "experts believe," "studies have shown," and "many believe" before a comment can indicate that this represents the newspaper's perception of dominant public opinion. Likewise, the phrase "some say" preceding a comment can mean that the journalist thinks that readers will believe it is a less common position or a less reasonable one. The placement and volume of quotations from different sources sometimes indicate a newspaper article's position on their relative importance.

Public service announcements, in contrast, strive to make every statement seem like common sense and rarely offer any contradictory opinions. Likewise, law and policy texts position themselves as authorized by the institution of democracy. While political rhetoric usually advocates a position, it is designed to and often claims that it represents public interests and opinions even while attempting to persuade. Policymakers routinely rely on anecdotes and statistics to make their arguments, but there are no norms or standards that prevent gathering evidence from dubious sources. For example, in his opening remarks as chair of a U.S. congressional hearing on the Deleting Online Predators Act, Representative Fred Upton, R-MI, commented: "It is estimated that at any given moment, 50,000 predators are prowling for children online, many of whom are lurking within social networks" (H.R. 5319, 2006). This seemingly accurate and widely disseminated crime statistic was actually culled from Dateline NBC's "To Catch a Predator," a television program that staged sting operations of alleged online predators and was invented by a consultant as a rough estimate: "A 'Goldilocks' number—not too hot, not too cold" (Kaplan, 2006). This book analyzes the role of such statistics ("50,000 predators"), terms ("lurking"), and assertions ("prowling for children") as common sense in debates about teen sexuality in mass media and policy.

I do not focus on the discourses of specialized organizations unless they are part of the dominant media and policy conversation about sexting. Focus on the Family, for example, is a mainstream Christian institution, and the participants comment on sexting on their website; however, their representatives appear infrequently—if ever—in media coverage of sexting or in policy discussions about online safety. In contrast, I examine the commentary, press releases, and policy papers of the National Center for Missing & Exploited Children because, while it is likewise a specialized organization, its representatives are commonly quoted as experts in media reports about sexting. They are a major voice in the conversation about online safety: They produce PSAs, fund research, issue press releases, and testify at congressional hearings about online safety.

Both Entman (2004) and Gitlin (1980) perceive frames not as ideology imposed from above but as a method or resource that journalists and others rely on to make sense of the world and use to produce their specific interpretation of an issue. Common sense is mainstream and dominant in that it consists of taken-for-granted ideas that seem natural, inevitable, and normal. But as this book's introduction explains, my purpose in studying common sense is to change it. By critiquing the existing assumptions about sexting and offering alternative ways of framing the issue, this book develops a new set of common sense ideas that are hopefully a resource for researchers, policymakers, activists, and youth educators.

APPENDIX 3

Sexting tips and recommendations

Common pitfalls to avoid

- Avoid the scare tactic of warning teens not to sext because all sexts will eventually be distributed.
  - Why? Teens already know distribution is a possibility, but they trust the people they share private images with. In fact, the existing data suggests that most teenage sexts are shared consensually among peers and are not distributed without permission.
- Don't ban mobile phones or try to monitor kids' technology use.
  - Why? This is an ineffective Band-Aid solution. It's impossible to keep up with every new app, and the most tech-savvy kids can easily get around monitoring applications. Violating young people's privacy with a monitoring app sets the wrong example.
- Don't tell people whose private images have been distributed that their future job and college prospects are ruined and that their images are being viewed by child molesters.
  - Why? This creates unnecessary fear and shame, and in cases in which images are distributed without permission, they are rarely if ever uploaded to public websites.

- Avoid the strategy of telling girls that abstaining from sexting proves and preserves their self-respect and self-esteem.
  - Why? This perpetuates slut-shaming and victim-blaming.

Recommendations for everyone

- Understand that not everything digital is meant to be public—never assume that the format of something private (an email or a digital photo, for example) means that it's ok to distribute it.
- Learn, use, and promote the affirmative consent model in your sexual relationships and among your peers. Think about sexting as a sex act and always make sure you have enthusiastic consent from your partner before you create or share a sexual image.
- Consider safer-sexting strategies. For exmple: crop or blur your face or other identifying marks out of suggestive photos; delete old photos often and ask your partner to do the same; and consider using an app that deletes photos automatically after they've been viewed.
- Avoid blaming the victims of privacy violations. Be aware of rape culture, slut-shaming, homophobia, and the sexual double standard. Speak out against gender- and sexuality-based insults when you hear them.

Recommendations for legislators and prosecutors

- Decriminalize consensual sexting. This means repealing any age-specific sexting misdemeanors and exempting all minors from prosecution under child pornography laws by adding age-span exemptions (to prevent, for example, the prosecution of an 18-year-old for consensual sexting with a 17-year-old).
- Develop a civil offense to address privacy violations. Because most victims have a relationship with the person who harmed them, they will be more likely to use laws that carry weaker penalties.
- Remember that young people are entitled to the same free speech rights as adults.
- Understand the difference between consensual sexting and privacy violations. The intent and effect of each are very different, yet many people think they are the same.

- Accept that eliminating sexting is simply not possible. Adopt a harm-reduction approach instead to deal with privacy violations and harassment.
- Demand that media companies build privacy protections into the design of their devices.
- Support and fund comprehensive sexual education programs. Require such programs to include a discussion of privacy and sexual information ethics.
- Support and fund programs in schools that work to reduce gender- and sexuality-based harassment and violence.

Recommendations for parents and educators

- Discuss the similarities between sexting and other sexual activities; talk about sexual ethics, consent, and respect between partners.
- Support comprehensive, consent-based sexual education programs and media literacy training for everyone. Collectively develop and support on-going strategies to resist gender- and sexuality-based harassment and bullying.
- Develop programs, strategies, and discussions to discourage privacy violations.
- Avoid using an incident of nonconsensual distribution as an occasion to advise youth to abstain from sexting—the risks are already clear, and this message authorizes blaming and shaming the victim. Focus instead on the forwarders who violated the victim's privacy. Ensure support services for the victim.
- Ask teens about their norms and expectations of privacy on the internet and mobile phones in different contexts. Discuss the challenges to privacy in digital media environments and the strategies youth currently use and might consider using to manage their online presence.
- Be a role model for the importance of digital privacy. Routinely monitoring kids' texts (or reading their diaries) sends the wrong message that privacy violations are ok.
- Discuss online reputation management as an optional strategy to achieve particular ends (such as getting a job or getting into college) rather than through shaming youth for revealing too much or "having no sense of privacy." Talk about practical steps, such as using privacy settings, which can help create an online identity that serves specific goals.

- Discuss how media companies collect, aggregate, and use individuals' personal information.
- Explain the state and federal laws that could apply to sexting. Discuss the disproportionate prosecution of consensual relationships between partners of the same gender or of different class backgrounds or racialization.
- Consider the potential legal consequences (to the consensual sexter and the privacy violator) before reporting incidents to police, recognizing that mandatory reporting requirements might complicate these decisions.

SAMPLE DISCUSSION QUESTIONS

- How do you know if an image you receive is intended to be private or if it's ok to pass on to your friends?
- If you want an image to be private, what's the best way to make sure your recipient knows?
- What kind of images are the most and least likely to cause problems if someone distributes them? Does the person's gender make a difference? Is that fair?
- How do you think others would feel if you shared private images they sent you? What could happen to them if their friends, teachers, and family members saw the images?
- Do you think sexting should be illegal for people your age? Compare your answers to state laws.
- What information and images do you have online that you think are important to keep private? How do you protect your privacy online?
- What could someone find out about you by searching public websites? Are you satisfied with your online presence?
- How do social network sites like Facebook make a profit? How is the site allowed to use personal information about its users?
- Should privacy laws be stronger?

Notes

Introduction

1. Though sexting is also discussed in many other countries, the scope of this project is limited to the United States. The "Sex and Tech" survey, by the National Campaign to Prevent Teen and Unplanned Pregnancy ("Sex and Tech," 2008), was widely reported in December 2008 and was mentioned, according to one study, in 55 percent of newspaper articles about sexting published through April 2009 (Lynn, 2010). U.S. news coverage of sexting first peaked in spring 2009 with extensive coverage of child pornography prosecutions and the sexting-related suicide of Jesse Logan (Podlas, 2011). See appendix 1 for a brief history of mass media coverage of sexting.

A range of studies since 2008 have found that by age 18, around one-third of young people have sent a nude or sexually suggestive image of themselves to someone else—responding to slightly different questions, approximately 25–40 percent of different populations of young adults report having sent a sext (Drake et al., 2012; Drouin & Landgraff, 2011; Englander, 2012; Strassberg et al., 2012). Like other sexual activities, sexting is more common among older teenagers, and it appears that it consists of sexually suggestive images more often than explicit ones. One study found that 1 percent of all surveyed youth (10–17 years old) reported that they created or appeared in an explicit image in the last year (Mitchell et al., 2012).

2. I use the terms *adolescent girls*, *teenage girls*, and sometimes simply *girls* to refer generally to people who identify or are identified as female and are 13 to 17 years old. I do not use these terms to refer to girls under 13; nor do I refer to people who are 18 or older and no longer minors as "girls," "teens," or "adolescents."

3. I use the terms *digital media, social media,* and *new media* interchangeably. None of these terms are completely adequate or accurate: *New* is a relative term; a few older media are technically digital; and nearly all media are social in some way. I use these terms to refer to a variety of new media, but primarily the internet, mobile phones, and the applications that are built for these platforms, such as picture messaging (MMS), Snapchat, Facebook, and YouTube.

4. Many studies have investigated sexting's links to behaviors identified as risky such as illegal drug use, alcohol consumption, casual sex, and unprotected sex (Benotsch et al., 2013; Dir, Cyders, & Coskunpinar, 2013; Drake et al., 2012; Rice et al., 2012; Temple et al., 2012; to online victimization (Reyns et al., 2013); and to psychological measures such as attachment anxiety (Drouin & Landgraff, 2011; Weisskirch & Delevi, 2011), impulsivity (Dir et al., 2013), and histrionic personality (Ferguson, 2011). However, one large-scale study found no correlations between sexting and sexual risk behaviors or psychological health (Gordon-Messer et al., 2013).

5. Any activity in which the production, distribution, or possession of a sexual image occurs without the consent of all the people involved could harm someone. This would include producing a sexual image of people without their knowledge or permission, coercing them to create or share a sexual image, sending a sexual image to people who do not want to receive it, and forwarding a private sexual image of someone without permission.

6. I use the term *normative* to describe something that reflects dominant mainstream social norms.

7. There is a need for qualitative research that asks young people to describe the content of the sexual images they create and receive and that examines their feelings about this.

8. The Ferber decision explained that child pornography should be categorically prohibited because: (1) the state has a strong interest in preventing the sexual exploitation of children; (2) child pornography maintains a record of abuse and later becomes part of a distribution network and market that promotes abuse; and (3) any possible literary, scientific, or educational value of permitting such performances or photos is "exceedingly modest" (*New York v. Ferber,* 1982, p. 762).

9. The law defines "sexually explicit conduct" as: (1) sexual intercourse, including genital-genital, oral-genital, anal-genital, or oral-anal, whether between persons of the same or opposite sex; (2) bestiality; (3) masturbation; (4) sadistic or masochistic abuse; or (5) lascivious exhibition of the genitals or pubic area of any person (18 USC § 2256).

10. In one case, a video of fully clothed children that focused on their genitals was prosecuted as child pornography (*United States v. Knox,* 1994). Legal scholar Adler (2001) notes: "If we pushed the definition in the evolving case law to the extreme, it seems to threaten all pictures of unclothed children, whether lewd or not, and even pictures of clothed children, if they meet the hazy definition of 'lascivious' or 'lewd'" (p. 240).

11. Like laws about child pornography, the crime of statutory rape is defined solely in terms of the perpetrator's actions. See chapter 4 for further discussion. This flexibility is useful for prosecutors aiming to convict the sexual assailants of minors, regardless of the age of the perpetrator. However, this means that these laws can also be used against

two minors involved in a consensual sexual relationship with each other. In one such case involving a 12-year-old and a 13-year-old, the court concluded that since there was no evidence of coercion or force, using statutory rape law against both of them would be absurd (Kimpel, 2010).

12. Twenty-three percent of people arrested for child pornography production in 2009 were 17 years old or younger (Wolak et al., 2012c). Moreover, a large proportion of arrests in 2009 for child pornography production (39 percent) were of adults involved in the creation of youth self-produced images (Wolak et al., 2012c). Some of these no doubt represent cases of abuse and exploitation, but others may be consensual relationships between young adults and minors. For example, an 18-year-old involved in consensual sexting with a 17-year-old would be included in this last category of arrests.

13. A body of media-effects research on female youth is concerned with investigating whether representations of sexuality in mass media cause young women to have sex (for example, Escobar-Chaves et al., 2005). In contrast to the concerns about girls' sexual relationships, the major fears about young men and mass media often focus on the promotion of violence in viewers (Wartella & Jennings, 2000).

14. Attorney Larry Walters explains: "It is a perpetuating thing that snowballs to the extent it is being discussed. Then, you have more authority figures in schools looking for it. More police and prosecutors realize it's an option to charge these kids in this way" (Richards & Calvert, 2009, p. 11).

15. A large body of scholarship analyzes panics about young, working class, and/or racialized men; welfare mothers; drug users; immigrants; and sex offenders (for example, Best, 1990; Chauncey, 1993; S. Cohen, 2002; S. Hall et al., 1978; P. Jenkins, 1998; Kohler-Hausmann, 2007; Reeves & Campbell, 1994; Springhall, 1999). A few studies examine the moral panics about sexually active teenage girls (Cocca, 2002; Freedman, 1987; Odem, 1995; Tapia, 2005).

16. There may be informal and professional ties between news and the law (for example, a journalist's connections to the state's attorney, or an organization's relationship to a particular newspaper). I am primarily concerned with the rhetorical and ideological connections between the two. Doing so helps to provide an account of both the production of media representations and the production of laws, especially in the context of a moral panic.

Chapter 1. The criminalization consensus and the right to sext

1. See chapter 5 for my discussion of potential solutions for dealing with privacy violations.

2. According to one focus group study, the view that the legal system should play a prominent role in responding to sexting is relatively uncommon among youth and parents and is more prevalent among legal and educational practitioners who are involved with youth (A. J. Harris et al., 2013).

3. In other instances, the ACLU of Pennsylvania can publicly support teens' freedom-

of-expression rights. For example, in a press release, the ACLU (2010) argues that the state's new summary offense criminalizing a wide range of electronically transmitted youth sexual images violates adolescents' First Amendment rights.

4. A few months after the restraining order was filed, Skumanick narrowly won the Republican nomination for district attorney, but after 20 years in office, he was defeated in the November 2009 general election by the Democratic candidate (J. Meyer, 2009).

5. I refer to this case as "the Miller case" because Marissa Miller's mother MaryJo is named first in the lawsuit, followed by Marissa and the two other mothers and their teenage daughters.

6. The ACLU's involvement in this case brought further national attention to sexting and the legal issues involved.

7. Lawyers also cannot publicly make arguments about a case that are beyond the scope of the legal arguments they present in court. However, any news commentator or other observer could have raised the freedom of expression issue.

8. In later statements about other cases, Walczak and the ACLU defend teens' right to sext on First Amendment grounds (Stiles, 2013).

9. An exception is Nebraska, where legislators decriminalized some child pornography offenses for minors in early 2009 around the same time as the legal reforms were being passed in Vermont. While it is not entirely clear why Nebraska escaped any national attention for this move, it may be because Nebraska's reform applies only to possession (not distribution to third parties) and covers only minors who are at least 15 years old; Vermont's cutoff was 13 years old ("Legislative bill 97," 2009; "Senate bill 125," 2009).

10. As feminist scholars have observed, new technologies can be deployed in ways that reassert social hierarchies, particularly if they can become mechanisms of surveillance (Gates, 2011; Magnet & Rodgers, 2012). Researchers also document how abusive intimate partners can use communication and locative technologies for stalking and harassment (Southworth et al., 2007). More broadly, many scholars critique the corporate, state, and institutional use of digital media and surveillance technologies for control and for profit (e.g., Andrejevic, 2007).

11. Many researchers have found systemic discrimination problems in the juvenile justice system (see, for example: Chesney-Lind & Irwin, 2008; Dohrn, 2004; Foulkes, 2008; Ruskola, 1996; Schaffner, 2006; Sullivan, 1996; Woodhouse, 2002).

12. In Englander's (2012) study, 9 percent of sexters who said they were coerced into sending the image reported getting in "trouble" with parents and 2 percent were caught at school, while among voluntary sexters, 4 percent said they got into trouble with parents and 0 percent at school. In a Cox Communications study (2009), which involved the National Center for Missing & Exploited Children, 14 percent of sexting teenagers report having ever been caught; of those who were, two-thirds were caught sexting by a parent.

13. The sexual double standard underlies the assumption that sexting is always wrong whether it is consensual or not and is evident in many cases, including the Miller case and the Seattle case (Blanchard, 2008), and is implicit in the educational messages about sexting that I discuss in chapter 3.

14. Queer youth are also more likely to enter the juvenile justice and foster care systems, especially if unsupportive parents abandon them, and once they are part of this system, their sexual behavior may be monitored and reported to authorities (Sullivan, 1996).

15. If the girls in the Miller case had completed the assignment by identifying only themselves as victims and refusing to accept any responsibility for harming the community, would Skumanick have accepted their answers?

16. This is also the case in a number of states that have passed new misdemeanor laws (Greenberg, 2010, 2011). Furthermore, the original bill proposing to decriminalize all types of sexting also did not account for the difference between consensual sexting and privacy violations.

17. Only public school officials (in their capacity as state actors) are bound by such limitations; private school students enjoy no protection from the Bill of Rights.

18. Additionally, officials can censor any "student speech in school-sponsored expressive activities so long as their actions are reasonably related to legitimate pedagogical concerns" (*Hazelwood School Dist. v. Kuhlmeier*, 1988, p. 273).

19. Images of illegal but consensual sex between young people would still be prohibited under this logic (for example, in some states a 15-year-old and an 18-year-old cannot legally have sex).

20. An age-span exemption would protect more young people than simply excluding all people under 18 years old from child pornography laws. For example, a 19-year-old would be protected from prosecution for consensual sexting with a 17-year-old only if the law included an age-span exemption.

Chapter 2. Beyond teenage biology

1. For example, Haraway (1989) demonstrates that primatologists' gender biases lead to false conclusions about animal behavior and social organization, and Fausto-Sterling (1985, 2000) demonstrates the faulty assumptions behind many scientific studies on biologically based gender differences.

2. Biologically determinist statements are a potent source of common sense, and I found in a previous study (Hasinoff, 2009) that whether they are attached to named experts or not, such statements are often positioned as obvious but legitimated with the weight of scientific authority. As Treichler (1999) contends in her research on scientific discourses of AIDS in popular culture, "There is a continuum . . . not a dichotomy, between popular and biomedical discourses" (p. 15).

3. I combined a search for *sexting* with specific search terms such as *biological, brain,* and *hormones* in order to gather hundreds of articles that used biological concepts to explain sexting. The examples in this chapter are drawn from that archive. Focus group research also indicates that many adults explain sexting by referring to narratives of development and to adolescent risk-taking and impulsivity. As A. J. Harris and coauthors (2013) explain: "Virtually all explanations of the motivations and contexts of teen sexting, either implicitly or explicitly, evoked themes related to adolescents' social, cognitive, sexual,

and emotional development" (p. 36). They also note that "parents and practitioners alike regularly invoked themes such as adolescent impulsivity, lack of judgment and failure to foresee long-term consequences" as reasons for sexting (p. 64).

4. When young people begin to acquire other (more valued) skills such as math or cooking, they are said to be practicing, learning, or gaining expertise—teenagers are not described as "experimenting with" algebra.

5. In the 1990s, queer theory coalesced around a collectivist politics of sexuality and social marginalization that stresses a shared relationship to power. These scholars and activists pushed the definition of *queer* to describe all sexual acts that are not legitimated by mainstream social and legal institutions. For example, Lisa Duggan (1992) calls for community organizing based on "shared dissent from the dominant organization of sex and gender" (p. 20), and Cathy Cohen (1997) advocates for prioritizing "one's relation to power, and not some homogenized identity" (p. 438).

6. Many queer theorists also criticize the model of sexual orientation as natural, unchanging, and genetically determined for limiting the radical potential of the movement to respond to broader inequalities and transform gender, sexuality, and family formations (e.g., L. Duggan, 1992; Terry, 1999).

Chapter 3. Self-esteem advice and blame

1. Albert is the chief program director of the National Campaign to Prevent Teen and Unplanned Pregnancy, the organization that published the first major report on sexting and sparked national debate about the issue.

2. According to some studies, higher self-esteem is actually correlated with more risk-taking (Goodson et al., 2006).

3. Indeed, some girls are highly critical of the PSAs I discuss in this chapter. For example, a 2007 Facebook groups page consisting of 13 members identified as teenage girls is set up to sarcastically mock the concept of the 2 SMRT 4U ring, which is part of a campaign I examine later in the chapter. The description of the group reads: "2SMRT4U rings are the shit. They also protect you from online predators so you can post all the information you want to about yourself without the fear of an online predator finding you and raping you. And they're free" ("Hell Yeah," 2007).

4. While some of the institutions involved in creating PSAs and the informal advice this chapter examines have specific agendas (such as NCMEC) and others operate under norms of journalistic objectivity (such as the *New York Times*), they are all part of a universe I define as the dominant, mainstream discourse about these issues. The institutions with an agenda typically speak in a monotone voice of common sense assertions, backed up with the occasional expert, while news sources often position some statements as controversial and uncommon and others as obvious and commonsensical.

5. Nearly three-quarters of NCMECs $51 million 2010 annual budget came from government grants (National Center for Missing and Exploited Children, 2012). John Walsh cofounded this organization in 1984. He gained national prominence and later became the host of *America's Most Wanted* after his son was abducted and murdered in 1981.

6. I chose specific texts and examples for this chapter from the campaigns and their press materials, major newspapers, and popular talk shows because they illustrate this dominant discourse.

7. For example, this narrative appeared in news reports and mass-market online safety books, sometimes in the context of a broader overview of online dangers, like spam or credit card scams (e.g., Baker, 2002; Quarantiello, 1997); in dozens of websites produced by the private sector and by national and local governments (e.g., netsmartz.com; xblock. isafe.org; wiredsafety.org); in pamphlets produced by the NCMEC (Magid, 1994, 1998); in personal narratives about girls duped by online predators (e.g., Tarbox, 2000); and in coverage of internet stings (e.g., Richter, 2001), including Dateline NBC's *To Catch a Predator*, which premiered in 2004.

8. Rupert Murdoch's News Corporation, the second-largest media company, purchased MySpace in 2005 for $580 million.

9. Prior to 2005, the only national media that addressed youth directly were educational curricula and websites, such as netsmartz.org, a safety website for youth launched in 2001 by NCMEC and the Boys & Girls Clubs of America.

10. As was the case before the internet, family members, intimate partners, and acquaintances rather than strangers from the internet commit the vast majority of sexual assaults against young people—whether it involves an online component or not (Mitchell, Wolak, & Finkelhor, 2001; Mitchell et al., 2005; Wolak et al., 2004; Wolak et al., 2008; Ybarra et al., 2007).

11. Some sexual violence prevention programs hold men responsible for preventing sexual violence, including some feminist anti-rape organizations and some groups that target men exclusively, such as "Men Can Stop Rape" and "Men against Sexual Violence" (Masters, 2010).

12. "2 SMRT 4U" was produced by the National Center for Missing & Exploited Children and the Postal Inspection Service in 2006.

13. This campaign was produced by the National Center for Missing & Exploited Children, the Ad Council, and the United States Department of Justice.

14. The online predator is typically depicted as a white, middle-aged, low-income male. In the two television PSAs from "Think before You Post," the final and most dangerous character (literally, a chilling "Anyone") is a janitor in one and a busboy in the other—both lower-income jobs that make these men physically dirty and, presumably, unattractive and even frightening to the well-scrubbed middle-class girls this campaign seems to target.

15. Note again that the final, most dangerous character is again marked as lower-income and as literally dirty.

16. Indeed, a Toronto police officer's public statement in 2011, "Women should avoid dressing like sluts in order not to be victimized," sparked an international protest movement known as "Slutwalk" ("Why," 2011).

17. The campaign was produced in partnership with the Family Violence Prevention Fund and a number of additional groups, such as Perry Aftab's WiredSafety organization, Liz Claiborne's Love Is Not Abuse, the National Teen Dating Abuse Helpline, and other nonprofit and corporate sponsors such as Facebook and MySpace.

18. The Family Violence Prevention Fund, the Ad Council, and the Department of Justice's Office on Violence against Women sponsored this campaign.

19. In another study, 11 percent of teens reported that they had experienced being "pressured by someone to send them naked pictures or videos" of themselves (Gatti, 2009). Likewise, another report finds that 8 percent of boys and 16 percent of girls say they sexted because of pressure or coercion (Englander, 2012).

20. The campaign was produced by the United States Postal Inspection Service and the National Center for Missing and Exploited Children; *Teen Vogue* was a promotional sponsor.

21. Feminists have been fighting for decades against the belief that sexual violence is the victim's fault if she is out late at night, or drinking, or wearing revealing clothing (and so on).

22. Ally, the girl in the MTV News story discussed earlier, used this strategy by sending a photo to her ex-boyfriend that did not depict her face. Though her identity was still readily identifiable to her peers, if such an image somehow became publicly available years later, it would be much more difficult to identify her than if she had included her face in the picture.

23. This strategy is sometimes used in anti-rape campaigns, such as one that targets men with the message, "My strength is not for hurting" (Masters, 2010).

Chapter 4. Sexualization and participation

1. The standard way to measure self-objectification is a questionnaire developed in the late 1990s (Fredrickson et al., 1998), in which participants rate how important various attributes are to their "physical self-concept." People who give higher importance to appearance attributes (weight, firm/sculpted muscles, measurements, physical attractiveness, and sex appeal) than ability attributes (energy level, physical fitness level, strength, health, and physical coordination) are described as higher in self-objectification. Hundreds of studies have since used this questionnaire to demonstrate that self-objectification is correlated to mental health problems in women, such as depression and eating disorders. However, in these correlational studies, it is not possible to know whether self-objectification is a discrete, causal agent, or whether the mental health problems and self-objectification are both caused by some third factor.

2. Most adults in a focus group study also thought sexting was caused by mass media and technology, including, "youth exposure to sexual content via the Internet, celebrity sexual misbehavior, graphically suggestive music videos and lyrics, and immodesty in fashion and clothing.... [In the focus groups there was also] a fairly common sentiment of 'downward drift' in the standards of modesty and respectability within popular culture. Additionally, these perceived negative influences on youth—particularly girls—were often framed as pervasive and inescapable" (A. J. Harris et al., 2013, p. 25).

3. The National Center for Missing & Exploited Children estimates, based on internal data that combines commercially circulated online child pornography and undistributed

images found in personal collections, that 14 percent of images were self-produced with no adult involvement (Lanning, 2010, p. 97). However, in these statistics, it is not clear what proportion of self-produced images came from minors who commercially or otherwise intentionally distributed them, how many were private images distributed by someone else without permission that ended up on the internet, and how many were held in the private collection of a minor's adult romantic partner.

4. Empirical research is still emerging, but surveys have found that around 10 percent of youth report that a private sexual image they created has been distributed to someone else without their consent, and around 1 percent of youth report that such an image has been uploaded to a website without their consent (Cox Communications, 2009; Gatti, 2009; Mitchell et al., 2012).

5. Based on multiple sources of justice agency data and victim surveys, Finkelhor and Jones (2012) state: "Our judgment is that the decline in sexual abuse [since 1990] is about as well established as crime trends can be in contemporary social science" (p. 3). Still, since sexual abuse is not accurately reported, is also possible that disclosure has precipitously declined while actual incidents have increased or remained the same, or alternatively, that without the new factor of online child pornography, the decline in incidents would have been greater.

6. Some legal scholars (Humbach, 2010; Wastler, 2010; Weins & Hiestand, 2009) argue that there is precedent that might support this position. A Supreme Court decision striking down a law banning virtual child pornography, in which no actual children are involved or depicted, explained that it is unconstitutional to prohibit images that are not the product of sexual abuse or proximately linked to it (*Ashcroft v. Free Speech Coalition*, 2002). In theory this could support decriminalizing consensual sexting, because this kind of sexting is neither the product of abuse nor closely linked to it.

7. Except in rare cases such as the uproar about 15-year-old Miley Cyrus appearing in a photograph with her back exposed (Barnes, 2008), models under 18 years old routinely appear in sexually suggestive fashion and advertising images without much public reaction, despite critiques from social conservatives and some feminists who take up the cause of sexualization (for example, Durham, 2008; Oppliger, 2008).

8. Moreover, many sex-positive feminists (including Susie Bright, Pat Califia, Avedon Carol, Betty Dodson, Carol Queen, Gayle Rubin, Carole Vance, and Tristan Taormino) argue that the best response to sexist representations of women in mass culture is not censorship, but to create better, nonoppressive representations of sexuality. However, this logic is rarely applied to teen girls and sex, since adolescents are explicitly prohibited from creating and sharing sexual representations of themselves.

9. There is a range of other female identity positions that offer an alternative to dominant models of femininity. But it is not at all clear how to embody femininity without any sexualization, and in some contexts (e.g., some high schools and some courtrooms that still forbid female attorneys from wearing pants) a nonfeminine female gender presentation would require considerable personal sacrifice.

10. For example, in one episode of *Dr. Phil* about a repeat sexter whose parents are

unable to control her, Dr. Phil insists that the girl needs to be medically evaluated for some kind of mental abnormality, and announces that he is sending her to a special facility where experts will "map her brain . . . [and] look at her hormonally, biochemically" (Dowdey, 2009). For Dr. Phil, a girl using sexuality to get attention or to attain power is so disturbing and incongruous that he believes she requires medical evaluation.

11. In different contexts, girls and women perform gender in many ways and for many reasons ranging from survival to pleasure.

12. White people are often presumed to follow "standard" rationality and morality, since they occupy the privileged normative position of having "no culture."

13. For example, the Moynihan report infamously blamed African American poverty and crime rates not on social and economic inequalities but on the "tangle of pathology" generated by a reportedly matriarchal culture that emasculated African American men and thus removed agency from its supposedly rightful place in the hands of the patriarch.

14. These researchers are well aware that the internet has not, as initially promised, ended gendered forms of oppression, but they examine how these communication technologies might offer some help.

15. These and other academics, activists, and sex educators position themselves against the antipornography feminism popularized in the 1980s by Catharine MacKinnon, Andrea Dworkin, and others.

16. For example, a Department of Justice report suggests that sexting is the direct result of the "participatory culture" that Henry Jenkins (2006) describes. The report explains: "Popular culture is no longer something that is 'out there' and transmitted to a passive audience, but rather something that is actively defined by those who embrace these new forms of communication and self-expression" (A. J. Harris et al., 2013, p. 72).

Chapter 5. Information and consent

1. In another peer-reviewed study, 25 percent of those who received a photo reported forwarding it, and 8 percent reported sending a sexually explicit photo they took of someone else to a third party, often without permission (Strassberg et al., 2012). Privately funded surveys have found that 2 percent (Cox Communications, 2009) and 14 percent (Gatti, 2009) of people who sent sexts report that they were later distributed.

2. In contrast, this study found that 36 percent of those who said they were pressured or coerced into sexting reported that the image was forwarded—of those, most respondents indicated that 1 or 2 other people saw the image (Englander, 2012). It appears from this study that people who send or create sexual images because of threats or coercion are more likely to be also victimized by privacy violations.

3. As recently as 1998, Mississippi was the last state to eliminate the once-common statutory rape defense that the young female was "of previously unchaste character," in which case both parties could be charged with the lesser crime of fornication (Cocca, 2004).

4. Wolak and Finkelhor's (2011) typology is derived from their study of arrests for youth-produced images. In this framework adult involvement is always an aggravating fac-

tor, meaning that young adults would still be viewed as victimizing their teenage partners. By calling consensual sexting "experimental" they may garner sympathy from prosecutors and convince them not to charge those youth with child pornography offenses. However, the rhetoric of "youthful experimentation" is a limited way of understanding consensual sexting. Adults who sext consensually for attention or romance are not seen as "experimenting" but as legitimately and purposefully expressing themselves. See chapter 2 for further discussion of the problems with adolescent development narratives.

5. The most significant criticism of the affirmative consent model is that it can potentially criminalize conduct with complex practices of consent, such as some BDSM practices (Khan, 2013). A few mainstream critics also worry that the affirmative consent model's standards are too rigid and unrealistic because it can criminalize the so-called "art of seduction." Neither of these concerns are particularly relevant in the context of applying an explicit consent standard to private media circulation.

6. Consenting to the same act under the same conditions with the same person might reasonably establish a precedent in which explicit verbal consent is no longer necessary. For example, a couple consensually posting new videos on Xtube together every weekend would be setting a fairly strong precedent.

7. In many cases, if both parties claim they consented, they can both be defined as perpetrators and charged with violating these laws.

8. These changes were largely based on the recommendations of feminist organizations promoting an affirmative consent model for sex (Gotell, 2010).

9. The Code says that 12- and 13-year-olds can only consent to sex with a person who is less than 2 years older, while 14- and 15-year-olds can only legally consent to sex with a person less than 5 years older. Any sexual activity with a person under 18 is unlawful if the older party is in a relationship of trust, authority, or dependence with the minor. For adults, it is unlawful only to abuse such a relationship to incite or counsel sexual activity.

10. This is not reflected in the Code in its entirety, because, unlike other sex acts, anal sex is specifically criminalized for unmarried partners if one or both are less than 18 years old or if the act is in public (defined as more than two persons taking part or being present). This unequal criminalization of a specific sex act has been declared unconstitutional in Ontario and Quebec.

11. However, sexters who hold the copyright to their images can issue takedown notices to websites and search engines. Indeed, one lawyer advises people who find their private images posted on a public website that they are best protected if they created the images of themselves and thus can file a copyright claim (K. Hill, 2011).

12. Digital images have fingerprints (such as a hash value, which is generated by an algorithm) that would make this a possible, if not always reliable, way of controlling an image.

Conclusion

1. As I explain in chapter 4, acknowledging girls' agency does not mean we must assume that every stated "yes" in every situation is valid. In that chapter, I refer to the Ca-

nadian Criminal Code on sexual assault as a possible framework for determining which mitigating factors would render a stated "yes" invalid, such as intoxication or a significant power imbalance between the two parties. The idea that teen girls have been influenced by mass media or biology is not a sufficient or specific enough reason to disbelieve their stated consent to a sex act.

Works Cited

2 SMRT 4U (2006). Retrieved from http://www.2smrt4u.com/

2 SMRT 4U: Safety net [advertorial] (2006). *Teen Vogue, 6.*

Abu-Lughod, L. (2002). Do Muslim women really need saving? Anthropological relativism and its others. *American Anthropologist, 104,* 783–790.

Adler, A. (2001). The perverse law of child pornography. *Columbia Law Review, 101.* 209–273.

Aftab, P. (2006). Testimony of Parry Aftab. *Hearing: H.R. 5319, the Deleting Online Predators Act of 2006, Subcommittee on Telecommunications and the Internet.* Retrieved from http://energycommerce.house.gov/108/Hearings/07112006hearing1974/Aftab.pdf

A. H. v. State, 949 So.2d 234 (Fla. Dist. Ct. App. 2007).

Ahonen, T. T. (2008). *Mobile as 7th of the mass media: Cellphone, cameraphone, iphone, smartphone.* London: futuretext Ltd.

Albanesius, C. (2011, March 22). German court: Google street view is legal. *PC Mag.* Retrieved from http://www.pcmag.com/article2/0,2817,2382412,00.asp

Albury, K., & Crawford, K. (2012). Sexting, consent and young people's ethics: Beyond Megan's story. *Continuum, 26*(3), 463–473.

Albury, K., Crawford, K., Byron, P., et al. (2013). Young people and sexting in Australia: Ethics, representation and the law [Report]. *ARC Centre for Creative Industries and Innovation/Journalism and Media Research Centre.* Retrieved from http://jmrc.arts.unsw.edu.au/media/File/Young_People_And_Sexting_Final.pdf

Albury, K., Funnell, N., & Noonan, E. (2010, July 7–9). *The politics of sexting: Young people, self-representation and citizenship.* Paper presented at the Australian and New Zealand Communication Association Conference, Canberra.

Alexander, M. (2010). *The new Jim Crow: Mass incarceration in the age of colorblindness.* New York, NY: The New Press.

Alexander, R. M. (1995). *The "girl problem": Female sexual delinquency in New York, 1900–1930.* Ithaca, NY: Cornell University Press.

Alexy, E., Burgess, A., & Baker, T. (2005). Internet offenders: Traders, travelers, and combination trader-travelers. *Journal of Interpersonal Violence, 20*(7), 804–812.

Allender, D. (2009). Applying Lawrence: Teenagers and the crime against nature. *Duke Law Journal, 58,* 1825.

Ambro, T., Chagares, M., & Stapleton, W. (2010, March 17). Maryjo Miller v. Jeffery Mitchell. *Recent precedential opinions.* Retrieved from http://www.ca3.uscourts.gov/opinarch/092144p.pdf

American Civil Liberties Union of Pennsylvania (2009, March 25). ACLU sues Wyoming county DA for threatening teenage girls with child pornography charges over photos of themselves. Retrieved from http://www.aclu.org/privacy/youth/39151prs20090325.html

American Civil Liberties Union of Pennsylvania (2010, June 29). ACLU of PA calls sexting bill passed by PA house unconstitutional [Press release]. Retrieved from http://www.aclupa.org/pressroom/acluofpacallssextingbillpa.htm

American Psychiatric Association (2013). *Diagnostic and statistical manual of mental disorders* (5th ed.). Arlington, VA: American Psychiatric Association.

Anderson, M. J. (2002). From chastity requirement to sexuality license: Sexual consent and a new rape shield law. *The George Washington Law Review, 70,* 51–162.

Anderson, M. J. (2003). Marital immunity, intimate relationships, and improper inferences: A new law on sexual offenses by intimates. *Hastings Law Journal, 54,* 1465–1574.

Andrejevic, M. (2004). *Reality TV: The work of being watched.* Lanham, MD: Rowman & Littlefield.

Andrejevic, M. (2007). *Ispy: Surveillance and power in the interactive era.* Lawrence, KS: University Press of Kansas.

Andrejevic, M. (2009). Exploiting YouTube: Contradictions of user-generated labor. In P. Snickars & P. Vonderau (Eds.), *The YouTube reader* (2nd ed.) (pp. 406–423). Stockholm: The National Library of Sweden.

Andrejevic, M. (2012, January 24). What has privacy got to do with SOPA? *Antenna.* Retrieved from http://blog.commarts.wisc.edu/2012/01/24/what-has-privacy-got-to-do-with-sopa/

Angelides, S. (2004). Feminism, child sexual abuse, and the erasure of child sexuality. *Gay and Lesbian Quarterly, 10*(2), 141–177.

Angelides, S. (2013). "Technology, hormones, and stupidity": The affective politics of teenage sexting. *Sexualities, 16*(5/6), 665–689.

Arney, W. R., & Bergen, B. J. (1984). Power and visibility: The invention of teenage pregnancy. *Social Science & Medicine, 18*(1), 11–19.

Arthur, C. (2011, April 29). Playstation network: Hackers claim to have 2.2m credit

cards. *The Guardian: Technology Blog.* Retrieved from http://www.guardian.co.uk/
technology/blog/2011/apr/29/playstation-network-hackers-credit-cards

Ashcroft v. Free Speech Coalition, 535 U.S. 234 (2002).

A Thin Line (2010). Sexting: What is it? *A Thin Line.* Retrieved from http://www.athinline
.org/facts/sexting

Attwood, F. (2006). Sexed up: Theorizing the sexualization of culture. *Sexualities, 9*(1),
77–94.

Bailey, J., & Hanna, M. (2011). The gendered dimensions of sexting: Assessing the ap-
plicability of Canada's child pornography provision. *Canadian Journal of Women &
the Law, 23,* 405–441.

Baker, L. (2002). *Protecting your children from sexual predators.* New York, NY: St. Martin's Press.

Balsamo, A. M. (1996). Myths of information: The cultural impact of new information
technologies. *Technology Analysis & Strategic Management, 8*(3), 341–348.

Balsamo, A. M. (2011). *Designing culture: The technological imagination at work.* Durham,
NC: Duke University Press.

Barbrook, R., & Cameron, A. (1996). The Californian ideology. *Science as Culture, 6*(1),
44–72.

Barlow, J. P. (1994). The economy of ideas: A framework for patents and copyrights in
the digital age. (Everything you know about intellectual property is wrong.). *WIRED
2.03.* Retrieved from http://www.wired.com/wired/archive/2.03/economy.ideas
.html

Barlow, J. P. (1996, February 8). A declaration of the independence of cyberspace. *Electronic Frontier Foundation.* Retrieved from https://projects.eff.org/~barlow/Declara-
tion-Final.html

Barnes, B. (2008, April 28). Revealing photo threatens a major Disney franchise. *New
York Times.* Retrieved from http://www.nytimes.com/2008/04/28/business/
media/28hannah.html

Barney, D. (2000). *Prometheus wired: The hope for democracy in the age of network technology.* Chicago, IL: University of Chicago Press.

Barney, D. (2010). "Excuse us if we don't give a fuck": The (anti-)political career of participation. *Jeunesse: Young People, Texts, Cultures, 2*(2), 138–146.

Barrigar, J. (2013). Time to care about reputation: Re-viewing the resonances and regulation of reputation. Unpublished LLD thesis, University of Ottawa, Ottawa.

Barry, J. L. (2010). The child as victim and perpetrator: Laws punishing juvenile "sexting."
Vanderbilt Journal of Entertainment & Technology Law, 13, 129–153.

Bartow, A. (2000). Our data, ourselves: Privacy, propertization, and gender. *University
of San Francisco Law Review.*

Bauerlein, M. (2008). *The dumbest generation: How the digital age stupefies young Americans
and jeopardizes our future (or, don't trust anyone under 30).* New York, NY: Tarcher/
Penguin.

Baumgardner, J., & Richards, A. (2000). *Manifesta: Young women, feminism, and the future* (1st ed.). New York, NY: Farrar, Straus and Giroux.

Before you text . . . (2012). *Texas School Safety Center*. Retrieved from http://beforeyou text.com/

Benedict, H. (1992). *Virgin or vamp: How the press covers sex crimes*. New York, NY: Oxford University Press.

Bennett, S., Maton, K., & Kervin, L. (2008). The "digital natives" debate: A critical review of the evidence. *British Journal of Educational Technology, 39*(5), 775–786.

Bennett, W. L. (2007). *News: The politics of illusion* (7th ed.). New York, NY: Pearson Longman.

Bennett, W. L. (Ed.). (2008). *Civic life online: Learning how digital media can engage youth*. Cambridge, MA: MIT Press.

Benotsch, E. G., Snipes, D. J., Martin, A. M., et al. (2013). Sexting, substance use, and sexual risk behavior in young adults. *Journal of Adolescent Health, 52*(3), 307–313.

Berlant, L. (1997). *The queen of America goes to Washington city: Essays on sex and citizenship*. Durham, NC: Duke University Press.

Best, J. (1990). *Threatened children: Rhetoric and concern about child-victims*. Chicago, IL: University of Chicago.

Bethel School Dist. No. 403 v. Fraser, 478 U.S. U.S. 675 (1986).

Beyer, M. (2000). Immaturity, culpability & competency in juveniles: A study of 17 cases. *Criminal Justice Magazine 15*(2).

Bijker, W. E., Hughes, T. P., & Pinch, T. J. (1987). *The social construction of technological systems: New directions in the sociology and history of technology*. Cambridge, MA: MIT Press.

Birke, L. (1986). *Women, feminism and biology: The feminist challenge*. New York, NY: Methuen.

Blanchard, J. (2008, November 21). Cheerleaders' parents sue in nude photos incident: Two were the only ones suspended. *The Seattle Post-Intelligencer*, A1.

Bobo, J. (1995). *Black women as cultural readers*. New York, NY: Columbia University Press.

boyd, d. (2008). Why youth (heart) social network sites: The role of networked publics in teenage social life. In D. Buckingham (Ed.), *Youth, identity, and digital media* (pp. 119–142). Cambridge, MA: MIT Press.

boyd, d. (2010). Making sense of privacy and publicity. *SXSW*, March 13 [Draft of a keynote address]. Retrieved from http://www.danah.org/papers/talks/2010/SXSW2010 .html

boyd, d., & Hargittai, E. (2010). Facebook privacy settings: Who cares? *First Monday, 15*(8).

Bradley, M. J. (2003). *Yes, your teen is crazy!: Loving your kid without losing your mind*. Gig Harbor, WA: Harbor Press.

Brand, S. (1987). *The media lab: Inventing the future at MIT*. New York, NY: Viking Penguin.

Bratich, J. Z., Packer, J., & McCarthy, C. (2003). *Foucault, cultural studies, and governmentality.* Albany, NY: State University of New York Press.

Braver, R. (2009, May 31). Targeting teens for sexting: More youngsters are transmitting racy photos of themselves via cell phones and the web, running afoul of child porn laws. *CBS News: Good Morning* [Article]. Retrieved from http://www.cbsnews.com/stories/2009/05/31/sunday/main5051909.shtml

Bray, A. (2009). Governing the gaze: Child sexual abuse moral panics and the post-feminist blindspot. *Feminist Media Studies, 9*(2).

Brockett v. Spokane Arcades Inc., 472 U.S. 491 (1985).

Brody, L. (2008, June 10). Porn gets students booted—used cellphones to trade photos of girls. *The Record.*

Brown, C. (2009, April 14). President Obama talks economy; pulling immigrant families apart. *Campbell Brown: No Bias. No Bull* [Transcript]. Retrieved March 1, 2012, from Factiva.

Brown, E. (2007, January 23). Sixteen-year-old girl criminally liable for child pornography. *Internet cases: Covering law and the internet since 2005.* Retrieved from http://blog.internetcases.com/2007/01/23/sixteen-year-old-girl-criminally-liable-for-child-pornography/

Brown, E. (2009, October 7). Group sex photos case heads to trial. *Internet Cases: Law and Technology.* Retrieved from http://blog.internetcases.com/2009/10/07/group-sex-photos-case-heads-to-trial/

Buchanan, C. M., Eccles, J. S., & Becker, J. B. (1992). Are adolescents the victims of raging hormones: Evidence for activational effects of hormones on moods and behavior at adolescence. *Psychological Bulletin, 111*(1), 62–107.

Buckingham, D. (2007). Introducing identity. In D. Buckingham (Ed.), *Youth, identity, and digital media* (pp. 1–24). Cambridge, MA: MIT Press.

Butler, J. (1990). *Gender trouble: Feminism and the subversion of identity.* New York, NY: Routledge.

Butler, J. (1997). *Excitable speech: A politics of the performative.* New York, NY: Routledge.

Calvert, C. (2009). Sex, cell phones, privacy, and the first amendment: When children become child pornographers and the Lolita effect undermines the law. *CommLaw Conspectus, 18*, 1–65.

Calvert, C., Murrhee, K. C., & Steve, J. M. (2010). Playing legislative catch-up in 2010 with a growing, high-tech phenomenon: Evolving statutory approaches for addressing teen sexting. *Pittsburgh Journal of Technology Law and Policy, 11*(1), 1–60.

Canadian Centre for Child Protection (2010). The 411: Guidelines for safe texting. *TextED.* Retrieved from http://www.texted.ca/app/en/the411

Carey, J. W. (1989). *Communication as culture: Essays on media and society.* Boston, MA: Unwin Hyman.

Carmody, M. (2005). Ethical erotics: Reconceptualizing anti-rape education. *Sexualities, 8*(4), 465–480.

Caron, C. (2006, June 3). *Too sexy to go to school: A discourse analysis of the recurring public debate on girls' dress*. Paper presented at the Canadian Communication Association Conference, York University, Toronto.

Caron, C. (2008, June 4). *Sexy girls as the "other": The discursive processes of stigmatizing girls*. Paper presented at the Canadian Communication Association Conference, University of British Columbia, Vancouver.

Carr, N. G. (2010). *The shallows: What the internet is doing to our brains* (1st ed.). New York, NY: W. W. Norton.

Cassell, J., & Cramer, M. (2008). High tech or high risk: Moral panics about girls online. In T. McPherson (Ed.), *Digital youth, innovation, and the unexpected* (pp. 53–75). Cambridge, MA: The MIT Press.

Cavoukian, A. (2009). Privacy by design . . . take the challenge. Retrieved from http://www.privacybydesign.ca/content/uploads/2010/03/PrivacybyDesignBook.pdf

Celizic, M. (2009, March 6). Her teen committed suicide over "sexting": Cynthia Logan's daughter was taunted about photo she sent to boyfriend. *TODAYshow.com* [Article and video]. Retrieved from http://today.msnbc.msn.com/id/29546030/

Center for Substance Abuse Prevention (2000). *Five steps to getting the media to cover girl power!* Rockville, MD: Department of Health and Human Services.

Chauncey, G. (1993). The postwar sex crime panic. In W. Graebner (Ed.), *True stories from the American past* (pp. 160–178). New York: McGraw-Hill.

Chesney-Lind, M., & Irwin, K. (2008). *Beyond bad girls: Gender, violence and hype*. New York, NY: Routledge.

Christen, K. (2011). Opening archives: Respectful repatriation. *The American Archivist, 74*, 185–210.

Christen, K. (2012). Does information really want to be free? Indigenous knowledge systems and the question of openness. *International Journal of Communication, 6*, 2870–2893.

Clark-Flory, T. (2008). OMG, teens r "sexting." *Salon.com*. Retrieved from http://www.salon.com/mwt/broadsheet/2008/11/25/sexting/index.html

Clark-Flory, T. (2009, February 20). The new pornographers. *Salon.com*. Retrieved from http://www.salon.com/mwt/feature/2009/02/20/sexting_teens/index.html

Clavier, R. (2005). *Teen brain, teen mind: What parents need to know to survive the adolescent years*. Toronto, ON: Key Porter Books.

Clifford, S. (2009, January 27). Teaching teenagers about harassment. *The New York Times*, B1.

CNN. (2009, January 15). Teens face porn charges [Video]. *Prime News*. Retrieved from http://www.cnn.com/video/#/video/bestoftv/2009/01/15/pn.sexting.teens.cnn

Cocca, C. E. (2002). From "welfare queen" to "exploited teen": Welfare dependency, statutory rape, and moral panic. *NWSA Journal, 14*(2), 56–79.

Cocca, C. E. (2004). *Jailbait: The politics of statutory rape laws in the United States*. Albany, NY: State University of New York Press.

Cohen, C. (1997). Punks, bulldaggers, and welfare queens: The radical potential of queer politics? *Gay and Lesbian Quarterly, 3,* 437–465.

Cohen, S. (2002). *Folk devils and moral panics* (3rd ed.). London: Routledge.

Colon, D. (2010, February 17). Is sexting right 4 u? :-). *AOL Personals.* Retrieved from http://personals.aol.com/articles/2010/02/17/is-sexting-right-4-u/

Comartin, E., Kernsmith, R., & Kernsmith, P. (2013). "Sexting" and sex offender registration: Do age, gender, and sexual orientation matter? *Deviant Behavior, 34*(1), 38–52.

Cook, T. E. (2005). *Governing with the news: The news media as a political institution* (2nd ed.). Chicago, IL: University of Chicago Press.

Corrigan, R. (2006). Making meaning of Megan's Law. *Law and Social Inquiry, 31,* 267–312.

Cox Communications. (2009). *Teen online & wireless safety survey: Cyberbullying, sexting, and parental controls* [Report]. Retrieved from http://www.cox.com/takecharge/safe_teens_2009/media/2009_teen_survey_internet_and_wireless_safety.pdf

Crawford, K. (2009). These foolish things: On intimacy and insignificance in mobile media. In G. Goggin & L. Hjorth (Eds.), *Mobile technologies: From telecommunications to media* (pp. 252–266). New York, NY: Routledge.

Cruikshank, B. (1996). Revolutions within: Self-government and self-esteem. In A. Barry, T. Osborne, & N. S. Rose (Eds.), *Foucault and political reason: Liberalism, neo-liberalism, and rationalities of government.* Chicago, IL: University of Chicago Press.

Cruikshank, B. (1999). *The will to empower: Democratic citizens and other subjects.* Ithaca, NY: Cornell University Press.

Cuklanz, L. M. (1996). *Rape on trial: How the mass media construct legal reform and social change.* Philadelphia, PA: University of Pennsylvania Press.

Cupples, J., & Thompson, L. (2010). Heterotextuality and digital foreplay: Cell phones and the culture of teenage romance. *Feminist Media Studies, 10*(1), 1–17.

Curtis, M. K., & Gilreath, S. (2008). Transforming teenagers into oral sex felons: The persistence of the crime against nature after Lawrence v. Texas. *Wake Forest Law Review, 43*(1), 155–222.

Davis, A. Y. (2003). *Are prisons obsolete?* New York, NY: Seven Stories Press.

Davis, A. Y. (2005). *Abolition democracy: Beyond prisons, torture, and empire* (1st ed.). New York, NY: Seven Stories Press.

Dawkins, R. (1976). *The selfish gene.* Oxford: Oxford University Press.

Dean, J. (2009). *Democracy and other neoliberal fantasies: Communicative capitalism and left politics.* Durham, NC: Duke University Press.

Debatin, B., Lovejoy, J. P., Horn, A.-K., et al. (2009). Facebook and online privacy: Attitudes, behaviors, and unintended consequences. *Journal of Computer-Mediated Communication, 15,* 83–108.

DeLea, P. (2009, April 15). Woman admits to relationship with girl, 14—minor says she is not a victim. *Harrisonburg Daily News-Record.*

D'Emilio, J. (1989). The homosexual menace: The politics of sexuality in cold war America. In K. Peiss & C. Simmons (Eds.), *Passion and power: Sexuality in history* (pp. 226–240). Philadelphia, PA: Temple University Press.

Department of Health and Human Services. (1997, June 23). Secretary Shalala unveils new girl power!—Girl Scouts partnership [Press release]. Retrieved from http://www .hhs.gov/news/press/1997pres/970623.html

Devlin, R. (1998). Female juvenile delinquency and the problem of sexual authority in America, 1945–1965. In S. A. Inness (Ed.), *Delinquents and debutantes: Twentieth-century American girls' cultures* (pp. 83–108). New York, NY: New York University Press.

Digital Millennium Copyright Act (1998), Pub. L. 105-304.

Dir, A. L., Cyders, M. A., & Coskunpinar, A. (2013). From the bar to the bed via mobile phone: A first test of the role of problematic alcohol use, sexting, and impulsivity-related traits in sexual hookups. *Computers in Human Behavior, 29*(4), 1664–1670.

Dobson, A. S. (2011). Hetero-sexy representation by young women on MySpace: The politics of performing an "objectified" self. *Outskirts, 25.* Retrieved from http://www .outskirts.arts.uwa.edu.au/volumes/volume-25/amy-shields-dobson

Dodero, C. (2012, April 4). Hunter Moore makes a living screwing you: The hated revenge-porn profiteer says he wants to teach a lesson with his web site. How long before the 26-year-old learns one himself? *Village Voice.* Retrieved from http://www.villagevoice .com/content/printVersion/3430751/

Dohrn, B. (2004). All ellas: Girls locked up. *Feminist Studies, 30*(2), 302–324.

Donohue, M. J., & Hailstone, A. J. (2009, October 23). Reply brief of appellant, George Skumanick, Jr. *Miller et al. v. Skumanick: Legal Documents.* Retrieved from http://www .aclupa.org/downloads/Skumanickreply.pdf

Döring, N. (2000). Feminist views of cybersex: Victimization, liberation, and empowerment. *CyberPsychology and Behavior, 3*(5), 863–884.

Döring, N. (2014). Consensual sexting among adolescents: Risk prevention through abstinence education or safer sexting?. *Cyberpsychology: Journal of Psychosocial Research on Cyberspace, 8*(1), article 9.

Dowdey, K. (2009, January 27). Crazy teen trends. *Dr. Phil* [Video]. Retrieved from http://www.youtube.com/watch?v=BfAm9saqAxo

Drake, J. A., Price, J. H., Maziarz, L., et al. (2012). Prevalence and correlates of sexting behavior in adolescents. *American Journal of Sexuality Education, 7*(1), 1–15.

Draper, N. R. A. (2012). Is your teen at risk? Discourses of adolescent sexting in United States television news. *Journal of Children and Media, 6*(2), 221–236.

Dretzin, R. (2010, February 2). Digital_nation: Life on the virtual frontier. *PBS: Frontline* [Video]. Retrieved from http://www.pbs.org/wgbh/pages/frontline/digitalnation/ view/

Driscoll, C. (2002). *Girls: Feminine adolescence in popular culture & cultural theory.* New York, NY: Columbia University Press.

Driscoll, C. (2008). Girls today: Girls, girl culture, and girl studies. *Girlhood Studies, 1*(1), 13–32.

Driver, S. (2007). *Queer girls and popular culture: Reading, resisting, and creating media.* New York: Peter Lang.

Drouin, M., & Landgraff, C. (2011). Texting, sexting, and attachment in college students' romantic relationships. *Computers in Human Behavior, 28*(2), 444–449.

Duggan, L. (1992). Making it perfectly queer. *Socialist Review, 22*(1), 11–31.

Duggan, M. (2013, October 28). Photo and video sharing grow online. *Pew Internet & American Life Project.* Retrieved from http://pewinternet.org/Reports/2013/Photos-and-videos.aspx

Duits, L., & Zoonen, L. v. (2011). Coming to terms with sexualization. *European Journal of Cultural Studies, 14*(5), 491–506.

Durham, M. G. (2004). Constructing the "new ethnicities": Media, sexuality, and diaspora identity in the lives of South Asian immigrant girls. *Critical Studies in Media Communication, 21*(2), 140–161.

Durham, M. G. (2008). *The Lolita effect: The media sexualization of young girls and what we can do about it.* Woodstock, NY: Overlook Press.

Effie Awards. (2008). 2 SMRT 4U internet safety campaign [Report]. *2008 Silver Effie Winner.* Retrieved from http://s3.amazonaws.com/effie_assets/2008/2644/2008_2644_pdf_1.pdf

Egan, R. D. (2013). *Becoming sexual: A critical appraisal of the sexualization of girls.* Malden, MA: Polity.

Egan, R. D., & Hawkes, G. L. (2008). Endangered girls and incendiary objects: Unpacking the discourse on sexualization. *Sexuality and Culture, 12,* 291–311.

Ehrenreich, B. (2009). *Bright-sided: How the relentless promotion of positive thinking has undermined America* (1st ed.). New York, NY: Metropolitan Books.

Eisenhauer, J. (2004). Mythic figures and lived identities: Locating the "girl" in feminist discourse. In A. Harris (Ed.), *All about the girl: Culture, power, and identity* (pp. 79–89). New York, NY: Routledge.

Elmer-DeWitt, P. (1993). First nation in cyberspace. *Time, 142*(24), 62–64.

Encrypt A Pic (2012). *Light Paint Pro.* Retrieved from http://www.lightpaintpro.com/?p=395

Englander, E. (2012). *Low risk associated with most teenage sexting: A study of 617 18-year-olds.* Bridgewater, MA: Massachusetts Aggression Reduction Center.

Entman, R. M. (2004). *Projections of power: Framing news, public opinion, and U.S. Foreign policy.* Chicago, IL: University of Chicago Press.

Epstein, D., & Sears, J. T. (1999). *A dangerous knowing: Sexuality, pedagogy and popular culture.* New York, NY: Cassell.

Epstein, R. (2007a). *The case against adolescence: Rediscovering the adult in every teen.* Sanger, CA: Quill Driver Books.

Epstein, R. (2007b). The myth of the teen brain. *Scientific American Mind, 17,* 68–75.

Eraker, E. C. (2010). Stemming sexting: Sensible legal approaches to teenagers' exchange of self-produced pornography. *Berkeley Technology Law Journal, 25,* 555–596.

Escobar-Chaves, S., Tortolero, S., Markham, C., et al. (2005). Impact of the media on adolescent sexual attitudes and behaviors. *Pediatrics, 116*(1), 303–326.

Estrich, S. (1987). *Real rape.* Cambridge, MA: Harvard University Press.

Estrin, J. (2013, November 23). Haitian photographer wins major U.S. Copyright victory. *The New York Times.* Retrieved from http://lens.blogs.nytimes.com/2013/11/23/haitian-photographer-wins-major-u-s-copyright-victory/

Eubanks, V. (2011). *Digital dead end: Fighting for social justice in the information age.* Cambridge, MA: MIT Press.

Fausto-Sterling, A. (1985). *Myths of gender.* New York, NY: Basic Books.

Fausto-Sterling, A. (2000). *Sexing the body: Gender politics and the construction of sexuality.* New York, NY: Basic Books.

Feinstein, S. (2007). *Parenting the teenage brain: Understanding a work in progress.* Blue Ridge Summit, PA: Rowman & Littlefield Education.

Feld, B. C. (1991). The transformation of the juvenile court. *Minnesota Law Review, 75,* 691.

Ferguson, C. J. (2011). Sexting behaviors among young Hispanic women: Incidence and association with other high-risk sexual behaviors. *Psychiatric Quarterly, 82*(3), 239–243.

Feyerick, D., & Steffen, S. (2009, April 8). "Sexting" lands teen on sex offender list. *CNN's American Morning.* Retrieved from http://www.cnn.com/2009/CRIME/04/07/sexting.busts/index.html

Fields, S. (2011, March 31). Teen sexting; in naive hands, cellphones can ruin lives. *Washington Times.* Retrieved from http://www.washingtontimes.com/news/2011/mar/30/teen-sexting/

Filler, D. (2004). Silence and the racial dimension of Megan's Law. *Iowa Law Review, 89,* 1535–1594.

Findholt, N., & Robrecht, L. C. (2002). Legal and ethical considerations in research with sexually active adolescents: The requirement to report statutory rape. *Perspectives on Sexual and Reproductive Health, 34*(5), 259–264.

Fine, M. (1988). Sexuality, schooling, and adolescent females: The missing discourse of desire. *Harvard Educational Review, 58*(1), 29–53.

Fine, M., & McClelland, S. (2006). Sexuality education and desire: Still missing after all these years. *Harvard Educational Review, 76*(3), 297–338.

Finkelhor, D., & Jones, L. (2012, November). Have sexual abuse and physical abuse declined since the 1990s? *Crimes against Children Research Center.* Retrieved from http://employees.achservices.org/images/stories/documents/havesapadeclined.pdf

Fischel, J. J. (2010). Transcendent homosexuals and dangerous sex offenders: Sexual harm and freedom in the judicial imaginary. *Duke Journal of Gender Law and Policy, 17,* 277–311.

Fischel, J. J. (2010). Per se or power? Age and sexual consent. *Yale Journal of Law and Feminism, 22,* 279–341.

Fisher, E., Getschmann, J., & Schwartz, T. (2005, June 8). New ads warn teens . . . "don't believe the type" [Press release]. Retrieved from http://www.adcouncil.org/newsDetail.aspx?id=31

Fishman, M. (1980). *Manufacturing the news.* Austin, TX: University of Texas Press.

Fitzgerald, E. (2009, April 16). Charge kids with "sexting"? Absolutely. *St. Albans Messenger* [Letter to the Editor]. Retrieved March 1, 2012, from NewsBank.

Fiveash, K. (2011, June 7). Facebook quietly switches on facial recognition tech by default: Tag, you're it. Zuckerberg amps up data-farming mission creep. *The Register.* Retrieved from http://www.theregister.co.uk/2011/06/07/facebook_facial_recognition _on_by_default/

Fortunati, L. (2002). The mobile phone: Towards new categories and social relations. *Information, Communication & Society, 5*(4), 513–528.

Foucault, M. (1980). Truth and power (C. Gordon, L. Marshall, J. Mepham & K. Soper, Trans.). In C. Gordon (Ed.), *Power/knowledge: Selected interviews and other writings 1972–1977* (pp. 109–133). New York, NY: Pantheon Books.

Foucault, M. (1990). *The history of sexuality* (R. Hurley, Trans.). New York, NY: Vintage Books.

Foulkes, R. K. (2008). Abstinence-only education and minority teenagers: The importance of race in a question of constitutionality. *Berkeley Journal of African-American Law & Policy, 10*, 3–51.

Frank, J. (2010, March 23). House bill eases up on penalties for "sexting"; recognizing youthful folly, legislators seek to decriminalize the first explicit offense. *St. Petersburg Times,* p. 1B.

Fredrickson, B. L., Roberts, T.-A., Noll, S. M., et al. (1998). That swimsuit becomes you: Sex differences in self-objectification, restrained eating, and math performance. *Journal of Personality and Social Psychology, 75*(1), 269–284.

Freedman, E. B. (1987). "Uncontrolled desires": The response to the sexual psychopath, 1920–1960. *Journal of American History, 74*(1), 83–106.

Freud, A. (1958). Psychoanalytic study of the child. *Adolescence, 15*, 255–278.

Friedman, J., & Valenti, J. (Eds.). (2008). *Yes means yes!: Visions of female sexual power & a world without rape.* Berkeley, CA: Seal Press.

Fruhwirth, J. (2008, March 3). Teens taking, distributing naked images of themselves a new battle for officials. *Ogden Standard-Examiner.*

Galanos, M. (2008, December 5). Kicked off cheer squad for "sexting": Girls' parents sue school over nude pics. *CNN Prime News* [Video]. Retrieved from http://www.cnn.com /video/#/video/bestoftv/2008/12/04/pn.cheerleader.trouble.cnn?iref=allsearch

Galanos, M. (2009, March 30). Is "sexting" a teen's right? *Prime News* [Video]. Retrieved from http://edition.cnn.com/video/#/video/bestoftv/2009/03/30/pn.sexting.right .cnn

Gantt, M. (2009, April 17). "Sexting" is pornography [Letter to the Editor]. Retrieved March 1, 2012, from NewsBank.

Garner, M. (2012). The missing link: The sexualisation of culture and men. *Gender and Education, 24*(3), 325–331.

Garrity, S. E. (2011). Sexual assault prevention programs for college-aged men: A critical evaluation. *Journal of Forensic Nursing, 7*(1), 40–48.

Gates, K. (2011). *Our biometric future: Facial recognition technology and the culture of surveillance.* New York, NY: New York University Press.

Gatti, J. (2009). The MTV-associated digital abuse study. *A Thin Line* [Report]. Retrieved from http://www.athinline.org/MTV-AP_Digital_Abuse_Study_Full.pdf

Gehman, L. M. (2006). Deleting online predators act: "I thought it was my-space": How proposed federal regulation of commercial social networking sites chills constitutionally protected speech of minors. *Loyola of Los Angeles Entertainment Law Review, 27,* 155–183.

Gerbner, G., & Gross, L. (1976). Living with television: The violence profile. *Journal of Communication, 26*(2), 172–199.

Geyer, H. (2009). Sexting: The ineffectiveness of child pornography laws. *Juvenile Justice E-Newsletter.* Retrieved from http://www.abanet.org/crimjust/juvjust/newsletterjune09/june09/pdfs/sexting.pdf

Giedd, J. N., Blumenthal, J., & Jeffries, N. O. (1999). Brain development during childhood and adolescence: A longitudinal MRI study. *Nature Neuroscience, 2*(10), 861–863.

Gill, R. (2007). Critical respect: The difficulties and dilemmas of agency and "choice" for feminism: A reply to Duits and van Zoonen. *European Journal of Women's Studies, 14*(1), 69–80.

Gill, R. (2008). Empowerment/sexism: Figuring female sexual agency in contemporary advertising. *Feminism & Psychology, 18*(1), 35–60.

Gill, R. (2009). Beyond the "sexualization of culture" thesis: An intersection analysis of "sixpacks," "midriffs" and "hot lesbians" in advertising. *Sexualities, 12*(2), 137–160.

"Girls gone wild" gets community service in underage video case. (2006, December 13). *USA Today.* Retrieved from http://www.usatoday.com/life/people/2006-12-13-girls-gone-wild-sentence_x.htm

Gitlin, T. (1980). *The whole world is watching: Mass media in the making & unmaking of the new left.* Berkeley, CA: University of California Press.

Glazer, E. (2008). When obscenity discriminates. *Northwestern University Law Review, 102,* 1379–1439.

Goggin, G. (2006). *Cell phone culture: Mobile technology in everyday life.* New York, NY: Routledge.

Goggin, G., & Hjorth, L. (Eds.). (2009). *Mobile technologies: From telecommunications to media.* New York, NY: Routledge.

Goldstein, L. (2009). Documenting and denial: Discourses of sexual self-exploitation. *Jumpcut, 51.* Retrieved from http://www.ejumpcut.org

Gonick, M. (2006). Between "girl power" and "reviving Ophelia": Constituting the neoliberal girl subject. *NWSA Journal, 18*(2), 1–23.

Goodkind, S. (2009). "You can be anything you want, but you have to believe it": Commercialized feminism in gender-specific programs for girls. *Signs, 34*(2), 397–422.

Goodson, P., Buhi, E. R., & Dunsmore, S. C. (2006). Self-esteem and adolescent sexual behaviors, attitudes, and intentions: A systematic review. *Journal of Adolescent Health, 38,* 310–319.

Gordon, A. (1999). Turning back: Adolescence, narrative, and queer theory. *Gay and Lesbian Quarterly, 5*(1), 1–24.

Gordon-Messer, D., Bauermeister, J. A., Grodzinski, A., et al. (2013). Sexting among young adults. *Journal of Adolescent Health, 52*(3), 301–306.

Gotell, L. (2008). Rethinking affirmative consent in Canadian sexual assault law: Neoliberal sexual subjects and risky women. *Akron Law Review, 41.*

Gotell, L. (2010). Canadian sexual assault law: Neoliberalism and the erosion of feminist-inspired law reforms. In C. McGlynn & V. E. Munro (Eds.), *Rethinking rape law: International and comparative perspectives.* New York, NY: Routledge.

Gram, D. (2009, April 14). VT may set aside harshest penalties for "sexting." *The Associated Press: Burlington Metro Area.*

Gramlich, J. (2007, July 16). New laws take "Romeo" into account. *Stateline.org.* Retrieved from http://www.stateline.org/live/details/story?contentId=224279

Gray, M. L. (2009). Negotiating identities/queering desires: Coming out online and the remediation of the coming-out story. *Journal of Computer-Mediated Communication, 14*(4), 1162–1189.

Greenberg, P. (2010, March 15). 2010 legislation related to "sexting." *National Conference of State Legislatures: Issues & Research.* Retrieved from http://www.ncsl.org/default.aspx?TabId=19696

Greenberg, P. (2011, March 31). 2011 legislation related to "sexting." *National Conference of State Legislatures: Issues & Research.* Retrieved from http://www.ncsl.org/default.aspx?tabid=22127

Grisso, A. D., & Weiss, D. (2005). What are gurls talking about?: Adolescent girls' construction of sexual identity on gurl.Com. In S. Mazzarella (Ed.), *Girl wide web: Girls, the internet, and the negotiation of identity* (pp. 31–49). New York, NY: Peter Lang.

Gye, L. (2007). Picture this: The impact of mobile camera phones on personal photographic practices. *Continuum: Journal of Media & Cultural Studies, 21*(2), 279–288.

Halberstam, J. (2005). *In a queer time and place: Transgender bodies, subcultural lives.* New York, NY: New York University Press.

Hall, G. S. (1904). *Adolescence: Its psychology and its relations to physiology, anthropology, sociology, sex, crime, religion and education.* New York, NY: D. Appleton and Company.

Hall, R. (2004). "It can happen to you": Rape prevention in the age of risk management. *Hypatia, 19*(3).

Hall, S. (1975). Introduction. In A. C. H. Smith, E. Immirzi, & T. Blackwell (Eds.), *Paper voices: The popular press and social change* (pp. 11–24). London: Chatto & Windus.

Hall, S. (1980). Encoding/decoding. In S. Hall, D. Hobson, A. Lowe, & P. Willis (Eds.), *Culture, media, language: Working papers in cultural studies 1972–79* (pp. 128–138). London: Hutchinson.

Hall, S., Critcher, C., Jefferson, T., et al. (1978). *Policing the crisis: Mugging, the state, and law and order.* New York, NY: Holmes & Meier.

Hallin, D. C. (1986). *The "uncensored war": The media and Vietnam.* New York, NY: Oxford University Press.

Hamilton, K., & Nakamura, L. (2010, April 23). The return of the digital native: Interfaces, access, and racial difference in district 9. *FlowTV*. Retrieved from http://flowtv.org/?p=4942

Haraway, D. J. (1989). *Primate visions: Gender, race, and nature in the world of modern science.* New York, NY: Routledge.

Haraway, D. J. (1991). *Simians, cyborgs, and women: The reinvention of nature.* New York, NY: Routledge.

Hargittai, E. (2008). The role of expertise in navigating links of influence. In J. Turow & L. Tsui (Eds.), *The hyperlinked society.* Ann Arbor, MI: The University of Michigan Press.

Harris, A. (2004). *Future girl: Young women in the twenty-first century.* New York, NY: Routledge.

Harris, A. J., Davidson, J., Letourneau, E., et al. (2013). *Building a prevention framework to address teen "sexting" behaviors* (Grant-sponsored report): Office of Juvenile Justice and Delinquency Prevention.

Harris, K. L. (2012). *Yes and no: Documenting consent and rape.* Paper presented at the National Communication Association.

Hartzog, W. (2014). Reviving implied confidentiality. *Indiana Law Journal, 89*(2), 763–806.

Hasinoff, A. A. (2009). It's sociobiology, hon! Genetic gender determinism in *Cosmopolitan* magazine. *Feminist Media Studies, 9*(3), 267–283.

Hasinoff, A. A., & Shepherd, T. (2014). Sexting in context: Privacy norms and expectations. *International Journal of Communication, 8,* 2932–2415.

Haynes, A. M. (2012). The age of consent: When sexting is no longer speech integral to criminal activity. *Cornell Law Review, 97,* 369–404.

Hazelwood School Dist. v. Kuhlmeier, 484 U.S. 260 (1988).

Heins, M. (2001). *Not in front of the children: "Indecency," censorship and the innocence of youth.* New York, NY: Hill and Wang.

Hell yeah i'm wearing my 2SMRT4U ring. What now online predators? (2007, August 30). *Facebook Groups.* Retrieved from https://www.facebook.com/group.php?gid=7743935195

Henderson, L. (2011). Sexting and sexual relationships among teens and young adults. *McNair Scholars Research Journal, 7,* 31–39.

Herring, S. C. (2007). Questioning the generational divide: Technological exoticism and adult constructions of online youth identity. In D. Buckingham (Ed.), *Youth, identity, and digital media* (pp. 71–92). Cambridge, MA: MIT Press.

Hewitt, J. (1998). *The myth of self-esteem: Finding happiness and solving problems in America.* New York, NY: St. Martin's Press.

Higdon, M. J. (2008). Queer teens and legislative bullies: The cruel and invidious discrimination behind heterosexist statutory rape laws. *University of California at Davis Law Review, 42,* 197–253.

Hill, K. (2011, November 22). How Hunter Moore could get into legal trouble for the revenge porn on isanyoneup. *Forbes.com: Tech.* Retrieved from http://www.forbes

.com/sites/kashmirhill/2011/11/22/how-hunter-moore-could-get-into-legal-trouble-for-the-revenge-porn-on-isanyoneup/

Hill, R. F., & Fortenberry, J. D. (1992). Adolescence as a culture-bound syndrome. *Social Science & Medicine, 35*(1), 73–80.

Himmelstein, K. E. W., & Brückner, H. (2011). Criminal-justice and school sanctions against nonheterosexual youth: A national longitudinal study. *Pediatrics, 127*(1), 49–57.

Hjorth, L. (2007). Snapshots of almost contact: The rise of camera phone practices and a case study in Seoul, Korea. *Continuum: Journal of Media & Cultural Studies, 21*(2), 227–238.

Hoad, N. (2000). Arrested development or the queerness of savages: Resisting evolutionary narratives of difference. *Postcolonial Studies 3*(2), 133–158.

Hoffman, J. (2011, March 27). A girl's nude photo, and altered lives. *The New York Times,* p. A21.

Hollenberg, E. (1999). The criminalization of teenage sex: Statutory rape and the politics of teenage motherhood. *Stanford Law and Policy Review, 10,* 267–278.

hooks, b. (1996). *Reel to real: Race, sex, and class at the movies.* New York, NY: Routledge.

H.R. 5319, The Deleting Online Predators Act of 2006, House of Representatives, 109th Cong. 2nd Sess. (2006).

Huff, C., Johnson, D. G., & Miller, K. W. (2004). Virtual harms and real responsibility. In L. L. Brennan & V. E. Johnson (Eds.), *Social, ethical and policy implications of information technology* (pp. 98–117). Hershey, PA: IGI Global.

Humbach, J. (2009). The censorship of love mail: "Sexting," the First Amendment and prosecuting teens [Manuscript]. Retrieved from http://law.pace.edu/jhumbach/

Humbach, J. (2010). "Sexting" and the First Amendment. *Hastings Constitutional Law Quarterly, 37.*

Hurdle, J. (2009, March 30). U.S. Judge rules for teen girls in "sexting" case. *Reuters.* Retrieved from http://www.reuters.com/article/domesticNews/idUSTRE52U0CX20090331

Illegal picture nets man 3 years. (2007, January 26). *Joliet Herald News,* p. A1.

Inbar, M. (2009, December 2). "Sexting" bullying cited in teen's suicide: 13-year-old Hope Witsell hanged herself after topless photos circulated [Video and article]. *TODAYshow .com.* Retrieved from http://today.msnbc.msn.com/id/34236377/ns/today-today_people/

Irvine, J. M. (2002). *Talk about sex: The battles over sex education in the United States.* Berkeley, CA: University of California Press.

Ito, M. (2005). *Intimate visual co-presence.* Paper presented at the Seventh International Conference on Ubiquitous Computing, Tokyo.

Jarvis, Jan. (2007, January 18). Teens' feeling of invincibility factor in posting nude photos. *Fort Worth Star-Telegram,* B1.

Jarvis, Jeff. (2011). *Public parts: How sharing in the digital age improves the way we work and live.* New York, NY: Simon & Schuster.

Jenkins, H. (2006). *Convergence culture: Where old and new media collide.* New York, NY: New York University Press.

Jenkins, H., Li, X., Krauskopf, A. D., et al. (2009, February 11). If it doesn't spread, it's dead. *Confessions of an Aca-fan.* Retrieved from http://henryjenkins.org/2009/02/ if_it_doesnt_spread_its_dead_p.html

Jenkins, H., Purushoma, R., Clinton, K., et al. (2006). *Confronting the challenges of participatory culture: Media education for the 21st century.* Chicago, IL: The MacArthur Foundation.

Jenkins, P. (1998). *Moral panic: Changing concepts of the child molester in modern America.* New Haven, CT: Yale University Press.

Johnson, S. B., Blum, R. W., & Giedd, J. N. (2009). Adolescent maturity and the brain: The promise and pitfalls of neuroscience research in adolescent health policy. *Journal of Adolescent Health, 45*(3).

Jones, L. M. (2010, June 14). The future of internet safety education: Critical lessons from four decades of youth drug abuse prevention. *Publius Project.* Retrieved from http:// publius.cc/future_internet_safety_education_critical_lessons_four_decades_ youth_drug_abuse_prevention

Kaplan, D. (2006, June 2). News mag dumps molest data. *New York Post,* 119.

Karaian, L. (2012). Lolita speaks: "Sexting," teenage girls and the law. *Crime Media Culture, 8*(1), 57–73.

Karaian, L. (2014). Policing "sexting": Responsibilization, respectability and sexual subjectivity in child protection/crime prevention responses to teenagers' digital sexual expression. *Theoretical Criminology 18*(3), 282–299.

Kasubhai, M. T. (1997). Destabilizing power in rape: Why consent theory in rape law is turned on its head *Wisconsin Women's Law Journal, 11,* 37–74.

Kearney, M. C. (2006). *Girls make media.* New York: Routledge.

Kehliy, M. J. (2004). Gender and sexuality: Continuities and change for girls in school. In A. Harris (Ed.), *All about the girl: Culture, power, and identity* (pp. 204–218). New York, NY: Routledge.

Kelly, J. (2011). Picture this: Congress doing the decent thing permitting the victims of their ex-lover's cyberbullying to go to court under a revised communications decency act. *Student Scholarship.* Retrieved from http://erepository.law.shu.edu/student_ scholarship/7

Kelly, L., Burton, S., & Regan, L. (1996). Beyond victim or survivor: Sexual violence, identity and feminist theory and practice. In L. Adkins & V. Merchant (Eds.), *Sexualizing the social: Power and the organization of sexuality.* New York, NY: St. Martin's Press.

Kennedy, H. (1998, July 12). Internet is peeking—so smile. *New York Daily News.*

Kerr, I. (2010). Digital locks and the automation of virtue. In M. Geist (Ed.), *From "radical extremism" to "balanced copyright": Canadian copyright and the digital agenda.* Toronto, ON: Irwin Law.

Khan, U. (2013). *Vicarious kinks: S/m in the socio-legal imaginary.* Toronto, ON: University of Toronto Press.

Kim, C. (2004). From fantasy to reality: The link between viewing child pornography and molesting children. *Child Sexual Exploitation Update, 1*(3).

Kimpel, A. F. (2010). Using laws designed to protect as a weapon: Prosecuting minors under child pornography laws. *New York University Review of Law & Social Change, 34.*

Kitrosser, H. (1997). Meaningful consent: Toward a new generation of statutory rape laws. *Virginia Journal of Social Policy & the Law, 4,* 287–337.

Kitzinger, J. (2006). Constructing and deconstructing the "gay gene": Media reporting of genetics, sexual diversity, and "deviance." In G. T. H. Ellison & A. H. Goodman (Eds.), *The nature of difference: Science, society, and human biology* (pp. 100–115). Boca Raton, FL: CRC Press.

Knowles, L. (2010, August 10). Parents advised to talk with kids about sexting. *Lancaster New Era/Intelligencer Journal.* Retrieved from http://lancasteronline.com/article/local/275181_Parents-advised-to-talk-with-kids-about-sexting.html?page=all

Kohler-Hausmann, J. (2007). "The crime of survival": Fraud prosecutions, community surveillance and the original "welfare queen." *Journal of Social History, 41*(2), 329–354.

Kunzel, R. G. (1993). *Fallen women, problem girls: Unmarried mothers and the professionalization of social work, 1890–1945.* New Haven, CT: Yale University Press.

Kupfner, A. M. (2001). *Reform and resistance: Gender, delinquency, and America's first juvenile court.* New York, NY: Routledge.

Lamb, S. (2009). Media effects and the sexualization of girls [Review of the book *The Lolita effect: The media sexualization of young girls and what we can do about it* by M. Gigi Durham]. *Sex Roles, 60,* 439–441.

Lamb, S. (2010). Feminist ideals for a healthy female adolescent sexuality: A critique. *Sex Roles, 62,* 294–306.

Lancaster, R. N. (2011). *Sex panics and the punitive state.* Berkeley, CA: University of California Press.

Lanning, K. V. (2010). Child molesters: A behavioral analysis for professionals investigating the sexual exploitation of children (5th ed.). *National Center for Missing & Exploited Children.* Retrieved from http://www.fitaba.com/resources/ABA-2/Child-Molestation.pdf

Lasén, A., & Casado, E. (2012). Mobile telephony and the remediation of couple intimacy. *Feminist Media Studies, 12*(4), 550–559.

Lawrence v. Texas, 539 U.S. 558 (2003).

Leary, M. G. (2007). Self-produced child pornography: The appropriate societal response to juvenile self-sexual exploitation. *Virginia Journal of Social Policy & the Law, 15,* 1–50.

Le Beau, E. (2009, February 10). Cellphone "sexting": How big a problem? Researchers study if sending nude photos by phone is a trend among teens or if parents are overreacting. *Miami Herald.* Retrieved from http://www.miamiherald.com/living/family/story/844893.html

LeCroy, C. W. (2004). Experimental evaluation of "go grrrls" preventive intervention for early adolescent girls. *Journal of Primary Prevention, 25*(4), 457–473.

Lee, C. (2002). The impact of belonging to a high school gay/straight alliance. *High School Journal* (February/March), 13–26.

Lee, D. (2012, 20 April 2012). Isanyoneup's Hunter Moore: "The net's most hated man." Retrieved from http://www.bbc.com/news/technology-17784232

Lee, D.-H. (2005). Women's creation of camera phone culture. *Fibreculture, 6.*

Lee, D.-H. (2009). Mobile snapshots and private/public boundaries. *Knowledge, Technology & Policy, 22,* 161–171.

Legislative bill 97, Nebraska Legislature, 2009/2010 Sess.(2009).

Lenhart, A. (2009, December 15). Teens and sexting: How and why minor teens are sending sexually suggestive nude or nearly nude images via text messaging. *Pew Internet & American Life Project.* Retrieved from http://pewresearch.org/assets/pdf/teens-and-sexting.pdf

Lenroot, R. K., & Giedd, J. N. (2006). Brain development in children and adolescents: Insights from anatomical magnetic resonance imaging. *Neuroscience and Biobehavioral Reviews, 30*(6), 718–729.

Lerum, K., & Dworkin, S. L. (2009). "Bad girls rule": An interdisciplinary feminist commentary on the report of the APA task force on the sexualization of girls. *Journal of Sex Research, 46*(4), 250–263.

Leshnoff, J. (2009, November). C*u*2nite: Sexting not just for kids. *Love & Relationships* section of *AARP.org.* Retrieved from http://www.aarp.org/content/aarp/en/home/family/love/articles/sexting_not_just_for_kids.print.html

Lesko, N. (1996). Denaturalizing adolescence: The politics of contemporary representations. *Youth & Society, 28*(2), 139–161.

Lesko, N. (2001). *Act your age!: A cultural construction of adolescence.* New York, NY: Routledge/Falmer.

Lessig, L. (2000). Code is law: On liberty in cyberspace. *Harvard Magazine.* Retrieved from http://harvardmagazine.com/2000/01/code-is-law-html

Lessig, L. (2006). *Code: Version 2.0.* New York, NY: Basic Books.

Levesque, R. (2000). *Adolescents, sex, and the law: Preparing adolescents for responsible citizenship.* Washington, DC: American Psychological Association.

Levick, M., & Moon, K. (2010). Prosecuting sexting as child pornography: A critique. *Valparaiso University Law Review(44),* 1035–1054.

Levick, M., & Shah, R. S. (2009, September 25). Brief of juvenile law center as *amici curiae* in support of appellees. *Miller et al. v. Skumanick: Legal Documents.* Retrieved from http://www.aclupa.org/downloads/Amicusmiller.pdf

Levin, D. E., & Kilbourne, J. (2008). *So sexy so soon: The new sexualized childhood and what parents can do to protect their kids.* New York, NY: Ballantine Books.

Levine, J. (2002). *Harmful to minors: The perils of protecting children from sex.* Minneapolis, MN: University of Minnesota Press.

Levine, J. (2009, February 2). What's the matter with teen sexting?: Sex and predatory adults are not the biggest dangers teenagers face online. Their main risk is garden-variety kid-on-kid meanness. *The American Prospect.* Retrieved from http://www.prospect.org/cs/articles?article=whats_the_matter_with_teen_sexting

Little, N. J. (2005). From no means no to only yes means yes: The rational results of an affirmative consent standard in rape law. *Vanderbilt Law Review, 58,* 1321–1364.

Livingstone, S. (2010, February 20). Youthful participation: What have we learned, what shall we ask next? *First Annual Digital Media and Learning Conference.* Retrieved from

http://www.scribd.com/doc/27906764/Sonia-Livingstone-2010-Digital-Media-and
-Learning-Conference-Keynote

Livingstone, S., & Helsper, E. (2010). Balancing opportunities and risks in teenagers'
use of the internet: The role of online skills and internet self-efficacy. *New Media &
Society, 12*(2), 309–329.

Luker, K. (1996). *Dubious conceptions: The politics of teenage pregnancy.* Cambridge, MA:
Harvard University Press.

Lynn, R. (2010). *Constructing parenthood in moral panics of youth, digital media, and "sexting."* Paper presented at the American Sociological Association. Retrieved from http://
www.potatochipping.com/wp-content/uploads/ASAFinal_081510.pdf

MacDonald, G. J. (2005, May 25). Teens: It's a diary. Adults: It's unsafe. Blogs are a
fun forum of self-expression for adolescents. But might blogging be dangerous? *The
Christian Science Monitor.*

Maddocks, T. (2014, August 21). New sexting laws to exempt young people from child pornography charges. *ABC News.* Retrieved from http://www.abc.net.au/news/2014–08
–21/australian-first-sexting-laws-to-be-introduced-in-victoria/5686166

Magid, L. J. (1994). Child safety on the information highway [Pamphlet], *National Center
for Missing & Exploited Children.* Silver Spring, MD.

Magid, L. J. (1998). Teen safety on the information highway [Pamphlet], *National Center
for Missing & Exploited Children.* Silver Spring, MD.

Magnet, S. (2011). *When biometrics fail: Gender, race, and the technology of identity.* Durham, NC: Duke University Press.

Magnet, S., & Rodgers, T. (2012). Stripping for the state: Whole body imaging technologies and the surveillance of othered bodies. *Feminist Media Studies, 12*(1), 101–118.

Mahaffy, K. (2004). Girls' low self-esteem: How is it related to later socioeconomic
achievements? *Gender & Society, 18*(3), 309–327.

Mahmood, S. (2005). *Politics of piety: The Islamic revival and the feminist subject.* Princeton,
NJ: Princeton University Press.

Males, M. A. (1996). *Scapegoat generation: America's war on adolescents.* Monroe, ME:
Common Courage Press.

Males, M. A. (1999). *Framing youth: Ten myths about the next generation.* Monroe, ME:
Common Courage Press.

Marchessault, J., & Sawchuk, K. (2000). *Wild science: Reading feminism, medicine and the
media.* New York, NY: Routledge.

Marks, A. (2009, March 30). Charges against "sexting" teenagers highlight legal gaps:
The growing trend of teenagers sending seminude photos of themselves over cellphone
presents a dilemma to parents and schools. *The Christian Science Monitor.*

Marwick, A. E. (2008). To catch a predator? The MySpace moral panic. *First Monday, 13*(6).

Marwick, A. E., Murgia-Diaz, D., & Palfrey, J. G. (2010, March 29). Youth, privacy and
reputation (literature review). *Berkman Center Research Publication No. 2010-5.* Retrieved from http://ssrn.com/abstract=1588163

Masters, N. T. (2010). "My strength is not for hurting": Men's anti-rape websites and their
construction of masculinity and male sexuality. *Sexualities, 13*(1), 33–46.

Mastronardi, M. (2003). Adolescence and media. *Journal of Language and Social Psychology, 22*(1), 83–93.

Mayer-Hohdahl, A. (2006, March 15). Myspace.Com: Teens love it. So do predators. *The Lowell Sun.* Retrieved from http://www.lowellsun.com/front/ci_3604910

Mayer-Schönberger, V. (2009). *Delete: The virtue of forgetting in the digital age.* Princeton, NJ: Princeton University Press.

Mazzarella, S. (2003). Constructing youth: Media, youth, and the politics of representation. In A. N. Valdivia (Ed.), *A companion to media studies* (pp. 227–246). Malden, MA: Blackwell.

McAuliff, M., & Bendery, J. (2011, June 16). Anthony Weiner resigns: Congressman announces resignation at press conference. *The Huffington Post.* Retrieved from http://www.huffingtonpost.com/2011/06/16/anthony-weiner-resigns_n_878229.html

McClurg, A. J. (2005). Kiss and tell: Protecting intimate relationship privacy through implied contracts of confidentiality. *University of Cincinnati Law Review, 74,* 887.

McCorkel, J. (2004). Criminally dependent? Gender, punishment, and the rhetoric of welfare reform. *Social Politics, 11*(3), 386–410.

McCullagh, D. (2007, February 9). Police blotter: Teens prosecuted for racy photos. *CNET News.* Retrieved from http://news.cnet.com/Police-blotter-Teens-prosecuted-for-racy-photos/2100-1030_3-6157857.html

McDonald, A. M., & Cranor, L. F. (2008). The cost of reading privacy policies. *I/S: A Journal of Law and Policy for the Information Society, 4,* 543.

McRobbie, A. (1999a). *In the culture society: Art, fashion, and popular music.* New York, NY: Routledge.

McRobbie, A. (1999b). More! New sexualities in magazines. *In the culture society: Art, fashion and popular music.* London: Routledge.

McRobbie, A. (2007). Top girls? Young women and the post-feminist sexual contract. *Cultural Studies, 21*(4–5), 718–737.

Mead, M. (1928). *Coming of age in Samoa: A psychological study of primitive youth for western civilisation.* New York, NY: W. Morrow & Company.

Meet 10-year-old Becky's 12-year-old internet friend (2003). *Campaign against Sexual Exploitation.* Retrieved from http://www.missingkids.com/en_US/documents/CASE_Internet_11x17.pdf

Meiners, E. R. (2011). Ending the school-to-prison pipeline/building abolition futures. *Urban Review, 43,* 547–565.

Mendoza, M. (2013, April 12). 3 teens arrested for assault after girl's suicide. *The Associated Press.* Retrieved from http://news.yahoo.com/3-teens-arrested-assault-girls-suicide-024221519.html

Meyer, E. (2009). *Gender, bullying, and harassment: Strategies to end sexism and homophobia in schools.* New York, NY: Teachers College Press.

Meyer, J. (2009, November 4). Long-time district attorney voted out. *WNEP 16: The News Station.* Retrieved from http://www.wnep.com/wnep-wyo-long-time-district-attorney-voted-out,0,3143925.story

Michels, S. (2008, October 10). Teen charged with sending nude pics of herself: Girl faces felony charges after allegedly sending photos of herself to classmantes. *ABC News*. Retrieved from http://abcnews.go.com/TheLaw/story?id=5995084

Miller v. Skumanick, 605 F. Supp. 2d 635 (United States District Court for the Middle District of Pennsylvania 2009).

Miller v. State of California, 413 U.S. 15 (1973).

Mitchell, K. J., Finkelhor, D., Jones, L. M., et al. (2012). Prevalence and characteristics of youth sexting: A national study. *Pediatrics, 129*(1), 1–8.

Mitchell, K. J., Finkelhor, D., & Wolak, J. (2001). Risk factors for and impact of online sexual solicitation of youth. *American Medical Association Journal, 285*(23).

Mitchell, K. J., Wolak, J., & Finkelhor, D. (2005). The internet and family and acquaintance sexual abuse. *Child Maltreatment, 10*(1), 49–60.

Morton, M. J. (1993). *And sin no more: Social policy and unwed mothers in Cleveland, 1855–1990.* Columbus, Ohio: Ohio State University Press.

MSNBC (2008, June 12). Survey: Teens sharing nude images online: Recent survey finds that sex, tech and teens make bad bedfellows. *Today Show* [Video and article]. Retrieved from http://www.msnbc.msn.com/id/28141513/wid/11915773

MTV launches "a thin line" to stop digital abuse: Shows, contests and online tools are aimed at halting the spread of sexting and cyberbullying. (2009, December 9). [Press release]. Retrieved from http://www.mtv.com/news/articles/1627487/20091203/story.jhtml

Munley, J. M. (2009, March 30). *Miller et al. v. Skumanick*. Retrieved from http://www.pamd.uscourts.gov/opinions/munley/09v540.pdf

Nathanson, C. A. (1991). *Dangerous passage: The social control of sexuality in women's adolescence.* Philadelphia, PA: Temple University Press.

National Center for Missing & Exploited Children (NCMEC). (2012). *BBB Wise Giving Alliance.* Retrieved from http://www.bbb.org/charity-reviews/national/children-and-youth/national-center-for-missing-and-exploited-children-in-alexandria-va-1907/financial

National Center for Missing & Exploited Children and the Ad Council. (2005). *Exchange* [Video]. Retrieved from http://www.adcouncil.org/default.aspx?id=56

National Center for Missing & Exploited Children and the Ad Council. (2007a). *Bulletin board* [Video]. Retrieved from http://www.adcouncil.org/default.aspx?id=56

National Center for Missing & Exploited Children and the Ad Council. (2007b). *Everyone* [Video]. Retrieved from http://www.adcouncil.org/page_column.aspx?id=56

NBC (2013, August 15). *Today Show*: NBC.

Newsom, J. S. (Director). (2011). *Miss representation.* In J. S. Newsom & J. Costanzo (Producers). USA: Girls' Club Entertainment.

Newton-Brown, C., Garrett, J., Carbines, A., et al. (2013, May). Report of the law reform committee for the inquiry into sexting. *Parliamentary Paper No. 230, Session 2010–2013.* Retrieved from http://www.parliament.vic.gov.au/images/stories/committees/lawrefrom/isexting/LRC_Sexting_Final_Report.pdf

New York v. Ferber, 458 U.S. 747 (1982).

Nissenbaum, H. (1998). Protecting privacy in an information age: The problem of privacy in public. *Law and Philosophy, 17*, 559–596.

Nissenbaum, H. (2004). Privacy as contextual integrity. *Washington Law Review, 79*, 119–158.

Nissenbaum, H. (2011). A contextual approach to privacy online. *Dædalus, the Journal of the American Academy of Arts & Sciences, 140*(4), 32–48.

North Dakota Century Code § 12.1-27.1-03.3 (2009).

Nunziato, D. C. (2012). Romeo and Juliet online and in trouble: Criminalizing depictions of teen sexuality (c u l8r: g2g 2 jail). *Northwestern Journal of Technology and Intellectual Property, 10*, 57–91.

Nussbaum, E. (2004, January 11). My so-called blog. *The New York Times Magazine*. Retrieved from http://www.nytimes.com/2004/01/11/magazine/11BLOG.html

Oberman, M. (2000). Regulating consensual sex with minors: Defining a role for statutory rape. *Buffalo Law Review, 48*, 703.

O'Brien, B. (2009, May 5). To deal with "sexting," xxxtra discretion is advised. *USA Today*. Retrieved from http://content.usatoday.com/topics/post/USA+TODAY+editorial/66374679.blog/1

O'Connor, K. M. (2010). OMG they searched my txts: Unraveling the search and seizure of text messages. *University of Illinois Law Review, 2010*(2), 685–718.

Odem, M. E. (1995). *Delinquent daughters: Protecting and policing adolescent female sexuality in the United States, 1885–1920*. Chapel Hill, NC: University of North Carolina Press.

Oliveri, R. (2000). Statutory rape law enforcement in the wake of welfare reform. *Stanford Law Review, 52*, 463–508.

Oppliger, P. A. (2008). *Girls gone skank: The sexualization of girls in American culture*. Jefferson, NC: McFarland & Company.

O'Reilly, B. (2004, April 4). Impact. *The O'Reilly Factor* [Transcript]. Retrieved December 3, 2008, from NewsBank database.

O'Reilly, B. (2008, December 8). Parents suing over suspension for nude photos. *The O'Reilly Factor* [Transcript]. Retrieved January 17, 2009, from NewsBank database.

O'Reilly, B. (2009, April 14). Pinheads & patriots: Jamie Foxx, emergency health care providers. *The O'Reilly Factor* [Transcript]. Retrieved March 1, 2012, from Factiva.

Ortner, S. (1996). *Making gender: The politics and erotics of culture*. Boston, MA: Beacon Press.

Ouellette, L. (2004). "Take responsibility for yourself": Judge Judy & the neoliberal citizen. In S. Murray & L. Ouellette (Eds.), *Reality TV: Remaking television culture* (pp. 231–250). New York, NY: New York University Press.

Outrageous distribution of private photos results in a plaintiff's verdict and punitive damage award (2009, November 9). *Smith, Coonrod, Mohlman, LLC: Legal Blog*. Retrieved from http://www.accidentlawyerkc.com/blog/outrageous-distribution-of-private-photos-results-in-a-plaintiffs-verdict-and-punitive-damage-award/

Palmer, M. (Director) (2012). *Sext up kids* [Video]. In R. LeGuerrier & T. M. Hogan (Producers). Halifax, Canada: CBC.

Papadopoulos, L. (2010). Sexualisation of young people: Review. Retrieved from http://webarchive.nationalarchives.gov.uk/+/http:/www.homeoffice.gov.uk/documents/Sexualisation-of-young-people.html

Patton, C. (1996). *Fatal advice: How safe-sex education went wrong*. Durham, NC: Duke University Press.

Pavia, C. J. (2011). Constitutional protection of "sexting" in the wake of *Lawrence*: The rights of parents and privacy. *Virginia Journal of Law & Technology, 16*(1), 189–220.

Peek: Sexting Awesome (2012). *Apple Online Store*. Retrieved from http://itunes.apple.com/us/app/peek-sexting-awesome/id517920149?mt=8&ign-mpt=uo%3D4

Pelham, T. (2010, February 26). "Sexting" can ruin lives, pure and simple. *Hartford Courant*. Retrieved from http://www.courant.com/features/hc-texting-sex-teens-column-feb26,0,2561998.column

People v. Klapper, 28 Misc 3d 225 (Criminal Court of the City of New York, New York County 2010).

Peters, J. D. (1999). *Speaking into the air: A history of the idea of communication*. Chicago, IL: University of Chicago Press.

Peterson, Z. D. (2010). What is sexual empowerment? A multidimensional and process-oriented approach to adolescent girls' sexual empowerment. *Sex Roles, 62*, 307–313.

Phillips, S. F. (2007). *The teen brain*. New York, NY: Chelsea House Publications.

Pineau, L. (1989). Date rape: A feminist analysis. *Law and Philosophy, 8*, 217–243.

Pitcher, K. (2006). The staging of agency in girls gone wild. *Critical Studies in Media Communication, 23*(3), 200–218.

Podlas, K. (2011). The "legal epidemiology" of the teen sexting epidemic: How the media influenced a legislative outbreak. *Pittsburgh Journal of Technology Law and Policy, 12*, 1–48.

Pollack, S. (2000). Reconceptualizing women's agency and empowerment: Challenges to self-esteem discourse and women's lawbreaking. *Women & Criminal Justice, 12*(1), 75–89.

Powell, A. (2010a). Configuring consent: Emerging technologies, unauthorised sexual images and sexual assault. *Australian and New Zealand Journal of Criminology, 43*(1), 76–90.

Powell, A. (2010b). *Sex, power, and consent: Youth culture and the unwritten rules*. New York, NY: Cambridge University Press.

Prensky, M. (2001). Digital natives, digital immigrants. *On the Horizon, 9*(5), 1–6.

Prensky, M. (2009). H. Sapiens digital: From digital immigrants and digital natives to digital wisdom. *Innovate, 5*(3).

Prickett, S. N. (2012, May 12). Speaking in tongues. *The New Inquiry*. Retrieved from http://thenewinquiry.com/essays/speaking-in-tongues/

Procunier v. Martinez, 416 U.S. 396 (1974).

Prøitz, L. (2005). Cute boys or game boys? The embodiment of femininity and masculinity in young Norwegians' text message loveprojects. *Fibreculture, 6*.

Projansky, S. (2001). *Watching rape: Film and television in postfeminist culture*. New York, NY: New York University Press.

Quarantiello, L. E. (1997). *Cyber crime: How to protect yourself from computer criminals.* Lake Geneva, WI: Tiare Publications.

Radway, J. A. (1984). *Reading the romance: Women, patriarchy, and popular literature.* Chapel Hill, NC: University of North Carolina Press.

Reeves, J. L., & Campbell, R. (1994). *Cracked coverage: Television news, the anti-cocaine crusade, and the Reagan legacy.* Durham, NC: Duke University Press.

Reimer, S. (2008, December 15). The brief indiscretion that never ends. *The Baltimore Sun.* Retrieved from http://articles.baltimoresun.com/2008-12-15/news/0812140120_1_young-adults-teens-and-young-20-somethings.

Reitz, K. (2008, February 13). Protocols needed in online child self-exploitation cases, says Leary. *News & Events* [Press release and MP3 file]. Retrieved from http://www.law.virginia.edu/html/news/2008_spr/online_exploit.htm

Reitz, S. (2008, June 4). Teens are sending nude photos via cell phone. *The Associated Press.*

Remick, L. A. (1993). Read her lips: An argument for a verbal consent standard in rape. *University of Pennsylvania Law Review, 141,* 1103–1151.

Renold, E. (2013). *Boys and girls speak out: A qualitative study of children's gender and sexual cultures (age 10–12)* [Report]. Cardiff University School of Social Sciences, the National Society for the Prevention of Cruelty to Children, and the Children's Commissioner's Office for Wales.

Reporting rates (2012). *Rape, Abuse & Incest National Network.* Retrieved from http://www.rainn.org/get-information/statistics/reporting-rates

Reyns, B. W., Burekb, M. W., Hensonc, B., et al. (2013). The unintended consequences of digital technology: Exploring the relationship between sexting and cybervictimization. *Journal of Crime and Justice, 36*(1), 1–17.

Rice, E., Rhoades, H., Winetrobe, H., et al. (2012). Sexually explicit cell phone messaging associated with sexual risk among adolescents. *Pediatrics, 130*(4), 667–673.

Richards, R. D., & Calvert, C. (2009). When sex and cell phones collide: Inside the prosecution of a teen sexting case. *Hastings Communications and Entertainment Law Journal, 32,* 1.

Richter, A. (2001, October 7). Setting the traps to snare online predators. *The New York Times,* 14LI.1.

Ringrose, J., Gill, R., Livingstone, S., et al. (2012). *A qualitative study of children, young people and "sexting": A report prepared for the NSPCC.* London: National Society for the Prevention of Cruelty to Children.

Ringrose, J., Harvey, L., Gill, R., et al. (2013). Teen girls, sexual double standards and "sexting": Gendered value in digital image exchange. *Feminist Theory, 14*(3), 305–323.

Rogers, M. (2008, April 1). Teens' nude-pics trading a growing trend, concern. *The Salt Lake Tribune.*

Romano v. Steelcase Inc., 30 Misc 3d 426 (New York Supreme Court 2010).

Rose, G. (2001). *Visual methodologies: An introduction to the interpretation of visual materials.* Thousand Oaks, CA: Sage.

Rosser, S. V. (2008). Endocrinology and hormones. In S. V. Rosser (Ed.), *Women, sci-*

ence, and myth: Gender beliefs from antiquity to the present (pp. 173–176). Santa Barbara, CA: ABC-CLIO.

Rubin, G. (1993). Thinking sex: Notes for a radical theory of the politics of sexuality. In H. Abelove (Ed.), *The lesbian and gay studies reader* (pp. 3–44). New York, NY: Routledge.

Rubinkam, M. (2009, March 25). Girls threatened with porn charge sue prosecutor: Pa. prosecutor calls it child porn; girls threatened with charges say no way. *The Associated Press.*

Rushkoff, D. (1994). *Media virus!: Hidden agendas in popular culture* (1st ed.). New York, NY: Ballantine Books.

Ruskola, T. (1996). Minor disregard: The legal construction of the fantasy that gay and lesbian youth do no exist. *Yale Journal of Law and Feminism, 8,* 269.

Russell, S. T., Muraco, A., Subramaniam, A., et al. (2009). Youth empowerment and high school gay-straight alliances. *Journal of Youth & Adolescence, 38*(7), 891–903.

Ryan, C., Huebner, D., Diaz, R. M., et al. (2009). Family rejection as a predictor of negative health outcomes in white and Latino lesbian, gay, and bisexual young adults. *Pediatrics, 123*(1), 346–352.

Ryan, E. M. (2010). Sexting: How the state can prevent a moment of indiscretion from leading to a lifetime of unintended consequences for minors and young adults. *Iowa Law Review, 96,* 357–383.

Sacco, D. T., Argudin, R., Maguire, J., et al. (2010, June 22). Sexting: Youth practices and legal implications. *Youth and Media Policy Working Group Initiative, Berkman Center for Internet & Society.* Retrieved from http://cyber.law.harvard.edu/sites/cyber.law.harvard.edu/files/Sacco_Argudin_Maguire_Tallon_Sexting_Jun2010.pdf

Salter, M., Crofts, T., & Lee, M. (2013). Beyond criminalisation and responsibilisation: Sexting, gender and young people. *Current Issues in Criminal Justice, 24*(3), 301–316.

Schaffner, L. (2006). *Girls in trouble with the law.* New Brunswick, NJ: Rutgers University Press.

Schlegel, A., & Barry, H. (1991). *Adolescence: An anthropological inquiry.* New York, NY: Maxwell Macmillan International.

Schlossman, S., & Wallach, S. (1978). The crime of precocious sexuality: Female juvenile delinquency in the progressive era. *Harvard Educational Review, 48*(1), 65–94.

Schulman, M. (2009, August 5). Sexting a world-wide epidemic: Problem hits home with "close call" in Polk County. *Spartanburg Herald-Journal,* p. C1.

Schwartz, P. (2004). Property, privacy, and personal data. *Harvard Law Review, 117*(7), 2055–2128.

Schwartz, T., & Donnellan, J. (2003, April 30). National Center for Missing & Exploited Children attacks "America's dirty little secret" with new campaign [Press release]. *National Center for Missing & Exploited Children: News and Events.* Retrieved from http://www.missingkids.com/missingkids/servlet/NewsEventServlet?LanguageCountry=en_US&PageId=1251

Searcey, D. (2009a, March 25). Does teens sending nude photos of themselves constitute a crime? *The Wall Street Journal Law Blogs.* Retrieved from http://blogs.wsj.com/law/2009/03/25/does-teens-sending-nude-photos-of-themselves-constitute-a-crime/

Searcey, D. (2009b, April 21). A lawyer, some teens and a fight over "sexting": Revealing images sent via cellphones prompt district attorney to offer seminars but threaten felony charges. *The Wall Street Journal*, A17.

Sears, R., & Mullin, K. (2009, April 15). Not condoning teen "sexting." *Rutland Herald*. Retrieved from http://web.archive.org/web/20090418193155/http://www.rutlandherald .com/article/20090415/OPINION02/904150333

Sedgwick, E. K. (1985). *Between men: English literature and male homosocial desire*. New York, NY: Columbia University Press.

Sedgwick, E. K. (1991). How to bring your kids up gay. *Social Text, 29*, 18–27.

Seeger, A. (2005). Who got left out of the property grab again? Oral traditions, indigenous rights, and valuable old knowledge. In R. A. Ghosh (Ed.), *Code: Collaborative ownership and the digital economy* (pp. 75–84). Cambridge, MA: MIT Press.

Senate bill 125: An act relating to expanding the sex offender registry (bill as introduced), Vermont Senate, 2009–2010 Sess.(2009).

Sex and Tech: Results from a survey of teens and young adults (2008). [Report]. *The National Campaign to Prevent Teen and Unplanned Pregnancy*. Retrieved from http:// www.thenationalcampaign.org/sextech/PDF/SexTech_Summary.pdf

"Sexting": High-tech flirting or serious sex offense? (2009, February 6) *FOX: America's Newsroom* [Video]. Retrieved from http://www.youtube.com/watch?v=hytYLxuTp-0

Sexting in America: When privates go public (2010, February 14). *MTV News* [Video]. Retrieved from http://www.mtv.com/videos/news/483801/sexting-in-america -when-privates-go-public-part-1.jhtml

Sexting: Naughty text ideas to try today. (2013). *Cosmopolitan*. Retrieved from http:// www.cosmopolitan.com/sex-love/advice/sexting

Sexual exploitation of children over the internet: What parents, kids and congress need to know about child predators: Hearings before the subcommittee on oversight and investigations of the committee on energy and commerce, House of Representatives, 109th Cong., 2nd Sess. (2006).

Shade, L. R. (2007). Contested spaces: Protecting or inhibiting girls online? In S. Weber & S. Dixon (Eds.), *Gro12wing up online: Young people and digital technologies* (pp. 227–244). New York, NY: Palgrave Macmillan.

Shade, L. R. (2011). Surveilling the girl via the third and networked screen. In M. C. Kearney (Ed.), *Mediated girlhoods: New explorations of girls' media culture* (pp. 261–275). New York, NY: Peter Lang.

Shanley, B., Lederer, L., & Spiegel, K. (2009, February 9). Ad council and family violence prevention fund launch innovative campaign to prevent digital dating abuse among teens [Press release]. Retrieved from http://www.adcouncil.org/newsDetail .aspx?id=262

Sherman, M. (2011). Sixteen, sexting, and a sex offender: How advances in cell phone technology have led to teenage sex offenders. *Boston University Journal of Science & Technology Law, 17*, 138–159.

Silverman, A. (2009, April 12). VT legislature considers legalizing teen "sexting." *Burl-*

ington Free Press. Retrieved from http://sexoffenderresearch.blogspot.com/2009/04/vt-legislature-considers-legalizing.html

Slack, J. D., & Wise, J. M. (2005). *Culture + technology: A primer*. New York, NY: Peter Lang.

Slane, A. (2009, March 9). Sexting, teens and a proposed offence of invasion of privacy. *IP Osgoode*. Retrieved from http://www.iposgoode.ca/2009/03/sexting-teens-and-a-proposed-offence-of-invasion-of-privacy/

Slane, A. (2010). From scanning to sexting: The scope of protection of dignity-based privacy in Canadian child pornography law. *Osgoode Hall Law Journal, 48*, 543–593.

Slovic, B. (2010, December 10). Sext crimes: Oregon has a name for teens who take dirty photos with their cell phones: Child pornographer. *Willamette Week*. Retrieved January 23, 2012. Retrieved from http://www.wweek.com/portland/article-16544-sext_crimes.html

Smith, C., & Attwood, F. (2011). Lamenting sexualization: Research, rhetoric and the story of young people's "sexualization" in the U.K. home office review. *Sex Education, 11*(3), 327–337.

Solove, D. J. (2004). *The digital person: Technology and privacy in the information age*. New York, NY: New York University Press.

Solove, D. J. (2007). *The future of reputation: Gossip, rumor, and privacy on the internet*. New Haven, CT: Yale University Press.

Solove, D. J. (2008). The end of privacy? *Scientific American, 299*(3).

Somerville, S. B. (2000). *Queering the color line: Race and the invention of homosexuality in American culture*. Durham, NC: Duke University Press.

Southworth, C., Finn, J., Dawson, S., et al. (2007). Intimate partner violence, technology, and stalking. *Violence against Women, 13*(8), 842–856.

Spade, D. (2012). Their laws will never make us safer: An introduction. In R. Conrad (Ed.), *Against equality: Prisons will not protect you* (pp. 1–12). Oakland, CA: AK Press.

Spigel, L. (1992). *Make room for TV: Television and the family ideal in postwar America*. Chicago, IL: University of Chicago Press.

Spinks, S. (2002, January 31). Inside the teenage brain. *Frontline* [Transcript]. Retrieved from http://www.pbs.org/wgbh/pages/frontline/shows/teenbrain/etc/script.html

Sprenger, P. (1999, January 26). Sun on privacy: "Get over it." *WIRED*. Retrieved from http://www.wired.com/politics/law/news/1999/01/17538

Springhall, J. (1999). Violent media, guns, and moral panics: The Columbine high school massacre. *Paedagogica Historica, 35*(3), 621–641.

Standage, T. (1998). *The Victorian internet: The remarkable story of the telegraph and the nineteenth century's on-line pioneers*. New York, NY: Walker and Co.

Stanley, E. A., & Smith, N. (Eds.). (2011). *Captive genders: Trans embodiment and the prison industrial complex*. Oakland, CA: AK Press.

Steele, M. F. (2008, June 1). Nude student photos spur internet warnings. *The New York Times*, CT1.

Sterne, J. (2012a). *Mp3: The meaning of a format*. Durham, NC: Duke University Press.

Sterne, J. (2012b). What if interactivity is the new passivity? *Flow, 15*(10).

Stiles, B. (2013, January 7). ACLU may sue over Greensburg teens' "sexting" charges. *Trib Total Media*. Retrieved from http://triblive.com/news/westmoreland/3239014-74/sexting-greensburg-charges

Stoerger, S. (2009). The digital melting pot: Bridging the digital native-immigrant divide. *First Monday, 14*(7).

Strassberg, D., McKinnon, R., Sustaita, M., et al. (2012). Sexting by high school students: An exploratory and descriptive study. *Archives of Sexual Behavior*, 1–7.

Strauch, B. (2004). *The primal teen: What the new discoveries about the teenage brain tell us about our kids*. New York, NY: Anchor Books.

Stuart, M. (2010). Saying, wearing, watching, and doing: Equal first amendment protection for coming out, having sex, and possessing child pornography. *Florida Coastal Law Review, 11*.

Subrahmanyam, K., Greenfield, P. M., & Tynes, B. (2004). Constructing sexuality and identity in an online teen chat room. *Journal of Applied Developmental Psychology, 25*(6), 651–666.

Sullivan, C. A. (1996). Kids, courts and queers: Lesbian and gay youth in the juvenile justice and foster care systems. *Law & Sexuality: A Review Of Lesbian, Gay, Bisexual, and Transgender Legal Issues, 6*, 31–62.

Sutherland, K. (2003). From jailbird to jailbait: Age of consent laws and the constructions of teenage sexualities. *Willliam and Mary Journal of Law, 9*, 313–349.

Sweeny, J. (2011). Do sexting prosecutions violate teenagers' constitutional rights? *San Diego Law Review, 48*, 951–991.

Szalacha, L. A. (2003). Safer sexual diversity climates: Lessons learned from an evaluation of Massachusetts safe schools program for gay and lesbian students. *American Journal of Education, 110*(1), 58–88.

Tallon, K., Choi, A., Keeley, M., et al. (2012). New voices/new laws: School-age young people in New South Wales speak out about the criminal laws that apply to their online behaviour [Report]. *National Children's and Youth Law Centre and Legal Aid NSW*. Retrieved from http://www.lawstuff.org.au/__data/assets/pdf_file/0009/15030/New-Voices-Law-Reform-Report.pdf

Tapia, R. C. (2005). Impregnating images: Visions of race, sex, and citizenship in California's teen pregnancy prevention campaigns. *Feminist Media Studies 5*(1), 7–22.

Tarbox, K. (2000). *Katie.Com: My story*. New York, NY: Dutton.

Teen faces charges for her own nude photos: An Ohio public defender is disputing the child pornography charges. (2008, October 14). *ABC News Now: Guilt or Innocence?* [Video]. Retrieved from http://abcnews.go.com/video/playerIndex?id=6034996

Teen girl charged with posting nude photos on internet. (2004, March 29). *USA Today*. Retrieved from http://usatoday30.usatoday.com/tech/webguide/internetlife/2004-03-29-child-self-porn_x.htm

Teens cautioned against nude photos. (2008, September 1). *The Bismarck Tribune*. Retrieved from http://bismarcktribune.com/news/state-and-regional/teens-cautioned-against-nude-photos/article_671fd5df-4dac-55d6-8094-928366fbe247.html

Teen sexting. (2009, March 25). *The Tyra Banks Show*. Retrieved from http://tyrashow
.warnerbros.com/showrecaps/archives/032009.php

Temple, J. R., Paul, J. A., Berg, P. v. d., et al. (2012). Teen sexting and its association with
sexual behaviors. *Archives of Pediatrics & Adolescent Medicine, 166*(9), 828–833.

Temporary restraining order hearing transcript. (2009, March 26). *Miller et al. v. Skumanick: Legal Documents*. Retrieved from http://www.aclupa.org/downloads/Transcript
TROhearing.PDF

Terranova, T. (2004). *Network culture: Politics for the information age*. Ann Arbor, MI:
Pluto Press.

Terry, J. (1999). *An American obsession: Science, medicine, and homosexuality in modern
society*. Chicago, IL: University of Chicago.

That's Not Cool (2009). Retrieved from http://www.thatsnotcool.com

Thiel-Stern, S. (2007). *Instant identity: Adolescent girls and the world of instant messaging*.
New York, NY: Peter Lang.

Thiel-Stern, S. (2009). Femininity out of control on the internet: A critical analysis of
media representations of gender, youth, and MySpace.com in international news discourses. *Girlhood Studies: An Interdisciplinary Journal, 2*(1), 20–39.

Thompson, H. (2006, November 14). Teen actress Hayden Panettiere and Teen Vogue
it girls™ speak out about internet safety and encourage teens to wear 2 SMRT 4U ring
[Press release]. *National Center for Missing & Exploited Children: News and Events*.
Retrieved from http://www.missingkids.com/missingkids/servlet/NewsEventServ
let?LanguageCountry=en_US&PageId=2880

Thurlow, C. (2007). Fabricating youth: New-media discourse and the technologization
of young people. In S. Johnson & A. Ensslin (Eds.), *Language in the media: Representations, identities, ideologies* (pp. 213–233). London: Continuum.

Tiidenberg, K. (2013). Bringing sexy back: Reclaiming the body aesthetic via body-blogs
and self-shooting. Unpublished article.

Todd, D. M. (2008, June 5). Dial "p" for porn: Explicit cell phone pics of underage teens
illegal. *Pittsburgh Post-Gazette*, p. EZ1.

Tolman, D. L. (1994). Doing desire: Adolescent girls' struggles for/with sexuality. *Gender
& Society, 8*(3), 324–342.

Tolman, D. L. (1999). Asking some unasked questions. *Frontline*. Retrieved from http://
www.pbs.org/wgbh/pages/frontline/shows/georgia/isolated/tolman.html

Tolman, D. L. (2005). *Dilemmas of desire: Teenage girls talk about sexuality*. Boston, MA:
Harvard University Press.

Tolman, D. L., Hirschman, C., & Impett, E. A. (2005). There is more to the story: The
place of qualitative research on female adolescent sexuality in policy making. *Sexuality
Research and Social Policy, 2*(4), 4–17.

Treichler, P. A. (1999). *How to have theory in an epidemic: Cultural chronicles of AIDS*.
Durham, NC: Duke University Press.

Treichler, P. A., Cartwright, L., & Penley, C. (1998). *The visible woman: Imaging technologies, gender, and science*. New York, NY: New York University Press.

Tynes, B. M. (2007). Internet safety gone wild? Sacrificing the educational and psychosocial benefits of online social environments. *Journal of Adolescent Research, 22*(6), 575–584.

United States v. Knox, 32 F.3d 733 (United States Court of Appeals for the Third Circuit 1994).

Vaidhyanathan, S. (2001). *Copyrights and copywrongs: The rise of intellectual property and how it threatens creativity.* New York, NY: New York University Press.

Vaidhyanathan, S. (2011). *The googlization of everything: And why we should worry.* Berkeley, CA: University of California Press.

van Dijck, J. (2009). Users like you? Theorizing agency in user-generated content. *Media Culture Society, 31*(1), 41–58.

Vanwesenbeeck, I. (2009). The risks and rights of sexualization: An appreciative commentary on Lerum and Dworkin's "bad girls rule." *Journal of Sex Research, 46*(4), 268–270.

Victorian government response to the law reform committee inquiry into sexting. (2013, December 10). Retrieved from http://www.parliament.vic.gov.au/images/stories/Govt_Response_Sexting_Inquiry.pdf

Vines, G. (1994). *Raging hormones: Do they rule our lives?* Berkeley, CA: University of California.

Visser, J. (2013, April 9). "The justice system failed her": Nova Scotia teenager commits suicide after being raped, bullied: Mother. *National Post.* Retrieved from http://news.nationalpost.com/2013/04/09/the-justice-system-failed-her-nova-scotia-teenager-commits-suicide-after-being-raped-bullied-mother/

Volpp, L. (2000). Blaming culture for bad behavior. *Yale Journal of Law & the Humanities, 12,* 89–116.

Vt. Stat. Ann. Tit. 13, § 2802b. (2009). Minor electronically disseminating indecent material to another person.

Walczak, W. J., Burch, V. A., & Kreimer, S. F. (2009, March 25). United States District Court for the middle district of Pennsylvania: Verified complaint. *Miller et al. v. Skumanick: Legal Documents.* Retrieved from http://www.aclupa.org/downloads/MillerComplaintfinal.pdf

Walczak, W. J., Burch, V. A., Roper, M. C., et al. (2009, September 11). Brief of appellees. *Miller et al. v. Skumanick: Legal Documents.* Retrieved from http://www.aclupa.org/downloads/Millerbriefappeal.pdf

Walczak, W. J., Rose, S., & Burch, V. (2010, March 17). *Miller et al. v. Skumanick*: United States District Court, middle district. *American Civil Liberties Union of Pennsylvania.* Retrieved from http://www.aclupa.org/legal/legaldocket/milleretalvskumanick

Walkerdine, V. (1984). Developmental psychology and the child-centered pedagogy: The insertion of Piaget into early education. In J. Henriques, W. Hollway, C. Urwin, C. Venn, & V. Walkerdine (Eds.), *Changing the subject: Psychology, social regulation and subjectivity.* New York, NY: Methuen.

Walkerdine, V. (1997). *Daddy's girl: Young girls and popular culture.* Cambridge, MA: Harvard University Press.

Walliker, A., & Critchley, C. (2007, December 28). Teen girls copy cyber sex acts, teen psychologist says. *Victoria, Australia Herald Sun.* Retrieved from http://www.heraldsun .com.au/news/victoria/teen-girls-copy-cyber-sex-acts/story-e6frf7kx-1111115202704

Wallis, C., & Park, A. (2004, May 10). What makes teens tick. *Time, 163,* 56–65.

Walsh, D. (2005). *Why do they act that way?: A survival guide to the adolescent brain for you and your teen.* New York, NY: Free Press.

Walsh, D. (2009, June 22). Ending the national panic on "sexting": Laws across different states are often draconian and unfair. Good parenting and common-sense law enforcement are better ways to address this teen behavior. *Los Angeles Times.*

Walters, L. G. (2010). Sexually explicit speech: How to fix the sexting problem: An analysis of the legal and policy considerations for sexting legislation. *First Amendment Law Review, 9,* 98–148.

Warren, S. D., & Brandeis, L. D. (1890). The right to privacy. *Harvard Law Review, 4*(5), 193–220.

Wartella, E., & Jennings, N. (2000). Children and computers: New technology—old concerns. *The Future of Children, 10*(2), 31–43.

Wastler, S. (2010). The harm in "sexting"?: Analyzing the constitutionality of child pornography statutes that prohibit the voluntary production, possession, and dissemination of sexually explicit images by teenagers. *Harvard Journal of Law & Gender, 33.*

Weber, S. (2012). What's wrong with be(com)ing queer?: Biological determinism as discursive queer hegemony. *Sexualities, 15*(5/6), 679–701.

Weekes, D. (2004). Where my girls at? Black girls and the construction of the sexual. In M. Fine & A. Harris (Eds.), *All about the girl: Culture, power, and identity* (pp. 141–154). New York, NY: Routledge.

Weeks, J. (1989). *Sexuality and its discontents: Meanings, myths, & modern sexualities.* New York, NY: Routledge.

Weins, W. J., & Hiestand, T. C. (2009). Sexting, statutes, and saved by the bell: Introducing a lesser juvenile charge with an "aggravating factors" framework. *Tennessee Law Review, 77,* 1–56.

Weintraub, A. N., & Yung, B. (Eds.). (2009). *Music and cultural rights.* Chicago, IL: University of Illinois Press.

Weis, L., & Fine, M. (2000). *Construction sites: Excavating race, class, and gender among urban youth.* New York, NY: Teachers College Press.

Weisskirch, R. S., & Delevi, R. (2011). "Sexting" and adult romantic attachment. *Computers in Human Behavior, 27,* 1697–1701.

Whatley, M. H. (1988). Raging hormones and powerful cars: The construction of men's sexuality in school sex education and popular adolescent films. *Journal of Education, 170*(3), 100–121.

What to type. (2006). *2 SMRT 4U.* Retrieved from http://www.2smrt4u.com/Tips

Why. (2011). *Slutwalk Toronto.* Retrieved from http://www.slutwalktoronto.com/about/ why

Willis, A. (2002). Nerdy no more: A case study of early Wired (1993–96). *Electronic Journal of Communication/La Revue Electronique de Communication, 12*(3–4).

Wolak, J., & Finkelhor, D. (2011). Sexting: A typology [Bulletin]. *Crimes against Children Research Center.* Retrieved from http://www.unh.edu/ccrc/pdf/CV231_Sexting%20Typology%20Bulletin_4-6-11_revised.pdf

Wolak, J., Finkelhor, D., & Mitchell, K. J. (2004). Internet-initiated sex crimes against minors: Implications for prevention based on findings from a national study. *Journal of Adolescent Health, 35*(5), 424.e411.

Wolak, J., Finkelhor, D., & Mitchell, K. J. (2009). Trends in arrests of online predators [Report]. *Crimes against Children Research Center.* Retrieved from http://www.unh.edu/ccrc/pdf/CV194.pdf

Wolak, J., Finkelhor, D., & Mitchell, K. J. (2012a). How often are teens arrested for sexting? Data from a national sample of police cases. *Pediatrics, 129*(1), 4–12.

Wolak, J., Finkelhor, D., & Mitchell, K. J. (2012b). Trends in arrests for child pornography possession: The third National Juvenile Online Victimization study (njov-3) [Bulletin]. *Crimes against Children Research Center.* Retrieved from http://www.unh.edu/ccrc/pdf/CV269_Child%20Porn%20Possession%20Bulletin_4-13-12.pdf

Wolak, J., Finkelhor, D., & Mitchell, K. J. (2012c). Trends in arrests for child pornography production: The third National Juvenile Online Victimization study (njov-3) [Bulletin]. *Crimes against Children Research Center.* Retrieved from http://www.unh.edu/ccrc/pdf/CV270_Child%20Porn%20Production%20Bulletin_4-13-12.pdf

Wolak, J., Finkelhor, D., Mitchell, K. J., et al. (2008). Online "predators" and their victims: Myths, realities, and implications for prevention treatment. *American Psychologist, 63*(2), 111–128.

Wolak, J., Mitchell, K. J., & Finkelhor, D. (2007). Unwanted and wanted exposure to online pornography in a national sample of youth internet users. *Pediatrics, 119*(2), 247–257.

Woodhouse, B. B. (2002). Youthful indiscretions: Culture, class, status, and the passage to adulthood. *DePaul Law Review, 51,* 743.

Worthington, N. (2005). Negotiating news representations of rape: Reporting on a college sexual assault scandal. *Media Report to Women, 33*(4), 6–14.

Ybarra, M. L., Mitchell, K. J., Finkelhor, D., et al. (2007). Internet prevention messages: Targeting the right online behaviors. *Archives of Pediatrics & Adolescent Medicine, 161,* 138–145.

Zabin, L. S., & Hayward, S. C. (1993). *Adolescent sexual behavior and childbearing.* Newbury Park, CA: Sage.

Zetter, K. (2009, March 25). ACLU sues prosecutor over "sexting" child porn charges. *Threat Level: Privacy, Crime and Security Online.* Retrieved from http://www.wired.com/threatlevel/2009/03/aclu-sues-da-ov/

Zurbriggen, E. L., Collins, R. L., Lamb, S., et al. (2007). *Report of the APA task force on the sexualization of girls.* Washington, DC: American Psychological Association.

Index

AMY ADELE HASINOFF is an assistant professor of communication at the University of Colorado Denver.

The University of Illinois Press
is a founding member of the
Association of American University Presses.

Composed in 10.75/13 Arno Pro
with Adrianna Extended display
by Jim Proefrock
at the University of Illinois Press
Manufactured by Cushing-Malloy, Inc.

University of Illinois Press
1325 South Oak Street
Champaign, IL 61820-6903
www.press.uillinois.edu